CHINESE POLITICS
FROM
MAO TO DENG

Professors World Peace Academy Books

World Social Systems Series
General Editor
Morton A. Kaplan

OTHER BOOKS AVAILABLE

*THE SOVIET UNION
AND THE CHALLENGE OF THE FUTURE*

Editors
Alexander Shtromas and Morton A. Kaplan

Vol. 1 *Stasis and Change*
Vol. 2 *Economy and Society*
Vol. 3 *Ideology, Culture and Nationality*
Vol. 4 *Russia and the World*

CHINA IN A NEW ERA

Series Editor
Ilpyong J. Kim

Chinese Defense and Foreign Policy

Editor June Teufel Dreyer

Chinese Economic Policy

Editor Bruce Reynolds

Chinese Politics From Mao to Deng

Editor Victor C. Falkenheim

Chinese Science and Technology

Editor Denis Simon

also planned:
LIBERAL DEMOCRATIC SOCIETIES

CHINESE POLITICS FROM MAO TO DENG

Edited by

Victor C. Falkenheim

Series Editor

Ilpyong J. Kim

A PWPA Book

PARAGON HOUSE
New York

Published in the United States by
Professors World Peace Academy
481 8th Avenue
New York, New York 10001

Distributed by Paragon House Publishers
90 Fifth Avenue
New York, New York 10011

A Professors World Peace Academy Book

The Professors World Peace Academy (PWPA) is an international association of professors, scholars and academics from diverse backgrounds, devoted to issues concerning world peace. PWPA sustains a program of conferences and publications on topics in peace studies, area and cultural studies, national and international development, education, economics and international relations.

Library of Congress Catalog-in-Publication Data

Chinese politics from Mao to Deng /
edited by Victor C. Falkenheim.
    p. 342. (China in a new era)
    "A PWPA Book."
    Includes index.
    ISBN 0-943852-71-4
    ISBN 0-943852-72-2 (pbk.)
    1. China—Politics and government—1976-
    I. Falkenheim, Victor C., 1940-
    II. Series.
DS779.26.C4743 1989
320.951—dc20
89-8438 CIP REV.

Table of Contents

PREFACE

This volume, comprised of 11 provocative chapters by prominent China specialists, analyzes Chinese politics from Mao Zedong to Deng Xiaoping, and their implications for China's future following a decade of reform programs. Initially, these chapters were presented at the Third Congress of the Professors World Peace Academy (PWPA) at Manila, the Philippines, on August 24-29, 1987. Under the conference theme of "China in a New Era: Continuity and Change," the congress addressed issues concerning the past, present and future development in China.

A total of 12 panels were organized with the participation of more than 98 China specialists from the five continents. Their research papers addressed various aspects of Chinese politics, economic development, law and society, industrial and rural reforms, and foreign and defense policies. The papers were subsequently revised by the authors and collected into five separate volumes, of which the present volume *Chinese Politics From Mao to Deng*, is the third book to come off the press.

The other volumes cover the fields of defense and foreign policy, economics, comparative reforms, science and technology, as well as Taiwan. It is our hope that these volumes will contribute to our understanding of China as it makes the great leap toward the 21st century under the "four modernizations" program. The organizing committee, which I chaired, attempted to organize the panels to be both interdisciplinary in scope and international in makeup.

I would like to express my heartfelt gratitude for the financial support the International Cultural Foundation provided for the convening of the Manila conference and the publication of these volumes. Gordon Anderson, General Secretary of PWPA, and his staff members as well as Kevin Delgobo, the program coordinator, and Robert Brooks, Publications Manager, have worked tirelessly for the conference and the publication of these volumes. However, the views expressed in these volumes are the sole responsibilities of the chapter writers, and do not represent the views of the organizers, sponsors, or editors.

Ilpyong J. Kim, Series Editor
Storrs, Connecticut

PART I

INTRODUCTION

ONE

CHINESE POLITICS IN TRANSITION

Victor C. Falkenheim

In the early spring of 1989, on the eve of the 40th anniversary of the founding of the People's Republic of China, the prospects for continued reform seemed to many outside observers to be bright. Over the preceding decade, Chinese politics had undergone a marked transformation, as the "open door" economic policy, market reforms, and overall liberalization reshaped the quality of political life. Clearly, many fundamentals had remained unchanged. Political power was still firmly in the grasp of the ruling Chinese Communist Party (CCP). Moreover, the party had continued to insist on fidelity to the "four cardinal principles," which called for a guiding role for Marxism-Leninism-Mao Zedong Thought under a party-led "People's Democratic Dictatorship."

But, within these limits, the changes were profound. The state had dramatically relaxed its repressive political controls, abandoning a revolutionary and mobilizational style of leadership for a more *laissez–faire* posture. And a wide range of institutional and personnel reforms had rationalized the system of government and administration. In the less turbulent political atmosphere of the 1980s, public debate had become more open and modest forms of social and economic pluralism emerged.

To critics, these changes were little more than cosmetic, limited by the party's retention of a monopoly of power. They see the emerging system as a rationalized form of authoritarianism, which though infinitely preferable to the radical totalitarianism of the late Mao era, was far from a significant step towards power sharing. To Chinese citizens, however, the state's efforts at deradicalization and depoliticization came as welcome changes. And many are guardedly hopeful that Deng Xiaoping's call for further efforts at political reform in the 1990s would bear fruit. While skepticism appeared warranted, the startling progress in political reform in Eastern Europe and the Soviet Union in the past year, and closer at hand, in Taiwan and Korea suggest the long-run potential for change.

For a brief, heady moment in April and May, 1989, it appeared that a popular, grassroots alliance of students, workers and ordinary citizens might spark even more rapid reform from below. The world watched in hopeful amazement as students and other citizens defied martial law to push for a change. The optimism was dashed by the violent and brutal suppression of the movement, which was quickly labelled a "counter-revolutionary rebellion," and by the repression and purge that followed. While the government has announced that political and economic reform are to continue, few observers expect a quick or easy return to Deng Xiaoping's reform agenda.

The chapters in this volume, which probe the Chinese leadership's efforts at political reform in the past decade, help to understand the cycle of reform and repression that have characterized the past ten years, most recently illustrated in the bloody events of 1989. The authors investigate the constraints and dilemmas that have bedeviled even the limited reforms undertaken to date. They explore the complex impact of such factors as intra-party conflict over the pace and extent of political reform, the growing strength and diversification of social and economic interests, and the impact of expanding market reforms and growing international contacts on this process. All these factors have generated a complex dynamic of change in which reform from above is propelled by demands for further reform from below. Faced with a choice between accommodating those demands or repressing them, the leadership has tended to waver, but invariably when confronted with mass political action has chosen to crack down.

THE REFORM AGENDA

The fact that the only successful reforms have been those which came from above underlines the importance of understanding the reform objectives of the Deng Xiaoping leadership. These not only shaped the reform agenda for the past decade, they also formed the basis of student demands in 1989. They remain even now the formal basis for continuing reform initiatives.

The most comprehensive and authoritative statement of the party's political restructuring goals is contained in the report delivered by the now deposed party Secretary General Zhao Ziyang to the 13th Congress of the CCP in October, 1987. While the document must be used with caution, reflecting the fact that it represents a compromise between competing conservative and liberal reform positions, it also reflects a consensus based on years of reform experimentation. Moreover, the document bears the clear imprint of Deng Xiaoping's own centrist views on reform.

The long-term objective of the reform is stated clearly: "To build a socialist political system with a high degree of democracy and a complete set of laws," as part of comprehensive political and economic restructuring. While bold in sentiment, the limited nature of the proposed package of reforms is evident in two of its key premises. One is Zhao's affirmation that as a "socialist country under the people's democratic dictatorship," China's "basic political system is good." The second is the document's insistence that China's distinctive political institutions, including its system of People's Congresses and its United Front organizations, have functioned well and are to be retained. These strengths acknowledged, Zhao also pointed out two "major defects" of the political system impelling reform: its "bureaucratiza- tion" and its "overconcentration of power." These problems originated in the course of the party's struggle for power and in its early years of post-1949 mobilization. In address- ing these problems, the overriding premise is the need to guarantee a "peaceful social and economic environment" for economic growth. This in turn means "advancing one step at a time." The limited and gradual intent of the pro- posed reforms is underlined in the explicit rejection of any western-style "separation of powers," or any system of competing political parties as possible models for Chinese reform.

Despite these limitations, the package of proposed struc- tural changes is cumulatively far-reaching in potential impact. Zhao's report specifies seven reform objectives. The first and most fundamental calls for the clearer separation of party and government operations, a longstanding prior- ity of Deng Xiaoping. Through the reform, the party is to relinquish its direct control over all aspects of economic and administrative operations, exercising its leadership pri- marily through setting policy priorities. Once party policy is embodied in legislative form, implementation and over- sight are to become the province of government. The party will retain the right to fill key governmental positions through recommendation. The goal of this reform is to re- duce political intervention in economic matters as well as to free the party from detailed routine tasks that blur its leadership role.

A second component of the reform calls for "appropriate decentralization" of power to lower administrative levels and to the "grassroots." The model for this reform is the successful agricultural reform which greatly enhanced the economic role of peasant households. In this reform, cities, localities, and enterprises are all to increase their autonomy and flexibility.

A third goal of the reform is government restructuring. This reform is to proceed in steps from the central government down to the localities, enhancing the efficiency of government operations by paring down staff and organizations, realigning functions, and clearly separating enterprise-type operations from administration. A linked, and critical reform is in the area of personnel systems. Zhao's report calls for the creation of a public service system. One notable feature of the planned system is the proposed distinction between public servants engaged in "political affairs," who will be recommended by the party, subject to public supervision and limited to specific terms in office; and those engaged in "professional work," who will be selected by competitive examination and will hold permanent tenure, subject to standardized procedures for demotion and promotion. The proposed timetable for this latter change envisages "a considerably long process to establish such a system," a clear acknowledgment of anticipated difficulties.

Two sets of reforms bear on the issue of democratization. One calls for a system of "consultation and dialogue" to facilitate communications between citizens and rulers. What appears intended is the strengthening and formalization of petitionary channels, feedback mechanisms, and grievance procedures of various sorts. A separate category of reform calls for strengthening further the formal instruments of socialist democracy, including the role of the legislature, the system of elections, and the system of united front organizations. Zhao's report acknowledges that "from time to time the rights of the masses are encroached upon," and calls for a "people's appeal system," and laws protecting rights of assembly, procession, public association, and the press.

The final, seventh area of reform calls for full estab-lishment of a socialist legal system to codify and institutionalize all of the proposed institutional changes, providing necessary guarantees and protections to in-dividuals and institutions in the exercise of their rights.

In presenting this package of reforms, Zhao called for both caution and boldness, balancing the requirements of effi-ciency and stability with the needs of groups and interests differentially affected by the process of economic and politi-cal change. Yet reconciling these competing values is not likely to be easy, as the record of the past decade makes clear.

THE RECORD OF REFORM
Legal Reform

Legal reform has long been a major priority of the post-Mao leadership. It has also been an area of substantial achievement. As Shao-chuan Leng documents in his chap-ter in this volume, the party's wide-ranging effort to extend the domain of law has resulted in a significant increase in the volume of new legislation, the creation of many new legal training institutes, the strengthening of the role of lawyers, and increasing reliance on law to resolve both civil and economic disputes. There has also been a major public education effort to increase citizen awareness and knowl-edge of law.

The problems and limitations of this effort are also evi-dent. From a human rights perspective, the failings are most glaring. James Seymour's chapter assesses the performance of the legal system in terms of compliance with human rights safeguards and finds evidence of pervasive and con-tinued abuses of police powers. Much of China's fledgling guarantees of protection against arbitrary arrest and deten-tion exist only on paper. In Seymour's view, the fundamental problem is that law in China remains more an instrument of control than a bulwark against state intru-

Communist revolution? These are the questions which this chapter probes.

MYTH AND CHARISMA

"The east is red
The sun rises
On the horizon of China
Appears the great hero Mao Tse-tung...
He is the great savior of the people."

Popular revolutionary song, circa 1949

REVITALIZATION

The Introduction began with the concepts of cultural crisis and cultural revitalization. These concepts flow from the notion that human beings create a world of symbols, culture, through which they attempt to understand the empirical world and their place in it, and through which they also attempt to ascribe value to themselves and their actions. Ernest Becker suggests that a part of this symbolizing involves the creation of transcendent explanatory systems—"hero-systems" he calls them— through which man attempts to deny the ultimate reality of his own death.[2] All this, of course, is expressed in the form of language. Becker in fact defines culture as the "linguistic psychological world the human animal learns from others."[3] The cultural historian Morse Peckham draws our attention to the performance or behavioral dimension of culture which he defines as, "those semiotic redundancy systems which maintain not merely behavior patterns but human behavior itself."[4] Or, as Peckham puts it more simply, culture provides "instructions for performance."[5]

On an individual level, if it is the job of culture to provide "instructions," I suggest that a primary source of human anxiety is the ever present possibility that culture may fail to provide adequate directions for performance in the empirical world. Peckham, in fact, sees this as the "fundamental and pervasive human anxiety."[6] Clifford Geertz expresses a similar view, suggesting that, "Man depends upon symbols and symbol systems with a dependence so great as to be decisive for his creatural viability and, as a result, his sensitivity to even the remotest indication that they may prove unable to cope with one or another aspect of experience raises within him the greatest sort of anxiety."[7] Or, more simply, as Becker puts it, "when culture falls down on its job...life grinds to a halt."[8]

Such a failure or breakdown can occur if the directions/performance system is invaded by massive negative feedback from the empirical world which threatens the coherence of an entire cultural or explanatory system. On a systemic level, such a breakdown or cultural "crisis" would occur, for example, as a result of the collision of two cultures, one of which is stronger or technologically superior to the other. It is this sort of crisis which occurred, I suggest, when China felt the full weight of the Western impact in the 19th century. The response to a cultural crisis will usually be a cultural revitalization movement, sometimes in the form of a political revolution, which seeks to construct a coherent new culture. Anthony Wallace describes such revitalization movements as, "a deliberate, organized, conscious effort by members of society to construct a more satisfying culture." Moreover, observes Wallace, this effort will attempt to "innovate not merely discrete items, but a new cultural system...."[9] And this, I suggest, is precisely what occurred in China.

While the May Fourth Movement and the intellectual ferment of the early decades of the century transformed Chinese culture to a considerable extent, these cultural innovations failed in the ultimate goal of a revitalization movement to achieve a new "steady state."[10] The incomplete Chinese revolution of the 1920s thus, in some measure, paved the way for the Communist revolution of the 1940s.

THE HERO AS SAVIOUR

It was Mao Zedong, I suggest, who finally succeeded in bringing all the disparate ideological elements together into a coherent system which explained the sorry state to which China had fallen and validated his revolution and the government which it established in 1949. In the years after 1949, as Mao's image was used by the new government to rally the people to its support, attention focused increasingly upon Mao himself, the Chairman, the Great Savior of the people. In its quest both for supportive behavior as well as supportive states of mind (legitimacy), the regime relied heavily on the growing cult of Mao which gradually assumed the appearance and functions of a religion.[11]

Mao's image soon adorned every home, school, public office, and work place. In many homes, it was said, Mao's image occupied the central place on the family altar and replaced the ancestor tablets as the principal object of worship.[12] Mao was regularly compared to the lifegiving forces of nature, especially the sun, and his "thought" was eventually cited as the guide to virtually all human activity. In all, Mao was an awe-inspiring figure, and awe, if we may return to the religion analogy, is perhaps the most central "sacred" emotion.[13]

It should not seem odd that the newly established government of the PRC should attempt to turn the growing cult of Mao into something like a political religion.[14] In its effort of constructing a polity, the new regime attempted to use the Mao cult in part to replace those institutions and attachments of the old order which it sought to uproot and eradicate. As David Apter has observed, "One cannot simply destroy primordial attachments and replace them with nothing."[15] Despite the bitter factional policy disputes which we know preceded the Cultural Revolution, all of the various political factions appear to have recognized the util-

ity of such a political religion focused on the powerful unifying figure of the Great Hero Mao Zedong.

And even greater claims were made for Mao as the charismatic prophet-leader of his revolution.

THE HERO AS PROPHET

Unlike his historical counterpart Washington, the
"indispensable man" of the American Revolution, much
greater claims were asserted for Mao than simply those of
a great historical figure around whom his countrymen
could rally. Mao also assumed the role of charismatic
prophet-leader of a cultural revitalization movement.

The term charisma has been given a wide variety of definitions, but always central to the charismatic leader is the
ability to reduce stress, anxiety, or cognitive tension associated with cultural disintegration. It is the function of
such a leader to resolve discontinuities and to explain the
world and its meaning to his followers in a new and more
satisfactory way. And, again, if we refer to the religious
analogy, the purest form of charismatic leadership being
found in religious movements, Mao's role was also that of
prophet, agent of the birth of New China, possessor of revealed truth.[16]

Religions, whether political or not, require prophets. Not
only does the prophet appear as the founder of the religion,
but as Apter suggests, if political religion is to serve the
needs of individuals, prophets must, "interpret immortal-
ity, identity, and purpose through their own personal gifts
of grace...[and] light a tinder of hope in the ordinary day-
to-day level of human demands."[17] The *People's Daily*
described Mao in this way: "Today in the era of Mao Zedong heaven is here on earth.... Chairman Mao is a great
prophet.... Each prophecy of Chairman Mao has become a
reality. It was so in the past; it is so today."[18]

Another account described Mao's charismatic role in this
way: "Comrade Mao Zedong is always able to see the es-

sence of things and future development, and able to point to the sun that is about to emerge from behind the clouds, to point to the coming of the dawn in the night, and to point to the correct direction in a maze of complex surroundings."[19]

The prophet, of course, is essentially a teacher to those who follow him. In this capacity, through his control and definition of the "Word," the rhetoric or verbal redundancies of the revolution, Mao attempted to create an explanatory system in which individuals could enjoy a sense of primary self-worth. The new explanatory system sought to redefine the meaning of life and to link human action to a new "invisible world"[20] of power and meaning. The Chinese Revolution, and, consequently, life and meaning for the Chinese masses, was linked to the Marxist engine of history, with Chairman Mao the Prophet-Teacher correctly forecasting and explaining the inevitable progress of his movement toward the millennium.

As suggested above, it is not uncommon for revolutionary regimes to rely on the unifying symbol of the revolutionary leader in order to endow their actions with legitimacy. They want individuals to follow directions for behavior because they believe those directions to be good, appropriate, or morally correct. The authority crisis which accompanies a cultural collapse, Lucian Pye suggests, by its nature, "means that power is limited by the suspicion that it lacks a proper moral base and hence lacks legitimacy."[21] Such a crisis, he notes, "calls for the creation of a myth of legitimacy for the new governmental institutions."[22]

The authorizing myth of the new revolutionary government was thus reinforced by the redundancies of the Mao cult—the Maoist political religion—and Chairman Mao, both the man and the symbol, was projected as the embodiment and exemplification of the value system supported by the government-maintained ideology. Without attempting to put too fine a point on the matter, I suggest that there is ample evidence that this effort enjoyed a fair measure of success in the years before Liberation, and to some extent in the early years of the PRC as well. Mao did seem to touch individual lives in a special way, to rekindle hope and reduce anxiety, and to offer new explanations which provided many individuals with a sense of self-worth. Mao linked human action to a new invisible world of power and called upon individuals to perform miracles by drawing power from this invisible dimension.

As I have suggested, it is no coincidence that the images of the Mao cult tend to be religious or pseudo-religious. Indeed, the literature of Mao's revolution, created by both participants and observers alike, abounds with religious imagery. Mao himself appears to have understood the compelling power of such a call. As he told Andre Malraux in 1966: "Revolution is a drama of passion; we did not win the people over by appealing to reason, but by developing hope, trust, and fraternity. In the face of famine, the will to equality takes on a religious force."[23]

But something happened to Mao's revolution on the way to the millennium. The revolution changed direction, aborted. As a cultural revitalization movement it failed to achieve the objective of a new "steady state." Indeed, many of the cultural problems which had given rise to the revolution in the first place remained to be solved.

The Setting of the Reddest Sun

One's theory or cognition is judged to be
true or untrue not by how it is
subjectively felt to be, but by what objectively
the result is in social practice.

Mao Zedong, *On Practice*

RITUALIZATION OF THE CULT OF MAO

"When the morning sun shed its shimmering rays over the city, throngs extending over dozens of *li* had already been converging on Tiananmen Square and the boulevard east of it. Basking in the early sunshine, the crowds recited quotations from Chairman Mao's works and read the paean dedicated to him: The red sun rises before us. Its splendor reddens the earth. Our great leader, Beloved Chairman Mao, may you be with us forever.

"The happiest moment had come! The square was astir, the military band struck up *The East Is Red* and then came Chairman Mao and his close comrade in-arms....

"The people thronged Tiananmen Square, which is 400,000 square meters in area, as well as the wide street east of it, and the Square became a roaring ocean of red. The shouting of slogans mingling with cheers sounded like spring thunder, unceasing and deafening.

"At this moment many jotted down these words in the fly-leaf of their *Quotations From Chairman Mao Tse-tung* [Mao Zedong] to commemorate this moment of great joy: 10 a.m. exactly, October 1, 1966."[24]

Perhaps the best evidence that something had gone wrong with Mao's movement was provided by the onset of the Cultural Revolution. It seems clear that Mao himself had come to the conclusion that his revitalization movement had gone off course, or at the least was far from complete and not getting any closer. On the eve of the Cultural Revolution, in an extraordinary interview, Mao told Andre Malraux: "The thought, culture, and customs which brought China to where we found her must disappear, and the thought, customs, and culture of proletarian China, which does not yet exist, must appear."[25]

Mao bemoaned the many major revolutionary "problems" which remained to be solved, and at the end of the interview, as the two walked alone toward Malraux's waiting car, Mao expressed his sense of isolation. "I am alone with the masses," he said. "Waiting."[26]

It is surely one of the great ironies of recent history that at the moment when the world discovered the cult of Mao, at a time when the mere sight of the Great Helmsman could bring tears of ecstasy to the faces of a million assembled young revolutionary fighters, at that moment of his apotheosis, Mao Zedong perceived his political difficulties within the CPC to be so intractable that he was moved to launch the desperate insanity of the Cultural Revolution. In fact, it seems plausible to assert, contrary to the popular opinion of the day, that the launching of the Cultural Revolution and the attendant growth and ritualization of the Mao cult—indeed, the deification of Mao Zedong—were indications of the weakness of the Great Helmsman, not of his strength.

Mao returned to Beijing on July 18, 1966, following his much publicized swim in the Yangtze on July 16. He had been absent from the capital and out of public sight since the previous November.[27] In view of the fact that Lin Biao had reportedly moved troops into the capital by late April, and that by early June the Maoists had reestablished control over the central party organization and propaganda machinery, Mao's failure to return to the capital until mid-July appears odd. If Mao was the Great Supreme Commander of the Cultural Revolution, why was he nowhere in evidence during the most crucial early stage of the struggle? I have argued at length elsewhere[28] that the evidence allows a strong suspicion that Mao may have been ill during his absence from Beijing and that it was not he but Lin Biao who was directing the Maoist counterattack.

It is impossible to defend this proposition with hard data, but one fact is clear: as the ceremonial importance of Lin Biao increased, the public role of Mao himself, the physical presence of the Chairman, became increasingly irrelevant. "Chairman Mao" the symbol and the Mao cult became political weapons manipulated by Lin Biao and Jiang Qing. This is not to suggest that Mao no longer wielded important political power. While he may not have exercised day-to-day control of the Cultural Revolution, his was certainly still the most important presence in the party, and on those policy questions about which he asserted himself, Mao was doubtless the most important voice in the soon to be shattered CPC. It was in his public role as Great Leader that Mao became increasingly symbolic and less substantial.

As the celebration of the Mao cult became ritualized, and as Lin Biao assumed greater importance as the spokesman for and manipulator of the Mao cult, the cult became depersonalized, and Mao grew less important as a living, breathing leader than as a spiritual presence. Thus it was soon possible for the *Peking Review* to produce a major article on party building composed entirely of Mao's past utterances.[29] Mao himself was no longer essential to the process of producing such an essay. It could be pieced together from fragments of his earlier work much as a Christian cleric might create a sermon from the recorded words of Jesus. Likewise, the Cultural Revolution brought a trend toward idolatry into the cult. Increasingly, the proper devotions were made not before the Chairman himself, but before his portrait or other likeness. Reports commonly described devotional activities such as an entire Army company taking a "solemn oath before Chairman Mao's portrait,"[30] or of a group of marchers converging on the Zhongnanhai "carrying pledges written on red paper" which they read "in front of the big portrait of Chairman Mao,"[31] or of a group of workers who "solemnly pledged before a portrait of Chairman Mao."[32]

But, in the end, this revolution failed as well. And all of the expressions of devotion to Chairman Mao created by the party Propaganda Department and dutifully recorded in the Chinese press proved to be not evidence of love for the great leader, but evidence of the weakness of a failed prophet. It was only after Mao's death that the horror of the Cultural Revolution was gradually revealed by those who had lived through it. Through these revelations we understand the depth of the feeling of betrayal and breach of trust by Chairman Mao experienced by the Chinese people.

It may well be that people's faith in Chairman Mao had begun to erode much earlier due to the failure of the Great Leap and the terrible famine which ensued. It is not important to fix a precise date for Mao's fall from honor. What is important to note is that faith in the Chairman, once vanished, could not be recreated. Mao had seen the heady enthusiasm of the early years replaced by intra-party bickering of the Great Leap period, his own forced resignation as Chairman of the PRC, and the gradual dismantling of his great visionary program by the "Capitalist Roaders" who came to control the day-to-day operation of his party. To be sure, they joined in the hymns of praise to the Great Helmsman, but they failed to share his revolutionary vision. They did, as Mao later accused them of doing, "wave the Red Flag to oppose the Red Flag." In response, finally, Mao conjured the Cultural Revolution, the terror and destructive violence of which he loosed against his party and his people in one last desperate attempt to transform China through an immense effort of human will.

In the end, though, the masses upon whom Mao was counting, and with whom he saw himself isolated from his party and "waiting," appear not to have been waiting for Chairman Mao, nor for another call to arms, but for the more seductive message of the capitalist roaders Mao had tried to banish.

HOW TO EXPLAIN THE "TEN YEARS OF DISORDER"?

"Comrade Mao Zedong, the esteemed and beloved leader of our party, our army, and the people of all the nationalities of our country, the great leader of the international proletariat and the oppressed nations and oppressed people, chairman of the Central Committee of the Communist party of China, chairman of the Military Commission of the Central Committee of the Communist party of China, and honorary chairman of the National Committee of the Chinese People's Political Consultative Conference, passed away at 00:10 hours, September 9, 1976 in Peking because of the worsening of his illness despite all treatment, although meticulous medical care was given him in every way after he became ill."[33]

The death of Mao Zedong brought to a close what the Chinese euphemistically came to call the "ten years of disorder." Though the violent phase of the Cultural Revolution had long been over, the more radical policies of the period modified, a measure of stability restored, and even some of the leading capitalist roaders such as Deng Xiaoping rehabilitated, there could be no effort to connect Mao directly with the violent excesses of the Cultural Revolution during his lifetime. Even at his death, a cadre of high-level supporters, including his wife, remained in power, and the issue of the future course of Chinese politics and of Mao's reputation remained to be settled.

The policy issues moved toward a fairly rapid settlement as Jiang Qing and the "Gang of Four" were arrested within the month of Mao's death. It took a bit longer, to the 3rd Plenum of the 11th Central Committee in December 1978, to dispatch Mao's chosen successor Hua Guofeng and his "two whatever" policies ["firmly uphold whatever policy decisions Chairman Mao made and unswervingly adhere to whatever instructions Chairman Mao gave"] to the rubbish heap of history. But, the other critical problem remained: how to explain the Chairman's role in the disaster of the Cultural Revolution. This was clearly no simple matter. As founder-prophet of the movement, as its "Great Leader" and Reddest Sun in the hearts of his countrymen, both Mao the man and "Chairman Mao" the symbol, were intimately connected with the entire fabric of the explanatory system which constituted the sanctioning ideology of the PRC; the sanctioning ideology which legitimized the position of the ruling Communist elite. It was with great care, therefore, that the matter was taken up at the 6th Plenum of the llth Central Committee in June 1981.

The "Resolution on Historical Questions" adopted by the 6th Plenum runs to thirty-eight single-spaced pages in translation. The Central Committee Resolution declared that, "Comrade Mao Zedong's personal leadership characterized by 'left' errors took the place of the collective leadership of the Central Committee, and the cult of Mao Zedong was frantically pushed to an extreme."[34] Nor did the Central Committee shy away from pointing the finger and fixing the blame. "Chief responsibility," said the Resolution, "for the grave 'left' error of the 'Cultural Revolution,' and error comprehensive in magnitude and protracted in duration, does indeed lie with Comrade Mao Zedong."[35] This is pretty strong stuff indeed for a leader who had been raised to the status of a god, or at least of a demi-god, and whose thought had been praised as *fa bao*, omniscient and free from error.

The new CPC leaders were, however, sensitive to the related issues of doctrine and legitimacy. Mao was too important; he could not be savaged the way Khrushchev had attempted to savage Stalin. Mao was China's Lenin, and as founder his role was too central to the legitimacy of Communist rule in China for him simply to be dismissed as "wrong." Mao himself might have made "mistakes" in his later years, but what of his "thought" which "advanced" and "developed" and added the Chinese dimension to Marxism-Leninism and brought it to its "highest stage" of development? What of this body of ideas which was so fundamental to the sanctioning ideology of the PRC? The Central Committee Resolution attempted to deal with this problem as well.

They declared that, on balance, Mao was a great Marxist and a great proletarian revolutionary: "It is true that he made gross mistakes during the 'Cultural Revolution,' but, if we judge his activities as a whole, his contributions to the

Chinese revolution far outweigh his mistakes."[36] As for his thought, they attempted to devise an entirely new formula: *"The Chinese communists,* with Mao Zedong as their chief representative, *made a theoretical synthesis* of China's unique experience in its protracted revolution in accordance with the basic principles of Marxism-Leninism. This synthesis constituted a scientific system of guidelines befitting China's conditions, *and it is this synthesis which is Mao Zedong Thought,* the product of the integration of the universal principles of Marxism-Leninism with the concrete practice of the Chinese revolution."[37] [Emphasis added.] Mao Zedong Thought, which was to remain one of the "cardinal principles" of Communist rule in China, was thus divorced from any particular "thoughts" Mao himself might have had and transformed into the collective historical wisdom of the "Chinese Communists" of whom Mao was only the "chief representative." The Central Committee thus seemed to have hit upon an extremely neat and innovative way of discarding all of the inconvenient or embarrassing aspects of Mao's body of theoretical work including, perhaps, the central thrust of his revolutionary vision while retaining the "scientific system" of Marxism-Leninism, Mao Zedong Thought as the keystone of the sanctioning and legitimizing ideology of the political system.

The only serious problem with this clever formula is this: if the central tenets of a body of doctrine can be so easily discarded, ignored, or, as was already happening, turned upside down—Mao, did, after all, stand for something— does the doctrine not cease to have meaning, at least the sort of meaning that anyone can believe in?

CHINA'S SEARCH FOR WEALTH AND POWER

It doesn't matter if the cat
is black or white as long as
it catches mice.

Remark attributed to Deng Xiaoping

HOW TO BE A GOOD COMMUNIST

"Socialism must possess...spiritual civilization with Communist ideology at its core. Without this, the building of socialism would be out of the question."[38] Thus was one of the main themes of the CPC 12th Party Congress articulated by then party General Secretary Hu Yaobang. If communist ideology is to be the "core," and if the program to build socialism is to be guided by this ideology, then it might seem reasonable to inquire as to the nature or content of this controlling ideology. We might also want to know the attributes of the category "spiritual civilization." That is, what does the CPC currently stand for? What are the values of the Chinese revolution under Deng Xiaoping? What sort of behavior does the leadership wish to promote and to stabilize? What is the model life which the good Communist should emulate in the post-Mao era?

The questions are easier put than answered; they go to the heart of the question of the nature of the culture or "hero-system" which the present leadership of China is attempting to construct. There was a time when we could point to the model of Lei Feng, the famous "ever rustproof screw," a young soldier of the PLA who died in 1962. Lei Feng's widely publicized diary revealed him to be the perfect Maoist new Chinese man, and his selfless, Mao-centered life as the perfect Communist life to be emulated.[39] It is my view, however, that in the post-Mao period, Lei Feng's appearance in the Chinese press has been principally an indication of conservative (if it is proper to call the more orthodox Maoists "conservatives") reaction to the thrust or pace of the Dengist reforms. Lei Feng made a prominent reappearance during the "spiritual pollution" campaign[40] and more recently he has resurfaced as a consequence of the drive against "bourgeois liberalization."[41] Indeed, on the twenty-fourth anniversary of Chairman Mao's famous inscription to "Learn From Comrade Lei

Feng" [March 5, 1963], all of the major newspapers in China carried articles on the need to "carry forward" the Lei Feng spirit. It is extremely difficult, however, to take this sort of thing seriously as moral instruction. For anyone who has lived and worked in China, the Lei Feng campaigns have a dream-like quality because they seem out of touch with the realities of the situation. It is simply impossible to find anyone over the age of five or six who would consider the life of Lei Feng an appropriate model to emulate. And when the government also sponsors admonitions such as "first get rich, then build socialism," the resulting confusion in values should probably foreclose the possibility of discovering any "living Lei Fengs of the eighties."

Nor are the instructions of Deng Xiaoping, the acknowledged ultimate leader, of much help in our effort to discover what the CPC now stands for. While it seems clear that the economic modernization of China is an important priority to the Deng leadership, the corresponding social or behavioral values to be promoted seem not clear at all. Deng has taken the vague high road in making his prescriptions. He has confined himself to calling on his fellow party members to have "lofty ideals and a sense of discipline,"[42] and to "earnestly practice Communist ideals and Communist ethics,"[43] without offering any guidance about the nature of these ideals. As a consequence of what I perceive to be considerable confusion in the consummatory values of the system, it has been extremely difficult for the party to issue clear directions for performance to those party members, for example, who have taken advantage of the enormously expanded opportunities for economic corruption which have accompanied the opening of the economy to hitherto forbidden private business activities. I suggest that much more than exhortations to "Serve the people!" and the like are going to be needed to eliminate the considerable venality in government in the PRC today.[44] It seems to me, in fact, even if one wanted to make the best good faith effort to follow the moral instruction of the CPC, it would be difficult to know how to be a good Communist in China today. And this situation is likely to continue in the face of persistent failure to develop what David Apter calls an "articulated moral element."[45]

WHATEVER HAPPENED TO CHAIRMAN MAO?

No less an authority than the *Beijing Review* has claimed that the spread of "liberalism" in China has caused people to suggest that the "root of alienation lies in the socialist system itself," and that this development is *"sowing distrust in the cause of socialism and Communism and the Communist party as well."*[46] [Emphasis added.] This hardly seems a trifling problem in a system which considers matters such as the final goals of the revolution and the leading role of the Communist party to be settled questions and not suitable topics for public discussion. On this count at least, then, the CPC at age sixty-five appears to have rather serious problems.

We suggested earlier that a breakdown in the directions/ performance system may occur if the system is invaded by massive negative feedback from the empirical world. Such seems to have been the case with the instructions for performance of the Marxist-Leninist system in China. Otherwise, how to explain the "distrust" in the cause of "socialism and Communism" and even of the Communist party itself? It is unrealistic, however, to expect that this breakdown will result in a breakup of the political system which this system of ideas supports. If Leninist state systems have proven nothing else, they have proven to be good at control. A breakdown in the directions/performance system, under these circumstances, may simply call forth a greater application of force, such as the rise in the number of mass public executions in the mid-1980s.

But the point of a regime's attempt to build a solid base of legitimacy is that killing is to be avoided if possible. Viewed from one perspective, killing may be an excellent method of social control, but at a systemic level, it is neither reliable nor durable in the long run. The ultimate aim of the regime is to see all members of the system follow instructions for performance because they believe it to be the right or proper thing to do. At the opposite end of the control continuum from "killing" we might place "seduction." This would include rhetorical seduction such as the Lei Feng campaigns, "model worker" or "labor hero" awards, and the like, which we have already suggested may be less than totally effective, as well as the manipulation of material rewards. The new open economic policies of Deng Xiaoping's drive for modernization certainly qualify as an attempt at this sort of economic seduction: if the peasants won't perform for "Communism" and the motherland, maybe they will perform to become 10,000 yuan households.

We should not be tempted, however, to conclude that this is likely to solve the legitimacy problem. David Apter issues this caution:

> No matter how much political leaders may manipulate material benefits in return for loyalty, the most equitably arranged society may fail to generate support without an articulated moral element.[47]

Once again, however, when we attempt to identify this "articulated moral element" we find only confusion, vague prescriptions, and conflicting directions.

What sort of behavior does a concept such as "socialist spiritual civilization" attempt to maintain and stabilize? What are the consummatory values of the PRC, and what are its sources of legitimacy as it pursues its goal of entering the modern world as a full participant? We do not seem to be significantly closer to an answer to these questions than we were at the outset.

I began this chapter with the suggestion that the early promise which many saw in the Chinese revolution is far from fulfilled, and along the way I have tried to indicate the sources of confusion in the belief system. Surely, one of the most important sources of confusion is found in the historical contradictions surrounding the now tarnished and shopworn image and reputation of Mao Zedong.

CONCLUSION

I suggested above that the founding of the PRC was closely linked to Mao's role as charismatic prophet-leader. Using Weber's formulation, we might suggest that the legitimacy of the new regime was based on the charisma of the Chairman, if we apply the term charisma broadly, and the authorizing myth of the new revolutionary government was reinforced by the redundancies of the Mao cult which projected Chairman Mao as the exemplification of the value system maintained by the government-supported ideology. So little of Mao's reputation, image, and charisma remain today, though, that something else must serve these important functions. Yet, as the Mao reputation has been destroyed (including self-destruction), there has been little meaningful development in the direction of institutionalization in the PRC and thus no meaningful development of a rational-legal basis of legitimacy.

Yet, many of the policies of the Deng Xiaoping leadership appear quite popular. Perhaps we could describe the present regime as based on a legitimacy of competence, combined with a policy of seduction based upon the manipulation of material benefits. In terms of competence, things certainly work better in the PRC today than they have at almost any time since 1949, and vast numbers of people, especially the peasants, are better off in their material lives than heretofore. Still, it is widely reported that the leaders of the PRC perceive their system to be suffering from some sort of "spiritual" problem; a fact of considerable importance in a Marxist-Leninist party which assumes for itself the right and responsibility for defining truth.

This may be, in fact, a problem which China's next generation of leaders will prove incapable of solving. We ought at least to acknowledge the possibility that Marxist-Leninist belief systems are inadequate to the tasks they have set for themselves. Complaining about the lack of belief in "scientific" Marxism-Leninism, Mao Zedong Thought, *The China Daily* observed that while farmers might use science in growing crops, in other matters, "concerning birth, death, age, illness, and marriage, many cling to feudal superstition and outmoded custom."[48] There may be more important human concerns than birth, death, age, illness, and marriage, but it is difficult to imagine what they might be. And, as Ernest Becker observes, "From a pragmatic point of view there must be something false about a belief system that stops short of all of man's empirical reality, and that fails when a segment of that reality fails."[49]

To what "invisible world of power," then, can the Chinese revolution be linked in the 1980s and beyond? Clearly the gutted, sanitized, and disembodied Mao Zedong Thought is no candidate at all. Nor, does the evidence hold out hope for the use of "Communism" or "History" either. In the end the CPC may decide that the best available candidate is "China," an extremely reliable and durable symbol of sentiment and identification.

When all is said and done, though, is this, will this become, the final result for which the young CPC fought and died, or a revolution which Chairman Mao would recognize, or be willing to claim for his own?

NOTES

1. James T. Myers, "The Fall of Chairman Mao," *Current Scene* (Hong Kong), Vol. VI, No. 10. June 15, 1968, pp. 15-16.
2. Ernest Becker, *The Denial of Death*, (New York: The Free Press, 1973), p. 27 and *passim*.
3. Ernest Becker, *The Birth and Death of Meaning*, 2nd edition (New York: The Free Press, 1971), p. 47.
4. Morse Peckham, *Explanation and Power—The Control of Human Behavior* (New York: The Seabury Press, 1979), p. 183.
5. *Ibid.*, p. xviii.
6. Morse Peckham, "The Arts and the Centers of Power," reprinted in Morse Peckham, *Romanticism and Behavior*—Collected Essays II (Columbia: The University of South Carolina Press, 1976, p. 336.
7. Clifford Geertz, "Religion as a Cultural System," in Michael Banton, ed., *Anthropoligical Approaches to the Study of Religion* (London: Travistock, 1966), pp. 13-14.
8. Ernest Becker, *Birth and Death*, p. 82.
9. Anthony F.C. Wallace, "Revitalization Movements," *American Anthropoligist*, Vol. 58, No. 2 (April 1956), p. 265.
10. *Ibid.*
11. James T. Myers, "Religious Aspects of the Cult of Mao Tse-tung," *Current Scene* (Hong Kong), Vol. X, No. 3, March 10, 1972.
12. Holmes Welch, "The Deification of Mao," *Saturday Review*, September 19, 1970, p. 25.
13. *Cf.* Elizabeth K. Nottingham, *Religion and Society* (New York: Random House, 1954), *passim*.
14. David E. Apter, *The Politics of Modernization* (Chicago: The University of Chicago Press, 1965), p. 223.
15. *Ibid.*, p. 213.
16. James T. Myers, "Religious Aspects Cult of Mao," p. 7.
17. David E. Apter, *Politics of Modernization*, p. 223.
18. *Renmin ribao*, Beijing, October 1, 1958.
19. *Renmin ribao*, Beijing, October 13, 1960.
20. Ernest Becker, *Birth and Death*, pp. 119-120.
21. Lucian W. Pye, *The Spirit of Chinese Politics: A Psycholocultural Study of the Authority Crisis in Political Development* (Cambridge, Mass.: The M.I.T. Press, 1968), p. 9.
22. *Ibid.*, p. 7.
23. Andre Malraux, *Anti-Memoirs* (New York: Holt, Reinhart and Winston, 1968), p. 360.

24. "Chairman Mao Reviews A Mammoth March-Past of One and a Half Million Paraders," *Peking Review*, No. 42, October 7, 1968, pp. 3-4.
25. Andre Malraux, *Anti-Memoirs*, p. 373.
26. *Ibid.*, p. 375.
27. There is a strange account of a meeting between Mao and the Albanian leader Mehmet Shehu during the latter's visit to China from May 3-11. The mysterious meeting and "banquet," for which no date or place were given, is the only reported appearance of Mao during the approximately eight-month period. For a fuller discussion of this period see James T. Myers, "Lin Biao and the Cult of Mao Tse-tung," *Issues & Studies* (Taipei: Institute of International Relations), Vol VI, No. 3, December 1969, pp. 56-58.
28. *Ibid.*
29. "Chairman Mao Tse-tung On Party Building," *Peking Review*, No. 15, April 11, 1969.
30. *Peking Review*, No. 15, April 11, 1969, p. 8.
31. *Ibid.*, p. 10.
32. *Ibid.*
33. "Central Organs Announce Mao's Passing," *Xinhua*, Beijing - English, September 9, 1976.
34. *Xinhua*, Beijing - English, June 30, 1981. In *Foreign Broadcast Information Service - China (FBIS-CHI)*, July 1, 1981, p. K16.
35. *Ibid.*, p. K18.
36. *Ibid.*, p. K25.
37. *Ibid.*, Emphasis added.
38. Hu Yaobang, "Create A New Situation In All Fields of Socialist Modernization," Report to the 12th National Congress of the Communist Party of China, September 1, 1982, *Beijing Review*, Vol. 25, No. 37, September 13, 1982, p. 21.
39. For a detailed account of this phenomenon see James T. Myers, "Socialist Spiritual Civilization and Cultural Pollution: The Problem of Meaning," in Yu-ming Shaw (Ed.), *Mainland China—Politics, Economics and Reform* (Boulder, CO: Westview Press, 1986), especially pp. 302-304.
40. *Ibid.*, *passim*.
41. See, for example, "Yu Qiuli Urges Emulating Lei Feng," *Xinhua*, Beijing, March 5, 1987. In *FBIS-CHI* March 9, 1987, pp. K5-K8; "Put Lofty Ideals Into Practice in the Course of Wholeheartedly Serving the People," *Jiefangjun bao*, Beijing, March 5, 1987. In *FBIS-*

CHI, March 18, 1987, pp. K22-K24; "Carry Forward Lei Feng's Spirit, Be Determined to Serve the People," *Zhunguo Qingnian bao*, Beijing, March 5, 1987. In *FBIS-CHI, March 19, 1987, pp. K6-K9*.

42. "Deng Reaffirms System of Public Ownership," *Beijing Review*, No. 11, March 18, 1985, p. 15.

43. "Ideals and Discipline are the guarantees of Reform," *Renmin ribao*, Beijing, March 12, 1985. In *FBIS-CHI*, March 15, 1985, p. K22.

44. James T. Myers, "China: Modernization and 'Unhealthy Tendencies,'" *Comparative Politics*, forthcoming; "Another Look At Corruption: Lessons of the Career of the 'God of Fortune,'" Yuming Shaw (Ed.), *Changes and Continuities in Chinese Communism Volume I: Ideology, Politics, and Foreign Policy*, Boulder, CO: Westview Press, 1988).

45. David E. Apter, *Politics of Modernization*, p. 271.

46. "Opposing Ideological Pollution," *Beijing Review*, Vol. 26, No. 44, October 31, 1983, pp. 6-7.

47. David E. Apter, *Politics of Modernization*, p.271.

48. *China Daily*, Beijing, November 10, 1982, p. 4.

49. Ernest Becker, *Birth and Death*, p. 191.

THREE

THE ORIGINS OF CHINA'S POST-MAO REFORMS

Lowell Dittmer

There has been a slowly accumulating body of literature describing and analyzing China's post-Mao reforms.[1] This is as it should be, for those reforms have been so comprehensive in their impact and so aleatory in their direction of movement that they must be expected to require close monitoring and commentary. There have also been attempts to infer from this experience the direction that the Chinese reform movement is likely to take in the foreseeable future.[2] But there have been few efforts to trace the ancestry of the reforms through the thicket of pre-1976 political cleavages.[3]

Inasmuch as such an attempt will here be undertaken, the presumption is of course that it will be a useful contribution to our understanding of the reforms. And useful not merely to an understanding of the recent past, but to provide at least a premonition of the future. Of course the past does not repeat itself, but nowhere else is George Santayana's dictum that those who do not understand the past are condemned to repeat it more applicable. For unlike the Cultural Revolution or the Great Leap Forward, the Chinese reform movement did not spring out of the mind of one great leader. It is rather the product of a confluence of thinkers and contradictory social forces that moves here in one direction and there in another without any master plan or predefined destination. In fact, China's reform movement is more clearly defined by the recent historical errors that it is trying to escape from than by any self-conscious vision of the future. It is among those historical phenomena without blueprint whose future must be found in a "tradition" constructed from its origins and historical development.

The thesis of this chapter is that the Chinese reform movement is of dubious origin in the sense that it can be traced back to at least three different births: the period of the First Five-Year Plan, the period of recovery from the Great Leap Forward, and the Cultural Revolution. For those who claim ancestry from the 1950s, the reform represents a restoration of the noble traditions of the founding fathers of party and state; for those who trace it to the Cultural Revolution, the reform movement represents the death of a bankrupt, moribund set of institutions and the dawning of new possibilities for political and economic development. Those features of the current reform movement that are derived from the early 1960s remain fatherless. Although Deng Xiaoping, Liu Shaoqi, and most other principals of that period have since been rehabilitated, their rehabilitation seems to have been controversial, and the "revisionist" episode in Chinese Communist Party (CCP) history remains in some ideological disrepute. A certain embarrassment is indicated by the fact that since 1979, the epithet "revisionism" seems to have disappeared from the Chinese political vocabulary, even in referring to the Soviet Union.

The origins of China's reform movement are still at issue at this writing. At stake is not only the past, but the future: By defining the tradition of this apparently open-ended movement, each party to the dispute seeks to grasp the historical dialectic implying its future. It will be worth our while to examine each of these perspectives more closely.

THE GOLDEN 1950s

For many of those who experienced it, the 1950s remain a golden age. After nearly a century of civil war and foreign invasion, the country was once again fully united and at peace. It enjoyed the protection of what seemed at the time a benign and powerful socialist motherland, and it could boast a young, unified, and relatively vigorous leadership. The CCP inaugurated not a proletarian dictatorship but rather a New Democracy, which promised a useful role to all patriotic classes in implementing a progressive but relatively moderate social program. The First Five-Year Plan was an outstanding success, revitalizing agriculture while forging ahead with industrialization to achieve overall economic growth rates without precedent. At the same time, socialization of the means of production was achieved in both agriculture and industry, expediting the transition to socialism in unexpectedly short order.

The 1950s were indeed a period of euphoria in many respects, but because they telescoped together so many divergent tendencies, it has proved difficult for the reformers to find a meaningful home for their policies here. Many of the more ambitious liberal reformers have been fascinated with New Democracy. For instance, the promise it seemed to hold for a democracy of the whole people within an economy containing a sizable private sector. This interest has been implicit, for example, in critiques of the land reform and collectivization policies as being too precipitous and forced. For those supporting a closer relationship with the Soviet Union, the 1950s, of course, represent the golden age of that alliance, when Soviet advisors selflessly helped the construction of Chinese industry and technology.

For party veterans, the decade of the 1950s is symbolized above all by the 8th Party Congress, when Mao Zedong thought was deleted from the CCP constitution for the sake of a more collective leadership. Then an accord seemed to have been reached that the class struggle had ended with the socialization of the means of production, leaving the leadership free to concentrate henceforth on rapid economic growth, which resolved the remaining "contradiction" between advanced productive relations and underdeveloped productive forces. For party veterans, the 8th Congress represented "rectification according to the norms" and the other attributes of wholesome party life before it had been poisoned by Lushan and the purge of Peng Dehuai, which first prefigured the rise of Mao Zedong's arbitrary, unilateralist decision-making style.

The problem with detecting echoes of this heroic age in the reform program is that wishful thinking may give rise to distorted perceptions of either the founding or later attempts at restoration. There is, however, no question that certain specific forerunners of important reform policies made their first appearance then. For example, the first prototype of the responsibility field system seems to have been introduced by Deng Zihui in the mid-1950s.[4] Yet it is unclear whether Deng was consciously presenting an alternative to the party "line," or simply a temporary, expedient fallback for households not yet prepared for full collectivization. This case illustrates the reformers' problem in trying to find a "home" for their policies in this period: There really was considerable consensus at the time about the need for a transition to socialism, as well as agreement as to what that would mean. This would have been incompatible with the willingness of the reformers to defer such questions indefinitely in the interest of more rapid growth under commodity socialism. Even the more conservative members of the reform leadership might not have felt fully at home in the 1950s. While there does seem to have been greater leadership consensus during this period, was that really because everyone played by the rules of collective leadership? Or simply because Mao's hand-picked crew of trusted subordinates continued to follow orders—why should they not, when everything was progressing satisfactorily?—or were dumped when they did not, like Gao Gang and Rao Shushi.[5] In other words, many of the failings that culminated in the Cultural Revolution—blind-sided utopianism, internal personal commitment to an all-knowing hero-leader, an intolerance of criticism that let the party lurch from one extreme to another—were already latent in the Golden Fifties.

REVISIONISM

"Revisionism" was the epithet used during the Cultural Revolution to characterize the policy platform introduced by Liu Shaoqi, Deng Xiaoping, and their followers during the early 1960s to facilitate recovery from the economic problems precipitated by the Great Leap Forward. Although this set of policies was first introduced as no more than an *ad hoc* collection of pragmatic responses to the problems of the day, closer examination reveals a certain systemic coherence to them. Thus it is not inappropriate to group them under the common rubric of "revisionism"—without, however, adopting the pejorative connotations of the term.

Liu Shaoqi was the theoretical weathervane and symbolic bellwether of revisionism. Liu's worldview was characterized by a certain moral elitism, just as his Red Guard critics claimed that it was—a belief that the political elite, specifically the CCP leadership, was morally superior to the masses. This impression can be readily corroborated by reading his classic *How to Be a Good Communist*.[6] Whether the criticism is altogether fair is another question, for it was Lenin who originated the doctrine of the "leading role" of the party. Be that as it may, nowhere else in the canon of CCP classics is the party's claim to moral superiority so articulately rationalized. In contrast, Mao's writings do not generally address themselves specifically to the elite. Mao preferred to think in terms of an elite that was indistinguishable from the masses it led. For the masses were the ultimate source of truth, and the tendency of the elite to "divorce" itself from the masses could only be considered a disturbing sign of "bureaucratism."[7] One of the most attractive features of revolution was that it permitted the "smashing" of all "frames" separating the elite from the masses.

To Liu Shaoqi, the touchstone of the party's superiority was its synoptic vision. Ordinary people might be able to discern and pursue their individual or even group interests, but only the party elite were capable of grasping the interests of the people as a whole. Only the elite had the theoretical ability to reason at such a high level of abstraction; only the elite had the moral self-discipline to renounce all personal advantage on behalf of the public interest. Such qualities had to be learned, carefully "cultivated" through years of service. Thus the party could be conceived as a vast hierarchy of moral efficiency, in which those best able to serve the interests of the whole and abnegate self-interest would provide leadership and cultivation to those who had not yet reached their "level" of consciousness. Moral efficiency and a vision of the whole would coincide with upward career mobility. By the time the qualified official had reached the top of the pyramid, personal and general interests would have become identical; they could have "merged":

> It must be understood that the interests of the party are identical with the interests of the people. Whatever benefits the people also benefits the party and must be carried out by every party member with heart and soul. Likewise, whatever injures the people also injures the party....The party has no interests of its own beyond the people's interests.[8]

Liu's elitism led him to embrace a socially differentiated concept of truth. Truth was, for example, not equally distributed even among the party elite, but tended rather to follow the hierarchy of authority. Nonetheless, the party as a whole had a monopoly on the truth. Freedom and necessity, theory and practice merged within the party. To be sure, outside its privileged confines other values could legitimately be pursued. There, political pragmatism was the rule—at best, this implied a situation ethic; at worst, *Realpolitik*.

This double standard—"value rationality" within, "purpose rationality" without—proved highly useful in facilitating underground operations in enemy–occupied or "White" areas during the first and second civil wars or the Sino-Japanese war, facilitating *les convenances des alliances*, the formulation of slogans to fit the audience, the systematic infiltration and manipulation of "front" (or "gray") organizations, and so forth.

Thus Liu was quite prepared to cater to the demands of client groups whom he in no way condoned as well as those he sanctioned, if expedient to winning their support. If an indigenous guerrilla group demanded booty as its price for collaboration in an expedition against Japan, they should get it.[9] Similarly, Liu was prepared "actively and energetically" to lead the labor union that he had helped organize in strikes for higher wages when he deemed their demands unwise, even "doomed to failure" under prevailing economic conditions, hoping thereby to rouse the workers to an awareness of shared interests.[10] Mao, in contrast, seems to have had a more absolute and monolithic concept of truth—certainly this was the case during the Cultural Revolution, when his moral standards were projected through Chinese history—but the tendency was also discernible before that.

Although Liu recognized as legitimate the pursuit of plural values (with certain qualifications), two seemed more fundamental than the others: politics and economics. Economics was essentially concerned with production for the improvement of living standards. Economic desires were "universal," and also most "important" for human existence; after all, people everywhere always need to eat, sleep, and clothe themselves. Yet political questions are "higher" than economic questions because they must encompass a wide range of discrete economic interests. In fact, the satisfaction of economic interests had no moral significance unless people were thereby brought to an understanding of the broader political ramifications. Thus, Liu says:

> All the economic demands of the masses must be integrated with political or cultural demands. When the masses begin to take action on one simple demand, we must lead the masses in fields related to their action on this simple demand so that they can better understand a series of problems and further push their actions to a still higher stage.

By "raising the economic demands to political demands, raising local demands to state and national demands," the masses are brought to a "higher" conception of their interests. Only the party is fully qualified to handle "political" questions, because only the party has the combination of synoptic vision necessary to aggregate diverse particular interests together with the moral self-discipline to renounce personal self-interest on behalf of the public weal. Contrary to the Red Guard accusations that Liu placed "economics in command," Liu was no less inclined than Mao to underwrite the primacy of politics. Although the two men's conceptions of politics differed, there were significant parallels.[11]

Liu's distinction between politics and economics and other apolitical pursuits contained two more far-reaching implications. First, his basically favorable attitude toward the division of labor inclined him to grant considerable autonomy to the economy, compared to other functional subsystems. Wide latitude could be permitted for the pursuit of avocational interests outside the party, provided such interests were not permitted to penetrate the party's sacred boundaries and thereby distort its synoptic vision of the whole. A "line of demarcation" thus had to be drawn, creating an insulated elite subculture known as "party life." Beyond that line, instrumentalism held sway: Deng's famous adage that whether a cat was black or white didn't matter as long as it caught mice is not a misleading paraphrase of the revisionist attitude.

To try to run the economy on the basis of political principles, Liu once declared, was a form of "feudalism." The economy should be run on the basis of economic principles, the press on the basis of sound journalistic principles (professionalized bylines, investigative journalism, feature articles). Scientists and artists should have ample ambit to function creatively within their respective spheres on the basis of principles appropriate to them. Such principles were assumed to be universal to artists, journalists, or scientists in all class structures, so learning from the experience of colleagues in other systems might thus be permitted or even encouraged. Liu seems to have been particularly interested in the applicability of managerial techniques from capitalist monopolies to socialist enterprises. In the name of subsystem autonomy, he at one time or another endorsed merit-based wage differentials, preservation of a private sector in industry, a lease-back arrangement similar to the "responsibility field system" in agriculture, expansion of markets, advertising and market research to promote retail sales, and even restoration of the stock market.

Second, tolerance outside the party implied discipline within it in order to preserve devotion to the public interest and unimpeachable personal morality. In fact, the more relaxed the party's socioeconomic regulation, the more rigorous its internal discipline had to be. This accounts for the paradoxical contrast between the relatively liberal economic and cultural policies pursued during the post-Leap recovery period and the draconian enforcement of cadre discipline during the same period. The most authoritative studies of the Socialist Education Movement (or "Four Cleans") find Liu Shaoqi to have consistently pursued a very hard line indeed ("apparently 'left,' but actually right," according to Mao).[12] The sanctions Liu endorsed did not include mass criticism, which would have violated the "line of demarcation" between mass and elite, but were very severe nonetheless. Based on his own field investigations and the more intensive involvement of his wife Wang Guangmei at Taoyuan Brigade, he concluded that two-thirds of the countryside had fallen under the sway of "bad people." To root out the corrupt, he advocated infiltration by outside work teams on a clandestine basis, confidential interviews with informants critical of the local leadership, intensive grilling of suspects, and the imposition of strict penalties (including fines) against those found to be "unclean." All this should proceed within a long-term time frame that foresaw continual pressure upon sequential adversaries for years to come. The movement was, however, prematurely brought to a close by Mao's decision in December 1965 to relieve pressure on lower-level cadres and turn the movement against the "small handful" at the top, including Liu Shaoqi himself—marking the onset of the Cultural Revolution.

Probably the main cause of the Cultural Revolution was Mao himself: He ignited the spark that started a prairie fire. This verdict of the Party Central Committee in its June 1981 Resolution on Party History is supported by a preponderance of available evidence. Mao's prestige was such that once he had publicly endorsed rebellion, it became legitimate for everyone with a grievance to join in, and the movement proliferated very rapidly. But to say that Mao was the main cause is not to say that he was the only cause; he was a necessary but not sufficient cause. A spark will not set a blaze without dry tinder. Actually, mass mobilization had already begun to get out of control during the "Fifty

Days" in June-July 1966, before Mao made his position public. True, the party would probably have brought the situation under control in the course of the summer if Mao had not repudiated the acting leadership of the CCP and endorsed the Red Guards. But the popular reaction to the opportunity to rise against the acting leadership was unexpectedly vigorous. Although Mao had been trying to mobilize the masses for a year, he was unable to do so until the Party Center sent out work teams. It seems fair to argue in that light that the "revisionist" regime, effective though it was in the regeneration of the economy, aroused widespread and combustible feelings of dissatisfaction.

The basis for that dissatisfaction was the elitism of Liuist revisionism already alluded to above. China had achieved levels of economic equality that were impressive in comparison with most other countries in the world, but politically it was a hierarchical society with strict penalties against dissent. That rankled, particularly in the light of the radicalized version of Mao's thoughts then being disseminated in his "little red book." The party's emphasis upon maintaining its purity behind a line of demarcation gave rise to arrogance and insulation from the masses, leading to polarization in a context of mobilization. The evidence for hypothesizing such submerged social strain is the enormous groundswell of support for the mass criticism of elites that ensued, resulting in easily the most sweeping purge since Liberation. This was particularly impressive in view of the fact that critics of authority still had to reckon with the possibility that their attack might fail, with the authorities surviving to retaliate. Second, the "revolutionary masses" themselves articulated this critique of Liuist revisionism—Mao himself remained publicly silent about Liu Shaoqi, and although it became possible to infer that he did not support him, it was the Red Guards themselves who articulated the critique. Although that critique was greatly exaggerated and often inaccurate or misleading, it was not without foundation.

It is not implausible to argue that the post-Mao reform regime represents a continuation of the revisionist tendency in Chinese politics. It was, after all, led by Deng Xiaoping, erstwhile "number two party person in authority taking the capitalist road," along with many other cadres who had been purged because they had been associated with Liu Shaoqi and the revisionist platform. The reformers went to the trouble to rehabilitate Liu posthumously and to republish a number of his best-known books, with particular application to party rectification. More than that, the same general posture toward innovation seems to have re-emerged, consisting of open-minded experimentalism with regard to the economy, but a much more cautious stance concerning the role of the party elite, which has once again tended to withdraw for internal rectification and "self-cultivation." Any form of political reform that might abridge the party's carefully insulated hegemony is pursued very cautiously. On the other hand, the economic reforms timidly experimented with in the early 1960s have been much more boldly implemented in Mao's absence, including the responsibility system in agriculture and to some extent in industry, the policy of opening to the outside world, the spread of the market. Revival of the idea of subsystem autonomy has given new hope to artists, scientists, and other professionals for protection against political interference in the pursuit of their chosen vocations.

THE CULTURAL REVOLUTION

As an event that has been compared to the Holocaust in its traumatic impact,[13] the Chinese Great Proletarian Cultural Revolution has continued to preoccupy the minds of those involved, giving an over-the-shoulder, reflexive character to the reforms introduced subsequently. Like the policies introduced during the iconoclastic euphoria of the

Cultural Revolution, many of the reforms seemed to need no justification other than the fact that they reversed the policies of the last ten years. But the wholly negative official depiction of the Cultural Revolution in post-Mao China belies the complexity of its impact on the reforms. That impact may be seen on at least two levels. On the obvious level, it provided a springboard for policies that reversed policies of scant intrinsic popularity that had been driven into the ground. On a much more implicit level, those relatively few Cultural Revolution policies that had successfully tapped a wellspring of popular support tended to be incorporated into reform policies.

In the absence of any effectively functioning mechanism for registering different popular options the foregoing propositions are difficult to demonstrate conclusively, and will instead be buttressed by an argument that is plausible but not irrefutable. That argument is that the "mass line" does provide a crude yet perceptible indication of the tenor of public opinion, which may move them to change their policies, provided their own interests are not adversely affected. The evidence for this is in the rhetoric used by those elites to justify policy changes and the absence of readily available alternative explanations for such changes. It is, of course, to be anticipated that those mass demands that coincide with elite interests will be responded to with greatest alacrity; those mass demands that conflict with elite interests may be expected to be ignored, unless they are very strong.

At the time Hua Guofeng came to power as Mao's personally designated successor in September 1976, there was every expectation, among both his supporters and his future political adversaries, that his tenure was secure and likely to be long. Deng himself said in a congratulatory letter that he looked forward to a long period of stability because of Hua's relative youth. As the first to occupy all three strategic positions in the party-state leadership—

Chairman of the party, Premier of the state, and chief of the Military Affairs Commission—his position seemed unassailable. Yet within about two years he had been pushed into a politically passive position, and within five he had been dismissed from the leadership altogether. The chief beneficiary of Hua's political demise was Deng Xiaoping, who had helped engineer it, as Hua himself correctly anticipated that he would. The way that Deng performed this feat of political legerdemain was to differentiate himself subtly from Hua on several key political issues, thereby appealing to unattached political constituencies (both cadres and masses) for their support. That he was successful in doing so is testimony to the fact that cadres and masses had emerged from the Cultural Revolution with some strong policy preferences, to which his rival failed to appeal.

The first of these issues concerned the role of the leader. Mao had encouraged a personality cult to develop around his public persona and role as an ideological fount; he then exploited that cult to purge any political actor who disagreed with him, and to raise high any whose services he deemed useful (e.g., the Gang of Four), regardless of whether his colleagues concurred. During the Cultural Revolution, his "thoughts" were encapsulated in a small book of epigraphs, and the sole criterion for political legitimacy became whether a given policy or set of political arrangements agreed with Mao's "thoughts" as expressed in his writings or in his "latest instructions." Hua Guofeng agreed with that criterion, as he publicly indicated in his February 1977 "two whatevers" formula: "Whatever decisions Chairman Mao makes we firmly support and whatever Chairman Mao instructs we unwaveringly follow"—with which Deng explicitly (albeit not publicly) disagreed at the time. In one of his first decisions upon seizing power from the Gang of Four, Hua also opted to build a large public mausoleum to house Mao's sarcophagus in the center of Tiananmen Square and placed himself in charge of the committee to edit the remainder of Mao's *Selected Works.* That Hua had a sincere personal devotion to the dead Chairman should not be denied, but he also expected to profit politically from such posthumous expressions of regard. By closely associating himself with Mao—in dozens of public portraits depicting the two chairmen together and in visits to places associated with Mao's legendary career—Hua made a clear bid to become the keeper of the sacred flame, high priest of the cult, and authorized exegete of Mao's thought. Not only was the fifth volume of Mao's *Selected Works* published in record time, with a proprietary foreword by Hua, but a large number of selections were published in the press.

Deng managed to identify himself as an opponent of the cult while avoiding any explicit opposition to Mao or his thought, which would have violated a persisting taboo. He did so by quoting Mao's words in support of a pragmatic rather than a dogmatic criterion of truth, and by explicitly confronting the supposition that Mao's thoughts were infallible to reasonable counterarguments.

These tactics succeeded in generating both cadre and demonstrable mass support. At the same time, Deng made his disinterest in either Mao's cult or position clear. While this disclaimer may not have been altogether sincere, Deng has at least assiduously avoided the trappings of the cult. Indeed, he made the restoration of collective leadership one of the top political priorities of the reforms, and that pledge has not been in vain. The institutions of collective leadership have revived, as indicated by the heightened frequency with which the Party Congress, the NPC, the CPPCC, and their various standing committees (the Central Committee, the NPC Standing Committee, and so forth) meet. New agencies of collective leadership—the Central Advisory Commission, the Central Disciplinary Inspection Commission—were created and staffed, and although the idea of introducing a check-and-balance relationship among them came to naught, their creation has perhaps resulted in a wider dispersal of power.

At least formally, executive power was also dispersed among several: Deng as chair of the Military Affairs Commission, Hu Yaobang (now Zhao Ziyang) as Secretary General of the CCP, Zhao Ziyang (now Li Peng) as Premier of the State Council, Li Xiannian (now Yang Shangkun) as Chief of State, Peng Zhen (now Wan Li) as Chairman of the Standing Committee of the National People's Congress. It must be conceded that a continuing discrepancy between formal position and informal power has meant that the collectivization of power has been more nominal than actual, but in time informal power may more closely approximate the formal distribution of offices.

Another issue in which there was a reversal of Cultural Revolution policy was the party's attitude toward intellectuals, formal education, and the cultural sector. All ruling Communist parties have perhaps harbored at least suspicions toward this sector, which characteristically threatens to challenge the party's claim to a monopoly on truth. But in China that suspicion was carried over to persecution that was particularly severe, reaching its acme during the Cultural Revolution. Partly because intellectuals were an elite during a period of emphasis on egalitarianism and mass conformity, partly because intellectuals tended to challenge Mao's infallibility claims, they were subjected to mass struggle and typically sent to the countryside to do manual labor, or even in some cases to labor reform camps. In parallel speeches to a national science conference in the spring of 1978, Hua expressed in milder form a continuation of Maoist suspicion of the intellectual community, while Deng implicitly called for emancipation of the intellectuals, making the novel claim that those who worked with their minds were also members of the proletariat. During the so-called Beijing Spring period from 1978 through much of 1979, the reformers voiced the slogan "emancipation of the mind" and called for a revival of the "double hundred." "Let a hundred flowers bloom, let a hundred schools of thought contend."

Certainly it must be conceded that the reformers have not remained altogether consistent in their attitudes toward the intellectual community. In fact, a cleavage has opened in the reform movement between those who place top priority on the "double hundred" and those who stress the "four fundamental principles." The less permissive group within the reform leadership continues to draw a direct causal connection between heterodox intellectual discussion and spontaneous mass movements deemed threatening to the established order—as became particularly clear during the December 1986 student protest movement and the elite backlash to it in the first three months of 1987. Despite such indications of continuing ambivalence toward the intellectual community, science and technology have been given much higher priority in the modernization program and formal school has been acknowledged as the necessary means to that end; educational credentials are even being gradually incorporated into the recruitment of party and state cadres. This represents a reversal of Cultural Revolution priorities and a revision to the prerevolution pattern in which educational and political upward mobility tended to correlate.

A third important ramification of the Cultural Revolution is the renunciation, with qualification, of class struggle and the mass movement. During the Cultural Revolution, the grand climax of all mass movements, class struggle was construed in a free-hand way that legitimated factional warfare, economic disruption, even assaults upon the party-state apparatus, all of which was extremely damaging to the interests, even the lives, of both masses and cadres. Class struggle has been retained in principle in order to justify the suppression of "enemies of the people" (i.e., political dissidents) and mass mobilization has occasionally been revived—as in the 1981 campaign against bourgeois liberalization, the brief 1982-1983 campaign against spiritual pollution, or the 1987 campaign against bourgeois liberalization—in order to repress certain social trends for which the regime has discovered no better antidote (although mass mobilization does not seem to be particularly effective either). Yet these recourses to class struggle and mass mobilization are perceptibly milder than in the past, perhaps because they are being managed by cadres who suffered their consequences in the past. Although the Cultural Revolution did not entirely discredit the mass campaign, it became such an embarrassment as to seriously complicate implementation.[14]

The shadow side of the Cultural Revolution consists of those elements of the movement that did succeed in tapping a reservoir of unmet needs for which there is continuing popular demand. According to subsequent interviews with former participants, conducted in Hong Kong, the main such element was a vague but real yearning for greater personal freedom, whose positive aspect has since been articulated in recurrent calls for greater democracy, and whose negative aspect has taken the form of a cleavage between masses and elites, or between the young and the old. This cleavage tends to erupt in spontaneous protest movements that inherit some of the anarchic iconoclasm of the Cultural Revolution, such as the fall 1985 demonstrations against the Japanese commercial invasion, or the protest movement in favor of democracy and reform that swept China's major cities and campuses in the fall of 1986. The reaction of the leadership to this unwelcome legacy has been to forbid—with imperfect success—the most disruptive features of such movements such as big-character posters, unofficial publications, or the notion that there are "people in the party taking the capitalist road"; to coopt other aspects (for example, the antibureaucratic animus seems to have been integrated into the campaign against cadre corruption), and to respond in good faith to still others. For example, the clampdown on Democracy Wall was immediately followed by the introduction of multiple-candidacy elections to local people's congresses, and there has been a considerable effort to retire aging veterans and replace them with younger cadres. Yet popular demand for the freedom once euphorically experienced in the chaotic melee of the Cultural Revolution has not been sated by the official response.

CONCLUSION

China's post-Mao reform movement, moving cautiously ahead without a clear picture of its ultimate destination, may look back at three homes: the Golden Fifties, when ideological and economic objectives seemed happily to coincide; the post-Leap revisionist period, when China began to experiment with its own eclectic blend of socialism; and the Cultural Revolution, which seemed to sound the death knell of Maoist socialism and open the way to much bolder experimentation than ever before with unorthodox alternatives.

The 1950s represent above all the sense of elite solidarity, vigor, and optimism that the party veterans would like to recover after ten years of catastrophe and the "three crises" of faith. More specific guidelines to the post-Mao era the fifties cannot provide, however, for any return to New Democracy would deny the need for socialization of the means of production and tend to give rise to a national identity crisis, and a return to the 8th Party Congress would succeed in recapturing only a fleeting moment of intra-elite calm without providing a clue to the solution of contemporary China's political and economic problems.

The revisionist period and the Cultural Revolution do furnish more substantative guidelines for the reformers, though they sometimes point in different directions. Whereas revisionist experiments provided many helpful suggestions to the economic reformers, post-Mao China has long since transcended revisionism and can no longer look back to those policies for specific suggestions. If the interpretation of the revisionist role in kindling the Cultural Revolution offered here is correct, however, the revisionist experience does provide a timely warning: economic modernization in the context of political rigidity and elitism is conducive to strain, which may explode under propitious circumstances. The shadow impact of the Cultural Revolution has been to reinforce that sense of strain by fostering a sense of popular entitlement and resentment of elites.

Yet the general tendency has been more and more to fall back into the revisionist pattern, willy-nilly. The elimination of mass mobilization, or at least the tendency in that direction, tends to exacerbate elite insulation by removing an occasion for elite-mass interaction on the level of values, outside of the daily, vocational, means-end context. There have been other attempts to permit feedback from the masses, first in the Beijing Spring or Democracy Wall movement, later in the introduction of multiple-candidacy elections. But these forums both proved too effervescent and unpredictable for the tastes of shell-shocked Cultural Revolution survivors, and the general tendency has been to reduce mass participation in politics to a purely ceremonial role. Deng's Four Cardinal Principles, introduced in response to cadre pressure in early 1979, are designed to protect the party, Mao's thought, socialism, the dictatorship of the proletariat—all of these hallowed institutions should be respected and obeyed without question. The party rectification movement launched at the 12th Party Congress in September 1982 thus spurned all Cultural Revolution innovations, such as open-door rectification or any form of mass monitoring of elites, to revert to a highly traditional approach involving elaborate preparations, rotational training classes held under the auspices of work teams, and the study of many central documents. While it must be conceded that there has been an attempt to breathe new life into the party through the appointment of younger and better educated cadres and the concomitant retirement of selected senior cadres, changes in the underlying structure have been minimal. The focus of innovation has passed from the party to the economy, placing the party in a relatively passive position.

The persisting belief in the party's moral superiority, in the context of the rising material prosperity of the masses outside the party, must pose a dilemma that the party has not had to face since Liberation: the prospect of a noncommunist upper class rivaling local party cadres in wealth, prestige, and perhaps even in power. There is obviously a mutual attraction between the two, with the new middle class needing party cadres to clear the way of political obstacles and facilitate economic growth, and cadres needing the new middle class as a source of dynamism. Yet such a symbiotic relationship is also filled with peril for a party that still defines virtue in terms of maintaining an undefiled elite subculture. Traditionally informal cadre contact with the independent middle class has been defined as corruption. There are, in fact, reports that many of the new rising middle classes are cadres or former cadres who saw their opportunity and took it.

One of the general tendencies of industrializing countries has been to obscure the distinction between politics and economics. Even in a free market system such as the United States, in which the doctrine of the "invisible hand" inhibits political meddling in the economy, interpenetration has grown like topsy-turvy since the Great Depression in the form of government regulation of fiscal and monetary policies, including taxes, wage-price control and so forth, while the private sector has in turn exerted its influence over relevant public policy through lobbies, PACs, and ad campaigns. State socialist systems have not been as troubled by this interpenetration as have been democratic political theorists. According to Marxist thinkers, it is to be assumed that politics is an expression—according to some, a mere reflection—of economic forces, and of course the government may be expected to manage the economy. In fact, in the classic centrally planned economy (CPE), the government has proprietary rights over the national economy and manages it like a large firm. The problem arises when a sizable private sector-and-market mechanism is introduced into a planned economy. In part it is a problem of definition and identity: What is capitalist? What is socialist? How far can the reforms go without trespassing the line of demarcation? The tactical problem is what Chinese leaders refer to as the bird-in-cage relationship—how can the economy be managed to unleash private incentive without loss of control? How can it be controlled without suffocating initiative?

Today's reformers are much more receptive to experiments in mixing market and plan than were the Maoists, or even their antecedent revisionists, and much more open-minded about learning from relevant Eastern European or even Western experiences. At the same time, their endeavor to limit the penetration of market-driven forces and mentalities to the economic realm seems as ill-fated as Zhang Zhidong's *fin de siècle* attempt to draw a distinction between Chinese values and Western instrumental knowledge. (*"Zhongxue wei ti, xixue wei yong."*) Spillover tendencies already abound. Technology transfer is, of course, officially encouraged, under the perhaps naive assumption that it can be detached from its cultural infrastructure. Lacking institutionalized avenues for interest intermediation, market spillover takes the form of bribes and other forms of "spiritual pollution." Cultural spillover takes the form of an influx of commercial consumerism and Western popular culture, which has made marked inroads into the elite subculture because of the elites' greater access to the West, but is noticeable at every social stratum.

In sum, the revisionist attempt to maintain a functional division of labor between politics and economics, between party elite and its social environment, will probably prove untenable in the long run. Three alternative lines seem open at this juncture. The first would be to abandon the functional division of authority and reassert "politics in command," reaffirming the party's special role and imposing it on the rest of society. This seems to be the preference of the party's ascendant left wing at this writing, but is likely to be short-lived in view of its predictably negative economic repercussions. The second, most challenging, alternative would be to redefine the party's mission and ideology to offer inspiring leadership to the rest of society while at the same time providing efficient and flexible economic management. Such an alternative might build on the party's vanguard traditions and quest for political virtue, taking advantage of the growing nexus between intellectuals and party cadres to foster a creative synthesis. There have been promising forays in this direction over the past several years, but typically they have been stymied by inhibitions against violating Marxist orthodoxy. The third, and perhaps the most likely; alternative would be for the party to attempt neither to fight nor actively to steer the perplexing socioeconomic transformation now under way, but rather to cling to its present status and attempt to adapt to changes on a pragmatic basis as that seems necessary. This would foresee the party's gradual decline over the long term from its vanguard role to a more passive position vis-a-vis society, managing crises as they emerge rather than seeking to maintain a distinct elite subculture and lead society toward some foreordained Valhalla.

NOTES

1. Only a few illustrative examples can be listed here: Richard Baum, ed., *China's Four Modernizations* (Boulder, CO: Westview Press, 1979); Elizabeth J. Perry and Christine Wong, eds., *The Political Economy of Reform in Post-Mao China* (Cambridge, Mass: Harvard University Press, 1985); Jack Gray and Gordon White, eds., *China's New Developmental Strategy* (London: Academic Press, 1982); Stephen Feuchtwang and Athan Hussain, eds., *The Chinese Economic Reforms* (London: Croom Helm, 1983); Bulletin of Concerned Asian Scholars, ed., *China from Mao to Deng* (New York: M.E. Sharpe, 1983); and Peter Moody, Jr., *Chinese Politics after Mao* (New York: Praeger, 1983).
2. See Ronald Morse, ed., *The Limits of Reform in China* (Washington, DC: The Asia Program, Wilson Center, Smithsonian Institution, 1982).
3. See, however, Tang Tsou, "The Historic Change in Direction and Continuity with the Past," *China Quarterly* (hereinafter *CQ*), 98 (June 1984): 320-47; also Stuart Schram, "To Utopia and Back: A Cycle in the History of the CCP," *CQ* 87 (September 1981): 420ff.
4. See the Editorial Board, "Shenqie Huainian Deng Zihui Tongzhi" [Deeply cherish comrade Deng Zihui's memory], *Nongcong Gongzuo Tongxin* [Agricultural work bulletin] 5 May 1981:7-9 Qiang Yuangan and Lin Bangquang, "Wo Guo Nongye Jitihua de Zhuozue Zuzhizhe Deng Zihui" [Our country's outstanding organizer of agricultural collectivization], *Xinhua Wenzhai* 7 (1981): 187-90; both as cited in Thomas Bernstein, "Reforming China's Agriculture," unpublished paper presented to the conference "To Reform the Chinese Political Order," Harwichport, Mass, June 1984.
5. See Roy Grow's unpublished manuscript, "Soviet Models in China: Kao Kang and the Politics of Economic Development" (Waltham, Mass: n.d.); also Lawrence Sullivan, "Leadership and Authority in the CCP: Perspectives from the 1980s," unpublished manuscript, 1985.
6. Liu Shao-Ch'i, "How to Be a Good Communist" (July 1939), in *Collected Works* [hereinafter *CW*] (Hong Kong: Union Research Institute, 1969), vol. 1.

7. In a characteristic aside when discussing the reform of medical services, Mao observed that "when making an examination, the doctor always puts on a gauze mask, regardless of what kind of patient he is dealing with....I think that the main reason is that he is afraid of being infected by other people." Mao, "Instruction on Health Work" (June 26, 1965), translated in *Current Background* 892 (October 21, 1969): 20.

8. Liu, "On the Party," *CW* II:41.

9. Liu, "Work Experiences in the North China War Zone" (1938), translated in Henry G. Schwarz, *Liu Shao-ch'i and "People's War"*: A Report on the Creation of Base Areas in 1938 (Lawrence, Kansas: Center for East Asian Studies, University of Kansas, 1969), 33-34.

10. Liu, "Training in Organization and Discipline," *CW* I: 400.

11. See Graham Young, "Liu Shaoqi on Party Leadership," (seminar paper, Australian National University, Contemporary China Center, May 8, 1979).

12. See Richard Baum and Frederick C. Teiwes, *Ssu-ch'ing: The Socialist Education Movement of 1962-66* (Berkeley: University of California, Center for Chinese Studies, 1968); and Richard Baum, *Prelude to Revolution* (New York: Columbia University Press, 1975).

13. "Many people in West Germany in the 1960s once asked their parents, 'What were you doing during the Nazi years?' We, who experienced the 'Cultural Revolution,' may well ask ourselves, 'What were we doing then?'" "'Cultural Revolution' Has Lessons for All," *China Daily* (Beijing), August 29, 1986, translated in *Foreign Broadcast Information Service: Daily Report, China* [hereinafter *FBIS-CHI,*] K5.

14. Thus, for example, the sponsors of the 1983 Spiritual Pollution-campaign avoided any comparison with the Cultural Revolution. As Deng Liqun put it, while answering questions raised at a meeting with *Associated Press* reporters, "There are worries among friends abroad that the party consolidation might be superficial or that it might take the form of the 'Cultural Revolution.'" But most of those leading the campaign had themselves been subjected to such methods during the Cultural Revolution and had suffered enough, he submitted: "We will not do unto others what they did unto us." *Xinhua,* 14 November 1983, in *FBIS-CHI,* November 2, 1983, K2.

FOUR

THE END
OF THE CHINESE
REVOLUTION
A LEADERSHIP DIVERSIFIES

Lynn T. White III

Revolutions do end. Less has been written, however, about their closings than their beginnings.[1] Maybe this is because they enter with bangs and leave with whimpers, or because people who like them are reluctant to see them die, or because people who dislike them are reluctant to give up such a fecund occasion for complaint. Since Crane Brinton and before, there have been many tomes about revolutions' temporal structure, but these pay less attention to their patterns of passing than to their birth and middle age.[2] Some revolutions (such as Mexico's) have had widely spaced periods of popular violence, punctuated by long doldrums (as under Porfirio Diaz). A revolution often comes in many convulsions separated by lengthy intervals, so that its unity as an event can fall into doubt. Yet as an ideal tradition, even while it winds down, it can still mean much to the revolutionaries. The literature on intentions in this field has a natural tendency to become dominant; and it needs to be balanced by studies of incentives, structures, and personnel—even though there is no reason to exclude any analytic approach, normative or behavioral, that throws light on the subject. Part of the difficulty in talking about revolutions, and most especially about their endings, arises from the need to talk about concrete factors, not just ideals, lest revolutions be mistaken for seminars.

This chapter, approaching the Chinese case, suggests a method to meet this need: Revolutions are defined in terms of their leading political institutions and elites. In revolutions, it is always possible to identify groups of politicians—sometimes disciplined by parties, sometimes more diffuse, often with differing structures along these lines—that conflict broadly and violently with each other, at both national and local levels. Maybe the difference between revolutions and other full-scale modern civil wars is the degree to which the winning elite calls itself leftist or "revolutionary."[3] Even when a traditionalistic, avowedly antirevolutionary radical elite seizes state power (as in Spain during the 1930s), such events involve fiscal and military centralization. They always involve conflicts between broad types of local leaders. The narrowing of officials' backgrounds, as they run stronger coercive and tax institutions, is similar in all these events. It is as important as the particular ideological banner the winning set of politicians decides to unfurl, attempting to explain the rightfulness of a claim to state power.

We can deal with revolutions as movements, not just philosophies, if we are willing to center attention on their institutional leadership. A revolution narrows, in the name of national discipline, the range of leaders in the state elite. Then evidence of an opposite trend, if it arises, is evidence that the revolution is ending. Such a change of institutional personnel does not presage the end of revolution, nor does it follow afterward. It is, instead, an essential part of the wide correlation that, taken together, means the windup of a revolutionary era. New types of institutional leaders are good data to show this political change directly; they do not show a factor that contributes in some subsidiary way to a new order. Any order is behavioral, as well as normative.

This chapter will use both kinds of data together, because it uses a definition of the event that includes them both.

Before concentrating on the Chinese case, to see whether elite change in the PRC is now ending revolution there, it will be useful to scan earlier cases. Revolutions and other modern civil wars may be centralizing, homogenizing events; but in complex modern situations, a variety of different kinds of leaders is needed for efficiency at specialized tasks.[4] Comparison of China's case with revolutions that seem to have ended can normalize the evidence relevant to assessing the Chinese future.

ELITE RECRUITMENT IN REVOLUTIONS WITH HISTORICAL AFTERMATHS

The English Revolution that climaxed under Cromwell is still one of the best examples. Although China's revolution has been compared too exclusively with Russia's (and the failure of Sinologists before 1978 to predict fast PRC change derives largely from overreliance on Soviet precedents), China's case should also be likened to the English, French, and other revolutions. In Britain too, iconoclastic violence was followed by a widespread reconciliation between local elites. Neither the Anglo-Catholics nor the Puritans were liberal by choice, but their mutual tolerance grew (eventually) from mutual exhaustion in fighting one another. Each of these large elites found it could not fully or finally repress the other, even with complete formal control of the state's coercive powers.

Just eleven years after chopping off one king's head in 1649, the Puritans restored his son to the throne. During those eleven years, the House of Lords had been abolished; and conflict between different kinds of British leaders certainly continued after the Restoration, even as the blood spilled in a civil war had taught them violence could not achieve their purposes. As G.M. Trevelyan writes, on this era when diversity became more legitimate than before:

> The hard-drinking fox hunters of the manor house hated the Presbyterians of the neighboring town not because they held the doctrines of Calvin, but because they talked through their noses, quoted Scripture instead of swearing honest oaths, and voted Whig instead of Tory.... Puritanism in the day of its power had not made for orthodoxy."[5]

Voltaire is famous for remarking that, "The English have a hundred religions but just one sauce." The aftermath of the Puritan's radical revolution restored hereditary rights to wider elites, but it also confirmed powers in a Parliament that irked the later Stuarts (until new kings were found in the House of Orange, arriving with less full divine rights). As Christopher Hill puts it, "Politics ceased to be ideological: the job of government was to increase the wealth of the country."[6]

The rise of companies, protected by new laws and charters, diversified power away from government in Britain. A system of knighthoods based on merit paralleled the hereditary recruitment of elites, and the Commons became more important than the Lords. As Lawrence Stone writes,

> Although the Revolution ostensibly failed, although Monarchy, Lords, and Anglican Church were restored, ...something of the Revolution nevertheless survived. There survived ideas about religious toleration, about limitations on the power of the central executive to interfere with the personal liberties of the propertied classes, and about a policy based on the consent of a broad spectrum of society.... A Bill of Rights, a Toleration Act, and an annual Mutiny Act effectively restrained the repressive powers of the executive, and, together with further gains won by the common law judges, made the personal and political liberties of the English propertied classes the envy of eighteenth-century Europe....something which could serve as a model in other times and places.[7]

America's revolution was a continuation of the English one. A Boston minister, preaching on the exact anniversary of the beheading of Charles I, and still happy about it, a century later, intoned that, "Rulers have no authority from God to do mischief."[8] America's revolution may have been less obviously structured by status groups or classes than those in Europe, but it can be largely understood in terms of the politics of the heads of leading families. Faced with Washington's victories, some local elites migrated (remigrated) to Ontario or other royal domains. Among the families that stayed, ideas of nationality became mixed with revolutionary notions. In these early cases, as in later ones, the revolutions helped centralize tax and army infrastructures, but that process, building new patterns of action with new resources, was much slower than the expressions of opinion for and against it.

Intolerance, based on the revolutionary tradition, reached an official peak in John Adam's Sedition Law of 1798, which imposed a fine and imprisonment for "writing, printing, uttering, or publishing any false, scandalous, and malicious writing or writings against...the President of the United States with intent to defame...."[9] This law expired under its own terms in 1801. When the Federalists were turned out of the presidency, in the first major transfer of power between political elites in the U.S., all who had been convicted under the Act were pardoned by Thomas Jefferson. Efforts to dampen intolerance between slaveholding and mercantile American elites continued for decades. A further revolutionary outburst during the 1860s—in which both the Union and Confederate heads claimed faithfulness to different aspects of the revolutionary tradition—finally transformed the main American political cleavage to one that separated business magnates from populist leaders.[10] Over many later years, as a maturing legal tradition moderated conflicts among these changed elites, the winding down of the revolution allowed more kinds of people to take roles in governmental and unofficial organizations of power. Especially after the introduction of civil service exams (based on Chinese models), the routes of recruitment to government offices were made more diverse at least at low levels, for efficiency's sake.

The French Revolution of 1789 has suffered more researches than any other.[11] One of the great debates in this literature roils between historians who emphasize social classes as actors and those who stress the role of superstructural variables, especially groups of politicians. Yet there is a consensus that diverse French elites (however defined) fought less with each other under Napoleon than before. Alfred Cobban, after offering a nonclass analysis, quotes, and for once agrees with, the main historian who stresses the centrality of social classes, Georges Lefebvre:

> If...we look with an open mind on the society that emerged from the revolution, we will be most struck by the permanent elements in the French social pattern. We will see a society with many new elements it is true, but bearing on it like a palimpsest the inadequately effaced writing of the *ancien regime*..."United to what remained of the old noblesse," says Lefebvre, "[the bourgeoisie] constituted henceforth a landed aristocracy powerful enough to hold down, under its economic dictatorship, that rural democracy which it had in part created."[12]

Mistakes under the new regime made the old one seem less bad. After the violence in France (as after the Cultural Revolution in China), many of the local leaders who bitterly remembered unfair attacks against them were also embarrassed by memories of unfair attacks they had launched against others. Victims and perpetrators, after a multiphase reordering of politics, are largely the same people. As a writer named Baroud put it, "Tout le monde est pardonable quand tout le monde a besoin de pardon."[13]

Revolution has been a way for large leaderships, including local notables and family heads, to identify themselves and claim more resources. This definition may be useful, even when the social violence in revolutions is relatively intense and brief. Frenchmen stormed the Bastille and cut off their king's head in a revolution that affected the lifestyles of identifiable social groups. But a few years later, they stormed all Europe together, led by French officers from many backgrounds—any who claimed the new tradition— not just under a king, but under an emperor.

The revolution created divisions that lasted long, even though most of the internal violence took place within six years, 1789-95. These splits still influence elections, most obviously in geographical terms. But the centralization and reconciliation of elites is now an even more obvious legacy of the intermission between Bourbons. As Ezra Suleiman shows, Napoleon institutionalized, especially in the *grandes ecoles*, methods of recruiting official elites that rivaled the older universities. Suleiman repeats a question of Marc Bloch's: "What is a faculty of letters, if not, above all, a factory for producing professors, much as Polytechnique is a faculty for producing engineering and artillery officers?"[14] State sponsorship of new means of recruitment diversified and modernized the elite-forming institutions inherited from the old regime, after the period of chaos. Francois Furet was right to announce, "The revolution has ended."[15]

Comparisons between China's revolution and those in England, America, or France are less common than comparison with the Russian case. The USSR and PRC share Leninist traditions, and these nations' two revolutions have some similarities. It is easy, however, to forget that earlier revolutionary parties such as Cromwell's also attempted, with some success, to instill party discipline. Also, Leninists are more unified in wanting unity than in achieving it. China's communications and transport system in 1949 was not notably better than Russia's in 1917. China's per-capita income was apparently lower. Above all, Mao did not so thoroughly achieve Stalin's feat of replacing older, nonrevolutionary elites with a single official leadership in each sphere of social life. As Soviet sinologists accurately claim, China's revolution has been less complete than Russia's.[16]

Stalin actually killed a greater portion of Russia's leaders not subject to his control than Mao did. Even Stalin's later critics, such as Khrushchev, prospered under his system before he died. Many of Mao's current critics suffered badly in the Maoist era, and now they are running the PRC government. Under Gorbachev, there is a move toward greater "openness" (*glasnost*), as in China (where it is called *kaifang*). But the Soviet system has taken much longer—a quarter century longer, if the clock starts in 1953, when the strongest centralizing Soviet leader died—to begin a broadly comparable change in a parallel direction. The recovery of political diversification after Russia's revolution, especially after Stalin's "second revolution,"[17] has been slower than in other cases. The main reason is the thoroughness of state violence in Russia's most centralist and taxing period. The Soviet case is atypical, different from other revolutions, because of Stalin's thoroughness in replacing old local elites with new ones.

"Cadres," as Stalin said with his usual subtlety, "decide everything."[18]

The USSR's *nomenklatura* is a roster of offices whose incumbents require party approval. In Russia (and to a lesser extent in China, where this system was imported during the 1950s) regular vetting of promotions assured party control of cadres. But nonofficial elites still received respect in particular local and functional circles; and in the USSR now (as in China), regional and patron-client bonds are highly relevant to recruitment decisions made by the party's organization departments. Political loyalty is not necessarily preferred over technical expertise; now, in both large Communist countries, many are promoted on the basis of both their educational attainments and having political patrons.[19]

Bohdan Harasymiw, who has done the most detailed work on cadre recruitment in the USSR, notes that under

Brezhnev affirmative action for blue collar workers created a blockage of circulation into the Soviet party:

> Party members with higher education experienced a notable deceleration in their rate of growth under Brezhnev (7.8 percent per annum in 1966-71, 6.2 in 1971-6, and 5.1 in 1976-81).... The intelligentsia should be developing expectations of occupying high status political positions, in such a way fulfilling a directive role politically as well as socially.[20]

Stephen Fortescue, a student of Soviet scientists, indicates that technicians' roles "in the Soviet policy making process" are not such that they:

> dominate it or can impose their will on the political leadership. One would not expect to find such power in any pluralist system. Their role in the policy making process is based on firmer foundations than the purely capricious good will of the party leadership, and to that extent it has a pluralist character.[21]

In the USSR, where Stalin's revolution repressed the diversity of leadership longer than in other countries, calls for modernity place constraints on totalitarian power. As Moshe Lewin shows, "the Gorbachev phenomenon" arises not just from the whim of a single man who took Russia's leadership in the mid-1980s, but from the political assertion, finally, of diverse, specialized, educated constituencies, whose development was long stunted by Stalinist police.[22]

RECRUITMENT OF BUREAUCRATIC ELITES IN THE 1980s

As in most countries where dictatorship remains a sometime ideal, the state in China claims a right to determine or approve all elite recruitment.[23] Official criteria for promotion have nonetheless differed at various times, places, and bureaucratic levels. Often these variations come from basic policy disagreements between leaders. More important, any recruitment (or other) policies that survive as maintainable over long periods are deeply influenced by unofficial forces, resources, and local intentions in society. The main point of this chapter is that in China, as in the other cases of revolution mentioned above, memories of violence have led to greater tolerance among leaders. Elite recruitment is the most obvious test of this change.[24]

The main slogan for cadre recruitment in recent years has called for "four changes" (si hua). These are policies to make cadres "revolutionary" (geming hua), "young" (nianqing hua), college-educated/"intellectual" (zhishi hua), and "professional" (zhuanye hua).[25]

All but the first of these four criteria for choosing new local leaders can be easily measured in quantitative terms: age to measure youth, the number of years of college to measure intellectual or "cultural" level, and the number of years a cadre has spent at a particular vocation to measure professionalism.[26]

A hard-line editorialist in 1986 could still write, "Revolutionization is the political standard for using people (yong ren). It is the prerequisite (qianti) of the remaining three, as regards the need for cadres' political direction, political standpoint, and habits of political virtue and thought."[27] But no serious editorials or speeches about cadre recruitment now emphasize the political criterion alone. It remains important—and it remains indistinguishable from family connection as a basis for recruitment—but it is no longer the only legitimate practical litmus test for leadership. The bureaucracy is a sprawling, gawky, halting, real-world organization, not a Platonic abstraction. It is diverse, and what some of its members do has no necessary identity with what other members say (or do). Its leaders see China's problems differently.[28] An articulate member of a reformist Beijing "think tank," who has extensive policy making experience, averred that "anything in accord with the Four Modernizations" must by definition also pass the political test. "If you turn your back on these [modernizations], everything is fake."[29]

Of the PRC's twenty million cadres by mid-1985, 90 percent had been trained after 1949.[30] Retirement of the remaining "old cadres" was greatly speeded by policies adopted in 1982. "New cadres" (*xin ganbu*) took their places. By 1984, one hundred thousand young cadres had been given positions at the county level or above. Self-recommendation (*zijian*) for cadre positions was encouraged in some cities like Guangzhou by late 1985; people could apply for posts.[31] In practice, political connections remained important, as in all countries, but youth and education were now concurrent prerequisites for most good jobs, too.

In the "leadership groups" (about five top cadres) at the "county level" and above, from early 1982 to the end of 1985, nearly half a million new cadres were employed.[32] An even larger number had retired at these high-intermediate levels, under two different plans: *lixiu* and *tuixiu*. "*Lixiu*" retirement was generally reserved pre-1949 cadres only, because it was practically a bribe-for-withdrawal and had to be limited because of its cost to the state budget. *Lixiu* usually meant highly favorable treatment: promotion-on-retirement of one grade in bureaucratic rank, higher and continued salary after active service finished, extended access to secret documents whose circulation is not public, and continued benefits in travel, housing, coal allowances, and medical care. *Lixiu* military officers retained their right to wear uniforms, which confer prestige.[33]

Tuixiu retirement generally involved no promotion and only 80 percent of previous salary, with fewer prerequisites. It was analogous to retirement for noncadre workers and staff. *Lixiu* cost the state far more than *tuixiu*, but politically influential cadres were apparently reluctant to retire, without more incentives.[34] The distinction between the two kinds of retirement (and a similar difference between the treatment of party and nonparty rightists, after their 1979 rehabilitation[35]) reveals a continuing ambiguity about the two, political and technical, elites that are still needed to run

China's state. The retirements, like the rehabilitations, show the revolution changing.

Retirements and new appointments have sharply lowered the average age of active cadres. Comprehensive statistics on crucial high and middle levels have been published to show this. From 1982 and 1985, top cadres' average age dropped from 62 to 53 at the province level, from 56 to 41 at the prefecture level, and from 49 to 44 at the county level.[36] The sample constituted the "members of leadership groups" (*lingdao banzi chengyuan*) in all high PRC government offices, both central and local, under the State Council.

New cadres at these same high levels were also well schooled. Of all 1985 province or ministry leaders, 62 percent had university or vocational college training. And 55 or 54 percent, respectively, had that much education at the prefecture or county levels. The *People's Daily* vaguely averred that for all three levels, the increase had been "about 45" percentage points since 1982.[37] If this is true, and if "third echelon" educated people counted in these positions actually serve as main unit leaders,[38] then the state's recent efforts to recruit younger and better-educated cadres to its top jobs are impressive.[39]

Quick retirement policies affected high officials more systematically than low ones. And they reached limits, when the supply of old cadres willing to accept retirement dwindled. By September 1985, the "youthfulization" (*nianging hua*) of China's provincial governors and party secretaries was reportedly "completed." The average age of provincial governors was 55.6 years then, and of their party secretaries, 58 years.[40] Almost three-fifths of these important leaders were between the ages of fifty and sixty (thus born circa 1925-35, and educated near the middle of the century). Another 16 percent were younger than fifty. Only 26 percent were older than sixty. Many cadres in lower offices that they "led," and many of their retired "advisors," how-

ever, had more grey hair, and the influence that is traditionally supposed to accompany age in China.

In a metropolis like Shanghai, where 1,300 high bureau-
level (*juji*) pre-1949 cadres still led the city even above the
urban district level, 840 of them had been retired to the "second line" (*er xian*) by mid-1985.[41] In the country as a whole,
more than half of the two million pre-1949 cadres working
in 1982 had taken advantage of *lixiu* treatment by the end
of 1985.[42] By late 1986, when about 2 million pre-1949 CCP-
member state cadres were still alive, 1.2 million of them had
"left the first line of work" (*tuigu diyi xian*).[43] They were assured they would not lose their stipulated benefits, even if
they went to live abroad.[44]

The 13th Party Congress, held in the autumn of 1987,
sharply confirmed the semiretirement of elites that had led
the climax of China's revolution. Although the party as a
whole has been told by its leaders to undertake less detailed
management of practically all organizations, we should obviously look at recent patterns for joining the CCP, as well
as those for changing the state bureaucracy.

RECRUITMENT OF PARTY ELITES IN THE 1980s

The party's national leadership is formally constituted at
meetings of new central committees (CCs), of which there
have been three since the death of Mao Zedong: the
Eleventh CC in 1977, the Twelfth in 1982, and the Thirteenth
in 1987. At these times, new secretariats, politburos, and
politburo standing committees have also been elected. The
trends in cadre background by age, education, and
professionalism have generally been more linear than
irregular in the 1977-87 decade, so that comparison between
the Eleventh and Thirteenth CCs shows the pattern of
change in party leadership clearly.

The average age of CC members in 1977 was 66 years, but
a decade later it had dropped to 55. In the 1982-87 period
alone, this decrease in the Secretariat was 64 to 56; in the

Politburo, 72 to 64; and in the Standing Committee, 74 to 64 years.[45] The portion of college-educated CC members rose, from 1977 to 1987, from 26 percent to 73 percent. In this same decade, the ratio of college-educated Politburo members rose from 23 percent to 67 percent. Three crucial members of the Standing Committee (Hu Qili, Li Peng, and Yao Yilin) hold university degrees in engineering.

These changes do not mean that the new, better-educated, and younger top cadres are Johnnies-come-lately to the party, or that they lack personal political connections that help, along with expertise, to lay claims on cadreships. A prominent example is Premier Li Peng, who was mentioned above for his engineering expertise but is also the adoptive son of Zhou Enlai. Among other 1987 CC members, Marshal Yang Shangkun's brother rose to head the Army's Political Department, Marshal Nie Rongzhen's son-in-law became a minister, and Marshal Ye Jianying managed to bequeath a governorship to his son, a ministry to his son-in-law, and even the directorship of the Central Weather Bureau to his son-in-law's brother.[46] In less anecdotal terms: Only one member (4 percent) of the 1977 Politburo was known to have joined the CCP after Liberation—but a decade later, only four members (22 percent) had joined after 1949. The new party cadres were indeed radically younger, better-educated, and more professional, even though their political connections and histories of personal commitment were no more dubious than those of the generation they succeeded.

This should not be surprising, because the party is not the government. Also, top CCP leaders tried to recruit a greater diversity of new members, especially among young educated people. In 1983, the *People's Daily* bemoaned that: "The party's policy on admitting intellectuals is far from being realized. The reality is that many intellectuals are applying for admission into the party, and they are being refused."[47] Yet by the next year, the CCP journal, *Red Flag*, claimed that the difficulty of intellectuals getting into the party (*"ru dang nan"*) had been solved, though evidence on this point is very mixed.[48] Even while reporting accomplishments, *Red Flag* still deplored that:

> Some comrades, when judging the applications of intellectuals to the party, look first not at their actual performances, but at the history of their [family] origins (*chushen lishi*). They are still using the old criteria. Influenced by "taking class struggle as the key link," they tend to check ancestry back three generations (*cha zuzong sandai*). If the applicants have some overseas connections, it is even more difficult for their applications to be approved...Some party cadres prevent excellent intellectuals from getting into the CCP because of their selfishness and jealousy. They fear that if intellectuals enter the party, these will be "like tigers with wings," difficult to control. They fear [the intellectuals] will threaten their iron chairs (*tiejiao yi*). Some even declare openly, "You have culture; I have a party card. You have knowledge; I have a distinguished history. No matter how great you are, so long as you are not in the party, you are still under my leadership."[49]

In the first half of the 1980s decade, however, 580,000 professionals and technicians joined the CCP. As a portion of the party's whole membership (reaching 44,000,000 by mid-decade), this number was unimpressive. The new-member intellectuals tended, however, to be disproportionately in urban and important units. Also, the rate of their recruitment increased sharply from 8 percent of the new members in 1978, to 24 percent in 1982, to 27 percent in 1983, and to 40 percent by the first half of 1984.[50]

In 1983, only 4 percent of all party members had college educations. Those who were illiterate (about 14 percent) or had education at only the primary level exceeded half the party's membership. Efforts to change this pattern, particularly in the party groups of modern units, were nonetheless important by the mid-1980s. Many, though not all, educated youths were eager to join the party. At "key-point" schools such as Beijing or Qinghua universities, whose students by this time had to pass highly selective academic admissions tests, the number of seniors in the party increased from less than 3 percent "a few years ago" to between 20 and 30 percent by 1985. By this time, about 30 percent of college students were applying for membership; whereas a few years earlier, only "a few" applied.[51] In a survey of the 1986 freshman class at People's University, 82 percent averred they wanted to join party or league activities.[52] Evidence suggests that the best students at the most prestigious universities were, on average, less eager to become CCP members than were other students[53], but editorials inviting more intellectuals to join also encouraged applications.

Rural cadres also deserve treatment here. Most of Chinese politics, in either the party or the government, occurs below the high, generally urban levels that have been discussed thus far. In county-level departments (*ke*, at *xianji*) and all inferior tiers by 1986, the party's Organization Department emphasized that "the popular masses" (*renmin Qunzhong*) should be able to "choose" their own cadres.[54] There is a tendency for researchers and governments outside China to emphasize leaders who have high ranks, as if local trends do not shape national politics, and as if legal sovereignty defines the only community worthy of scholars' attention or important to people. This approach is too narrow. (Alfred Cobban, studying the French Revolution for instance, insists that larger sets of leaders—though not economically defined social classes—are the people to see as important in revolutionary politics.)[55] Relevant elites include local notables whose names seldom appear in print.

Party organization departments used many pressures, and few incentives, in the 1980s to oust low-level cadres. These departures of officials were generally not voluntary—and when compensation of the lixiu sort was too expensive even for old cadres (lao ganbu, i.e., pre-1949 officials), some of them refused to retire. In some jurisdictions, such as Chongqing city, the "youthfulization" policy was bolstered by mass dismissals (*mianqu*) of cadres for bad performance. In that city, by November 1986, two hundred cadres at the bureau, county, and section levels were ousted from their "iron chairs" (*tie yizi*) and only 5.6 percent of these were "new cadres."[58] Some were demoted; others left government service entirely.

At still lower levels, this policy (like others coming from Beijing for decades) meant little. The rules for retirement worked better in urban work units than in rural or agricultural places. A 1986 report offers a revealing anecdote on the difficulty of encouraging withdrawals: A village in 1986 got a "new" party branch with five members; but they had, among them, just eight teeth.[57] The moral of this story, reported nationally, was that old people should withdraw from power, but clearly, the situation did not always turn out that way. What was happening at high political levels, as the revolution began to wind down, was crucially important for China's future, even though it does not fully reflect what was happening everywhere.

RECENT RECRUITMENT OF ARMY OFFICERS AND ECONOMIC MANAGERS

Top soldiers, who in China are all party members, are surely of greater political import than other party members at equivalent ranks, and top managers of state companies increasingly have more independence and resources than other officials to influence politics in China's many localities. These two groups deserve special attention because of their special powers, even though they often also fall into types that are covered above.

June Dreyer's recent research on the demobilization of leaders from the Army, suggests that far fewer officers retired than Beijing wished.[58] Exhortations to superannuate old officers did not lead to their universal departure; where there was policy smoke, there was not necessarily much behavioral fire. But organizational changes in the Army created occasions for high planners in Beijing to encourage the old soldiers to fade away.

The merger of China's eleven military districts (*da jun qu*) into only seven, in October 1985, was supposed to accompany a reduction, by half, of personnel in their "leading groups."[59] The average age of the new districts' groups of leading officers was reduced from 65 to 57 years (from 1982 to 1986).[60] Fully 51 percent of these new officers had college educations, and within a year, further inducements had raised this educated portion to 55 percent. The average age of top officers in these military districts dropped, between 1982 and 1986, from 65 to 57.

In the General Staff, Political Department, Logistics Department, and the commission that runs China's defense industries, the average age was lowered by 11 years (to an unspecified average). The establishment of China's National Defense University (*Guofang Daxue*) helped to raise the educational standards of many officers. In 1981, only 11 percent of cadre-level officers[61] had some military, vocational, or regular college instruction, while another 39 percent had high school degrees, and half of all PLA leading cadres had less education than high school. But by 1986, 28 percent had college educations, 64 percent were high school graduates, and only 8 percent had less schooling. It is hard to say whether this sharp change of background among active officers has as much implication for policy as might be expected because "retired" cadres not counted in the statistics may remain politically important.[62] Also, the average age of new military district officers implies that these soldiers were in their early twenties just after mid-century (and most were fighting then in Korea). Whatever influence the shift among China's officers may have on politics, there clearly has been a change.

Economic managers are at least as vital to the Four Modernizations program as any of the categories mentioned above and cadre turnover has been widespread in state companies. Already by 1982-83, 60 percent of the pre-1949 leadership groups of the most important 3,000 "core enterprises" (*gugan qiye*) withdrew to retirement, mainly a *lixiu* basis. This change, affecting about 1,200 managers nationwide, meant a circulation of elites in three or four of the top six posts in a typical large state company.[63] The evidence suggests that demobilized soldiers, who joined such firms during the Transition to Socialism in the 1950s, were often targeted for cold storage—and sometimes they accepted that role (along with attendant *lixiu* benefits).

By 1986, people below the age of fifty had assumed 83 percent of the leadership posts in these large core firms, and the average age among them was 45 years. Three-quarters of economic cadres in this high sample had tertiary educations. The striking concentration of such cadres, in a relatively narrow age cohort, may be seen in the distribution of China's university-educated persons by age, which is given in Table 1. There is a bunching of experts (as certified by colleges) trained during the Great Leap Forward and in surrounding years.

MID-LEVEL REVOLUTIONARIES
RESIST MODERN RECRUITMENT POLICIES?

Beijing's policies for China's elite are surely more effective because they promote members of families that were locally important in prerevolutionary times. These families never fully lost their informal social positions, despite attacks against them in 1957 and 1966. Declarations from on high of new tolerance, however, do not ensure compliance below, even from party members. Also, as William Parish has shown, China's urban areas showed social destratification during the quarter century after 1950.[64] As in the aftermaths of other revolutions, the emerging elite is a composite of groups from both before and after the main upheavals. Political struggle between elite types becomes moderated and institutionally channeled as the revolution "ends," but such conflict does not entirely disappear, especially in recruitment.

Middle levels of leadership, which set the country's direction because of their resources, may change less surely than national leadership. Beijing's policies for the whole country's cadres are documented above, but they are not followed automatically at these middle levels. In small units, especially rural ones, the conversion from communes to traditional households was possible early (as data from "Chen Village" suggests[65]), precisely because urban elites never fully controlled the millions of peasants. In Beijing and most high provincial posts, the writ of the center is strong. But for crucial mid-sized groups, reforms of elite recruitment have been slower.

As the *People's Daily* complained in 1986, mid-level officials are nepotistic and distort the new policies, "promoting their own children or relatives" (*'tipa ziji de zinu chinyou'*).[66] This is hardly a new problem for Chinese bureaucracies, whether revolutionary or not. As Etienne Balazs wrote about the traditional empire, "Protectionism and nepotism exist in all latitudes, but nowhere have they found more fertile soil than in China."[67] In the second half of the 1980s, high party editorialists still railed against the continuing power of patron-client relations (*guanxi wang*) that have a "family color" (*zongzu secai*):

> It is reported that when some leaders open meetings, they brazenly refer to "second uncle" or "third uncle" and think it just fine. "In the tent of the general, everyone's a family soldier."[68]

The state and lineages use each others' institutions and symbols.[69] This is not unique to China; there are shades of the habit in places as various as Louisiana, Italy, and India. Its pervasiveness shows how hard the goal of totalitarianism would be to achieve. The revolution has affected these relationships but has not overcome them, and in recent years they have been obvious. Some of the "new" recruitment policies have been highly compatible with the regionalism and clientele-ism inherited from prerevolutionary times. For example, affirmative action in appointing cadres from minority nationalities has been surprisingly successful; over 400,000 new minority officials were appointed at all levels of the state in the first half of the 1980s.[70] Non-Han minority representation on the CC also rose, in 1977, 1982, and 1987 respectively, from 6 to 8 to 11 percent.[71] Ethnic diversification of China's elite has clearly increased in recent years, despite the country's national homogeneity (it is 94 percent Han). A first, skeptical view of this change might attribute it "merely" to strategic concerns rather than decreased Han ethnocentrism. But growth of toleration in other countries have often correlated with contexts, not just majority changes of heart. The more accommodating political approach to minorities in China need not be belittled, because it makes rational sense as a reform-period policy.

Affirmative action for women cadres, which has scant traditional basis, was, however, slowed in the early reform era. Although the first woman top Party Secretary in any Chinese province, Wan Shaofen, was named for Jiangxi in June 1985,[72] most high administrative appointments of women have involved outreach more than important functions.[73] Female representation on the last three CCs has been unstable among alternate members: 18, then 9, then 11 percent (in 1977, 1982, then 1987). Among full members, the portion has been lower, as well as erratic: 6.9, then 5.2, then 5.7 percent.[74]

Part of the reason for this slowness comes from a shortage of university-trained women. As a 1984 source noted, less than one-quarter (24 percent) of China's college students were female. But the portion in America was 52 percent; in the USSR, 50 percent; and in the Philippines, 53 percent.[75] Postrevolutionary elite recruitment policies seem to work best when they mesh with old, mid-level social groups, and traditional cultures, as well as pressing concrete needs.

They have less effectiveness, when they do not call on such interests.

SPECIALIZED ELITES
AND EDUCATIONAL CERTIFICATIONS

Technical modernization and mass schooling nonetheless slowly create new social interests, and the slow action of these changes now affects Chinese elite recruitment more strongly than ever. The crucial importance of educational modernization has been stressed by scholars of politics after other revolutions, notably the French and Russian ones;[76] but work on this subject is just beginning for the Chinese case. As in all countries, the portion of China's university-educated people has differed in various professions. The 1982 census showed that 13 percent of all teachers, and 10 percent of industrial managers, had college degrees.[77] The portions in other large fields were lower. Only 7 percent of state cadres, and only 4.6 percent of party employees, had college degrees in 1982; but other evidence presented above suggests these figures must have risen in the five years through 1986.

Functional differentiation for efficiency, in the decade after Mao's death, created large new categories of cadres that had scarcely existed before. A striking example of this change has been the creation in the PRC of a new "troop of lawyers" (lushi duiwu). Between 1957 and 1979, China effectively had no lawyers, and it had only 2,800 before the Anti-rightist Campaign. But by late 1985, China for better or worse boasted 26 province-level bar associations, 2,900 law offices (lushi zhiwu so), with 11,000 practicing lawyers and 9,000 more in training.[78] These serve more than a million commercial businesses and 400,000 firms in industry and transport, as well as individuals, because people in the PRC now face increasingly complex criminal and civil codes.

Durkheimian "technical organization," designed to integrate Chinese society because of differences rather than ideology, certainly did not erase the older legitimacy of "human organization" based on common social consciousness and political will.[79] But to improve the productivity in China's economy, Deng's regime has emphasized the recruitment of expert cadres more than Mao's regime did. College-educated staff, available for this grand economic project in the 1980s, was distributed by age in an awkward manner.

Table 1

CHINA'S SUPPLY OF UNIVERSITY-EDUCATED EXPERTS, 1982

Age Cohort	Number Of People (m.)	Number Of Experts (m.)	% Of Cohort Who Are Experts	% Of All Experts In This Cohort	Approx. Years Of College Education	% Of Women Among Experts
75+	666	6.02	0.9	100		25.7
60+	77	.241	.31	4	1940-	14.6
55-59	34	.213	.63	3.5	1941-45	15.7
50-54	41	.387	.95	6.4	1946-50	18.8
45-49	47	.763	1.6	12.7	1951-55	21.3
40-44	48	1.062	2.2	17.6	1956-60	24.9
35-39	54	.774	1.4	12.9	1961-65	28.3
30-34	73	.567	.77	9.4	1966-70	28.7
25-29	93	.755	.81	12.5	1971-75	30.1
20-24	74	.656	.88	10.9	1976-80	28.7
15-19	125	.602(+)	.48(+)	10.0(+)	1981-85	26.4

Source: *Xinhua wenjai* (New China Digest), Beijing, July 1984, p. 6, especially calculations based on the data there. The terms "university-educated," "expert," and "intellectual" all refer to persons who graduated from university-level institutions or at any time studied in tertiary schools. These data came from the 1982 national census. Note the weight of the cohorts educated in 1956-60 and surrounding years. Figures on the higher education of the youngest cohort were still incomplete as of 1982.

Less than half of China's supply of experts in the early 1980s was educated during periods of considerable Soviet influence over the curricula in China's universities, i.e., in the first decade and a half of the PRC. By the late 1980s, a much larger, and much younger, cohort had its formative years of higher education since the death of Mao. (The group educated before 1949 is small, though important.) It is not easy to draw conclusions about political outlooks from data of this sort, because some students educated in the 1950s may nonetheless have somewhat liberal values; and some who received their training in the 1980s may be politically conservative. But the table shows an uneven distribution of China's experts by age, and it suggests the possibility of widespread differences between two generations of experts, centered on those who were trained in the late 1950s and in the early 1980s.[80]

Potential modern leaders are unevenly distributed by geography, too. The portion of university-educated persons in the 1982 populations of province-level units was over one percent only in Beijing (4.9 percent), Shanghai (3.4 percent), Tianjin (2.4 percent), and Liaoning (1.1 percent). In Henan, Guangxi, Qinghai, and Tibet, only 0.3 percent of the population had any higher education in 1982. The national ratio for tertiary education was 0.6 percent.[81]

The uneven distribution of leadership by age is a signal fact of political life in contemporary China. Toward the end of the 1980s, people in their middle and late thirties are still to some extent a "lost generation" or "confused generation."[82] Even young students had at least heard of the trouble that an emphasis on politics had brought to their country during the Cultural Revolution; and they were more inclined than their predecessors in earlier generations to withdraw from active politics.[83] *Beijing Youth News* did a survey of middle schools in 1984 and reported that nearly 95 percent of the students disliked their politics course more than any other subject they took. The surveyed students reportedly thought that politics textbooks were dull, the teachers in those classes offered too many fulsome monologues, and the exams discouraged thinking and encouraged parroting.[84]

Other kinds of education, however, had become more viable roads to careers for these students than for their predecessors. But top planners in government were more committed to the results of specialized education than to extensive financing for it. A 1983 article in the journal of a teacher's college pointedly calculated that of 151 countries in the world, China ranked 149th in per-capita educational expenditures. This magazine averred that the Ministry of Education cared only that schoolrooms should not collapse, that each class should have a room, and that each student should have a chair and desk space. And these academic standards were listed to stress that they were basic.[85]

Even for university-level schooling, the age-cohort ripples caused by the Cultural Revolution (and maybe a continuing high official ambiguity about students) created an uneven pattern through 1982 at least. Recruitment rates into higher education fluctuated sharply after Mao's death. The number of college admissions, in thousands, have been: 1977, 273; 1978, 402; 1979, 275; 1980, 281; 1981, 279; 1982, 315; 1983, 391; and 1984, 430 (a planned enrollment).[86] The trend of admissions was up, but the range of fluctuation from 1977 to the mid-1980s was high, almost half the average for these years. By 1986, fully 1,914,000 students took the college entrance tests, and one-third were promoted. Only 42,000 were exiled to television universities, and 543,000 went to ordinary universities and vocational colleges. The promotion rate of 30 percent was, by the late 1980s, higher than in the late 1970s and early 1980s, when it ran between 5 and 11 percent, both because the cohorts that had missed a chance at education in the Cultural Revolution were no longer sitting for exams, and because allowable university enrollments were doubled in the first six years of the decade.[87]

Once students got into universities, they were solidly on the escalator to cadredom. This was, in any case, the future dispensation widely expected by the mid-1980s. Practically no one was kicked out of college. Among all 120,000 students in 76 Beijing colleges during 1985, the enforced withdrawal rate was less than four-tenths of one percent.[88] Less than half as many of the withdrawn students left for bad behavior as for academic failure, but the scholastic standards were not stringent. A grade of sixty was sufficient to pass any course, and this was easy to achieve. In good university tradition, the students contrived a slogan, "Long live sixty points!" (*Liushi fen wansui!*), to express their pleasure at this.[89]

Some youths, who could not hop onto this escalator into China's local and national elites usually because their test scores were too low, might study on their own, pass regular exams (about twenty of them at a university, or a dozen at a vocational college), and finally receive degrees. Between 1981 and 1986, non-matriculated students sat for such tests over three million times, and 44,600 earned baccalaureates.[90] This was only a small portion (about 2 percent) of the graduates from regular programs, but the potential leaders produced in this way had proved their tenacity. They had received certification without having to clear either the academic or political admissions hurdles.

The quasi-traditional pressure for education, and for the elite status it was presumed to bring by the mid-1980s, was so strong that whole new schools developed outside of the state-financed system. By the end of 1985, various non-CCP "democratic parties" had established 974 vocational colleges, enrolling 550,000 students who were clearly not Communists.[91] Whether this pattern is pre- or post-revolutionary is less clear than that some urban groups were willing to pay for it, and the state now acquiesced.

OCCUPATIONAL STRUCTURE
AND NEW NORMS IN THE MODERNIZING PRC

By the middle of the decade, surveys of Chinese youths suggested that their perceptions of likely future incomes from different employments correlated negatively with their perceptions of the social desirability of jobs.

Table 2

1986 YOUTH ON OCCUPATIONS' SOCIAL STATUS AND INCOME STATUS

Occupation	Perceived Ranks in	
	Social Status	Income Status
University students, researchers	1	9
Administrative cadres	2	7
Professionals	3	8
Enterprise cadres and technicians	4	2
Secondary school teachers	5	10
Commercial and service personnel	6	3
Workers (in state enterprises)	7	6
Collective or private firm employees	8	4
Individual entrepreneurs (geti hu)	9	1
Farmers	10	5
(Youths awaiting jobs/occupations	11	11)

Source: *Shijie jingjie daobao (World Economic Herald), February 3, 1986,* p. 8.

Another survey of three Shanghai high schools produced similar results. Interviews of 150 graduates in four different classes of two ordinary and one "key-point" high school in 1982 elicited the youths' evaluations of 38 occupations. The top three (with much higher average rankings than other jobs) all required training that would give them independence in work units: engineers, doctors, and technicians. But cadres (*ganbu*) came in eighth.[92] Office clerks ranked tenth. Manual workers in railroads, construction, textiles, steelmaking, and shipping were low on the list. "Self-employed workers" were deemed in 1982 to have the lowest occupational status, according to the survey. This author's conversations in Shanghai during late 1988 suggest that the perceived social status of private entrepreneurs had risen somewhat by then; and expectations of their higher income had proven true.

Cadre and technical jobs in state enterprises, according to the early-1980s surveys, were seen as serving the best combination of social and individual values. A great part of China's emerging elite aim for such jobs, which require both specialized competence and party membership. Most such enterprises still have collective responsibility systems in the late 1980s, but there has been a trend toward more independence for local economic leaders. In Shanghai by the end of 1985, for example, 633 state enterprises had "single head systems" (*yizhang zhi*), so that one person took full credit or blame for operations.[93] High national leaders encouraged this trend for the sake of efficiency.

When the "single head" achieved his position because of individual or family power over official resources, however, another result could be corruption.[94] Reproduction of the ruling party in families, which continued the recruitment of elites over generations like a class, became a major issue of the 1980s. On several occasions, notably December 1984, the State Council and party Central Committee prohibited official cadres and agencies from running companies which private enterprise laws sometimes made lucrative. Public funds easily provided risk capital, however; and official positions still provided general power in many localities. Abuses of the rules against corrupt forms of "joint state-private" and collective enterprises therefore continued. Acknowledging this, the State Council and Central Committee have passed further regulations: Cadre dependents and retired officials were forbidden to take positions in any kind of private firm. Those who had state or party posts as well as enterprise jobs were supposed to resign the former. They were prohibited from continuing as officials, even if they gave up their salaries (*ting xin*). Retired cadres were supposed to wait two years before taking private posts. And then, they could legally do so only in industries unassociated with their former units and only if they were willing to lose their retirement pay and benefits. Criminal punishments were established for disobeying these rules. Above all, family dependents of cadres could not join private firms. If the dependents already had official jobs, they were prohibited from resigning to do private work.[95]

These rules, repromulgated from time to time, have been widely honored in the breach. Chinese interviewees, once safely abroad, make specific accusations against particular relatives of well-known national leaders. These can seldom be confirmed from inside China. Many of the best-documented cases of economic crime involve foreign trade, such as a massive import of autos by Hainan officials that became an infamous scandal.[96] In the mid-1980s, a former Minister of Aviation and a Vice-Minister were responsible for extensive imports of TV sets, on an outdated import license, issued to another office, but in the event, they were not even arrested. Only the former head of the party in the ministry was "suspended" from membership and "put under surveillance" for two years.[97] A survey of 785 economic crimes in the early 1980s showed that at least two-thirds of them involved cadres taking advantage of their positions.[98]

To a surprising extent, top CCP cadres, even those thought to be hard-line in domestic politics and potentially pro-Soviet in foreign policy,[99] now send their offspring to Western countries for study and business. This may be evidence of the CCP elite's broadening scientific and cultural interests, as the revolution matures and becomes nonviolent. China is in a period of changing occupational statuses and changing norms. A new recruitment of elites comes, unsurprisingly, at the same time the ideology justifying their leadership becomes more technocratic, cosmopolitan, and mixed.

CONCLUSION: OPEN DECISIONS IN QUICK CHANGE

Political struggles are not about to end in China, any more than in any other country. Such struggles could conceivably reignite the flame of China's revolution, but the forces working to lower that probability are many. They include newly technocratic state organizations in Beijing and provincial capitals, as well as legions of social clusters to which the state has lost some influence. Many people and groups in China are now, still recalling the Cultural Revolution, apparently weary of fighting each other. The balance of evidence from the last decade suggests a winding down of revolution and a wide diversification of elites in China.

This is entirely typical of past similar patterns in countries like England and France, after their revolutionary upheavals. The partial exception (different mainly because Stalin's "second revolution" slowed political development there) is Russia. China still has a Leninist party and could become a medial case between the Soviet and other examples. But recent diversification, even within the CCP itself, suggests that Leninist parties are not omnipotent and unchangeable, despite their implicit claims, despite the interesting ideologies of their leaders, and despite all the footnotes their newspapers give us. They operate along with other social forces and memories, which in China are powerfully influencing CCP policies at present.

Answers to the question "Is China's revolution ending?" are likely to depend on whether one emphasizes the continued viability in China of revolutionary ideas and groups, or instead the new pressures on them. The revolution will wind down, insofar as revolutions ever do, at some time. The evidence for a typical evolution in China is extensive, if incomplete. Scholarship can provide no absolutely sure answer for such a question, but it can frame the issue in terms of the historical examples that underlie any theory to answer it.

Thus the CCP's recent stress on expert specialization will not necessarily pluralize Chinese politics at any sure pace. Technocratic trends (mixed with old-fashioned Chinese political connections) are much easier to show in recent data than are democratic-competitive trends. Nor can we be certain that specific functions, much less institutions, will become divided in China along the same lines they have in any other country.[100] But cultural and elite diversity are twin aspects of the change now in China, both because of high government policy and because of many interests in smaller political communities and individuals there.

China's past provides symbols, nonrevolutionary in most cases, that are still of interest to local leaders. A striking example is the Confucius Foundation, whose head Kuang Yaming was respectfully quoted by the *People's Daily* in 1986 to the effect that,

> Confucius cannot be struck down. As for the world's three famous men—Jesus, Buddha, and Confucius—two have already become gods. But Confucius remains human, struggling for humanity all his life. I think Confucius is the greatest of them.[101]

Any major culture provides enough options to make either revolution or its termination handy, in the right season.[102]

China's universities now train potential elites in a broader range of interests than before. At Shanghai, university students now organize associations for debate, architecture, arts, the study of Lu Xun, and other activities. Forty-nine colleges in that metropolis had 294 such associations by late 1986.[103] Such clubs helped to organize students at that time for street demonstrations. Few students' associations existed in previous years, and they reflect a hope to explore a greater variety of options than in the past. A younger writer put it in terms that could not have been public in Mao's decades: "Our ideal person is not just [socially] creative, but also enjoys life."[104]

Deng Xiaoping puts the political corollary plainly:

> It is apparent that our party's prestige is not as high as it used to be.... When over twenty million workers were sent down to the rural areas [after the failure of the Great Leap Forward], we followed the mass line and explained things clearly and nobody complained. Things are not so easy today.[105]

A late 1986 poll of 3,000 college students in Wuhan confirmed Deng's appraisal. Half the respondents said individuals should think independently and have personal opinions about politics. Almost all (90 percent) said it was inappropriate to stick with the party line on all political issues.[106]

Aside from the diversity that arises from China's different generations and huge geography, even the few old men at the top of the CCP are not obviously unified on the fundamental questions that face the country. The partial, uncertain retreats from reformist policies associated with Hu Yaobang and then Zhao Ziyang provide recent evidence of this, but their policies have certainly not been abandoned. Earlier, the fizzling of the Campaign to Eliminate Spiritual Pollution climaxed in a September 1984 meeting, where Deng Xiaoping and Hu Yaobang prevailed (at least temporarily) over Deng Liqun and Hu Qiaomu.[107] Such defeats of the hard-liners can prevent struggles of the old revolutionary sort. Such events also showed that most top and local leaders are now wary of having too many exciting conflicts.

After the 1986-87 student demonstrations, the Criticism of the Tide of Thought of Bourgeois Liberalization[108]—not officially a "campaign" (*yundong*)—had a name too long to sing in the shower. Chinese leaders at many levels apparently felt ambiguous about it. Important intellectuals were temporarily silenced and reassigned in the name of this non-campaign. Some were only asked to resign their party memberships (but declined to do so). This movement did not lead to imprisonments or violent, revolutionary struggle meetings. After astrophysicist Fang Lizhi was sent back to observatories and out of politics, in the wake of the student demonstrations he had supported, the president of his previous unit was also fired. High party politicians decided on a new president, whose appointment should have been announced by Lu Jianxi, the Chair of the Chinese Academy of Sciences. But Lu reportedly refused to make the announcement.[109] He soon lost his job too, but his social standing among many leaders was not lessened, nor was that of the main targets like Fang Lizhi, Wang Ruowang, or Liu Binyan (who had to leave the CCP) or Su Shaozhi (who declined the request that he do so). The antibourgeois criticism proved too familiar to arouse much ardent interest.

Many other cases of lukewarm revolutionary feeling within high party ranks might also be cited. In late January 1987, Minister Wang Meng held a meeting to criticize bourgeois liberalization, and Deng Liqun (the senior party figure most clearly identified with such criticism) was invited to attend and to speak. Wang introduced the session with a speech against the dangers of excessive liberalism. Gradually, members of the select cadre audience left, to do other business. By the time Wang had finished, most of them were no longer in the room. Deng Liqun was so upset, reportedly, that he refused to give his own address. According to an interviewee, Deng tried to shake hands with other officials on the podium, but the first three he approached pretended not to notice him and also left.

The *People's Daily* has editorialized that disdain for Marxism is too widespread in China now. Even Hu Yaobang, while he headed the party, pointed to Marxism's limits, but his departure has apparently not restored universal respect for this official state ideology. The newspaper urged people not to laugh at concepts like "family background."[111] Yet clearly, such editorials would be unnecessary if the revolution in its previous, exclusive sense still retained its cachet among articulate Chinese. Instead, "democracy" has become a more salient topic to debate and define than revolution.[112] And economic growth is seen by many as the touchstone of legitimacy in today's China.

A reformer associated with Zhao Ziyang spoke in practical terms of three tutelary stages for the development of real democracy: a first stage that combines reform with elite democracy (*jingying minzhu*), a second era involving democracy among broad social groups, and a third involving democracy for individuals.[113] Such views articulate important trends of thought in China's leadership.

Among many other cadres, especially at middle levels and in rural areas, many leaders' hopes may be fundamentally different from this. A survey of young party members in a county outside Shanghai showed that in 1981, fully 72 percent of these youths had joined the CCP during the Cultural Revolution. Most of these had leadership posts and 40 percent were demobilized servicemen.[114] The views of ex-radical CCP members are important and official, as are the opposite views expressed by reformers, such as the one quoted in the paragraph above. Which will prevail? Events such as the 13th Party Congress help us answer, mainly because of changes in personnel and institutions.[115] In the long run, the kind of politics stirred by China's new technocratic leaders will be less violent than were the decades of revolution under Mao.

China scholars before 1978 did not predict the speed of change that the reform period has brought. Such failures are nothing new in our trade. After the Liberation of 1949, a dozen years passed before a coherent scholarly debate about its causes developed. On the Great Leap Forward, several years passed before Schurmann, Skinner, and others gave the Leap the organizational definition that now frames arguments about it. On the factors behind the Cultural Revolution, there are still varying definitions of what that event was, although recent publications may give somewhat more coherence to these debates.[116] In the Deng era since late 1978, the speed of trends toward more diversity in China has surprised our field. No one can be absolutely certain such trends will continue, and it is tempting to overstate their strength. There are mild counter trends, such as those of 1983 and 1987. But the speed of diversification since 1978 is a phenomenon to be explained, and historical precedents of leadership change help to explain it.

Are these current changes merely refining the revolutionary system, or are they basically altering it? The premise of the question is that China's policy has some single, unalterable essence, as might be posited as a concept in a conference or editorial. Yet China is not an idea but a country, with people in it. Their intentions have been sensibly flexible, never immutable, in the past. Their leaders at many levels will keep talking in terms of the revolution. They will also modernize. The quickness of change has surely been the most striking fact about the PRC during recent years.

NOTES

1. There is no space here for a full bibliography on revolutions. A recent book whose critical zing has brought much debate is Theda Skocpol, *States and Social Revolutions* (Cambridge: Cambridge University Press, 1979), which contains a forty-page bibliography. For the classic positive view, see Karl Marx and Frederick Engels, *The Communist Manifesto* (Beijing: Foreign Languages Press, 1970), or a recent application to China in Maurice Meisner, *Mao's China and After* (New York: Free Press, 1987). For a classic negative view, see Edmund Burke, *Reflections on the Revolution in France*, Thomas Mahoney, ed. (Indianapolis: Bobbs-Merrill, 1955); or a recent application to China in Simon Leys [Pierre Ryckmans], *The Burning Forest* (New York: Holt, Rinehart, and Winston, 1985). Lucien Bianco, *The Origins of the Chinese Revolution, 1915-1949*, tr. M. Bell (Stanford: Stanford University Press, 1971), summarizes conflicting ideas about the causes in China and suggests a changing definition for the word "revolution" (which is not tied, as in this chapter, to changes of elites).
2. See Crane Brinton, *The Anatomy of Revolution*, rev. ed. (New York: Vintage, 1966).
3. This implies great similarity between revolutions and self-proclaimed conservative movements such as those of the Meiji reformers, Hitler's Nazis, or Franco's Nationalists. This chapter need not detail all these, but books like Marius Jansen, *Sakamoto Ryoma and the Meiji Restoration* (Princeton: Princeton University Press, 1961);David Schoenbaum, *Hitler's Social Revolution: Class and Status in Nazi Germany, 1933-1939* (New York: Norton, 1966); and Paul Preston, *The Coming of the Spanish Civil War: Reform, Reaction, and Revolution in the Second Republic* (London: Methuen, 1978) would be relevant. Rightist centralizations are like leftist revolutions in their organization of some elites to oppose others; their difference may be in name more than reality. See suggestive Chinese parallels in Edward Friedman, *Backward Toward Revolution* (Berkeley: California, 1974); and in Frederick Wakeman, Jr., on pro-Ming, proto-revolutionary reaction in *Strangers at the Gate* (Berkeley: California, 1966), esp. chap. XI. Despite the uncertain implications for China, see also Paul Preston, *The Triumph of Democracy in Spain* (London: Methuen, 1986); Raymond Carr and Juan Pablo Fusi, *Spain: Dictatorship to*

Democracy (London: George Allen & Unwin, 1981); Kenneth Maxwell, ed., *Portugal in the 1980s: Dilemmas of Democratic Consolidation* (New York: Greenwood, 1986); and the interviews in Hugo Gil Ferreira and Michael W. Marshall, *Portugal's Revolution: Ten Years On* (Cambridge: Cambridge University Press, 1986). Political scientists and historians not only have a record of failing to predict revolutions and their constituent convulsions, they also have just as bad a record in predicting the starts of post-centralization democracies. The Iberian peninsula has offered two surprising examples in the past decade. After the systems created by Franco and Salazar fell, most analysts predicted successor dictatorships of Left or Right. The cultural and economic arguments for such judgments seemed overwhelmingly strong: A study on illiberal Catholicism in "Todas las Espanas" (even if it skipped intolerance between Basques, Catalans, Andalusians, and other Spaniards) or a treatise on Portugal's poverty might have footnotes alone to fill a shelf of books, and the same understanding for China would fill more shelves. Yet in Iberia, none of that would describe what recently happened. Social scientists should admit plainly they have scant idea why democracies actually begin—no more than why revolutions do. These problems seem to be linked. Books like Robert Dahl, *Polyarchy* (New Haven: Yale, 1971) help somewhat, but not enough to be true crystal balls.

4. This relies on Durkheim and later functionalist writings, as well as on distinctions between the traditional politics of pomp and the modern politics of efficiency. For more, see Ikuo Kabashima and Lynn White, eds., *Political System and Change* (Princeton: Princeton University Press, 1986), especially the chapters by White and Kabashima, "Systematic Definitions for Development Politics," pp. 3-19, and Harry Eckstein, "The Idea of Political Development: From Dignity to Efficiency," pp. 311-46. For an application, see Li Cheng with Lynn White, "Technical Elites and Modern Change in Taiwan and Mainland China: Data on the Theory of Technocracy," (forthcoming), as well as forthcoming works by Melanie Manion, Hong Yung Lee, and others.

5. G.M. Trevelyan, *English Social History* (New York: McKay, 1942), p. 256.

6. Christopher Hill, *Reformation to Industrial Revolution* (Harmondsworth, Eng.: Pelican, 1969), p. 161.

7. Lawrence Stone, *The Causes of the English Revolution 1529-1642* (New York: Harper, 1972), p. 147.

8. Rev. Jonathan Mayhew in Nicholas N. Kittrie and Eldon E. Wedlock, Jr., *The Tree of Liberty* (Baltimore: Johns Hopkins University Press, 1936), p. 34.

9. Reprinted in *ibid.*, pp. 86-87. By now, Americans are schizophrenic on revolutions, especially their own. On one hand, they think well of a principled event to start a nation. On the other, warlike patriots in Vietnam, Nicaragua, and elsewhere come in for resistance. Civics textbooks (maybe even American political scientists, though not historians) tend to downplay the violence of the American revolution, with its tarrings-and-featherings and guerrilla attacks. But U.S. liberalism arose largely from illiberal experiences, as in other countries.

10. See E.E. Schattschneider, *The Semi-Sovereign People: A Realist's View of Democracy in America* (Hindsdale, IL: Dryden, 1960). Another classic, which uses similar categories of elites for business and for government in a British economic history, is Karl Polanyi, *The Great Transformation: The Political and Economic Origins of Our Time* (Boston: Beacon, 1944).

11. George Rude, *Revolutionary Europe, 1973-1815* (London: Fontana, 1964), pp. 317-28, provides a selected bibliography, emphasizing the spread of the French example to other parts of Europe, a subject this present chapter has to ignore.

12. Alfred Cobban, *The Social Interpretation of the French Revolution* (Cambridge: Cambridge University Press, 1964), pp. 169 and 172.

13. Quoted in Norman Hampson, *A Social History of the French Revolution* (London: Routledge & Kegan Paul, 1963), p. 249.

14. See Ezra N. Suleiman, *Elites in French Society: The Politics of Survival* (Princeton: Princeton University Press, 1978), p. 63 and *passim*.

15. Quoted in Brian C.J. Singer, *Society, Theory, and the French Revolution* (New York: St. Martin, 1986), p. 202.

16. See Gilbert Rozman, *A Mirror for Socialism: Soviet Criticisms of China* (Princeton: Princeton University Press, 1985), e.g. p. 143.

17. We need not start a new "Sino-Soviet split," like the one between the conservative Kremlinologist and the conservative Sinologist, each arguing that Communism in "his" country was worse, to see that Stalin's second revolution is aberrant in the general pattern of revolutionary events in England, France, and even China. For fresh insights on the causes of the Soviet uniqueness, documented from newly found sources, see Michal Reiman, *The Birth of Stalinism: The USSR on the Eve of the "Second Revolution,"* tr. George Saunders [from German], (Bloomington: Indiana University

Press, 1987). Recent studies of the results of Stalinism are collected in G.R. Urban, ed., *Stalinism: Its Impact on Russia and the World* (Cambridge: Harvard University Press, 1986), which includes a chapter by China specialist Roderick MacFarquhar. Another collection, which has greatly influenced the current author (rapporteur at the conference where the papers were given), is Robert C. Tucker, ed., *Stalinism: Essays in Historical Interpretation* (New York: Norton, 1977), especially chapters by Tucker on "Revolution from Above" and Stephen F. Cohen on "Bolshevism and Stalinism." See also Cohen's *Rethinking the Soviet Experience: Politics and History Since 1917* (New York: Oxford University Press, 1985) and Moshe Lewin's *The Gorbachev Phenomenon: A Historical Interpretation* (Berkeley and Los Angeles: University of California Press, 1988).

18. See T.H. Rigby and Bohdan Harasymiw, eds., *Leadership in USSR and Yugoslavia* London: George Allen & Unwin, 1983), p. 1. Lest it be thought Stalin was dull, he must be quoted again: "Gaiety is the most salient trait of Soviet culture."

19. For more on this in the Chinese case, see Li Cheng with Lynn White, "Technical Elites...."

20. Bohdan Harasymiw, *Political Elite Recruitment in the Soviet Union* (New York: St. Martin's 1984), pp. 189-91.

21. Stephen Fortescue, *The Communist Party and Soviet Science* (Baltimore: The Johns Hopkins University Press, 1986), p. 174.

22. Lewin, *The Gorbachev Phenomenon.*

23. Doak Barnett, Ezra Vogel, Michel Oksenberg, Harry Harding, and many others provide earlier discussions of PRC elite recruitment; but the literature on this topic during the past few years is less direct than one might expect. See, however, Roberta Martin, *Party Recruitment in China: Patterns and Prospects* (New York: Columbia University East Asian Institute, 1981), and Melanie Manion, "The Cadre Management System, Post-Mao: The Appointment, Promotion, Transfer, and Removal of Party and State Leaders," *China Quarterly* 102 (June 1985), pp. 203-33. Hong Yung Lee is finishing the draft of a book on this topic.

24. The same transformation, however, can also be shown in many other areas. This whole phenomenon, especially its development in 1980s journalistic media and in "horizontal" economic links uniting East China, will be the subject of this author's next book, whose title expands the Chinese word for "reform" (*gaige*): *Changing the Revolution.*

25. *Renmin ribao (People's Daily*, Overseas Edition) [herafter *RMRB*], June 29, 1986, and other sources.
26. "Cultural level" (*wenhua chengdu*) is expressed by PRC sources in fastidious terms: the number of years of education. Both the generality of the meaning, and the notion it can be captured this way, are Chinese and not only mainland. After the Kuomintang's 1988 Thirteenth Congress, more than a quarter (26 percent) of the KMT Central Committee members have Ph.D. degrees. See Li Cheng with Lynn White, "Technical Elites and Modernization in Taiwan and Mainland China" (forthcoming).
27. *RMRB*, March 14, 1986.
28. The best general documentation on recent policy splits in English is John P. Burns and Stanley Rosen, eds., *Policy Conflicts in Post-Mao China* (Armonk: Sharpe, 1986).
29. Interview with "Shao Din," a pseudonym for an official whom the present author has also interviewed, published in *Zhengming* (Contend and Bloom) [hereafter *ZM*], August 1986, pp. 34-37.
30. *RMRB*, August 16, 1984. Actuarial pressures, not just policy, speeded layoffs in the 1980s, but such pressures are typical of other countries whose revolutionary generations also found the state was easier to control than the Grim Reaper.
31. *RMRB*, November 22, 1984.
32. *RMRB*, June 29, 1986. The figure was 469,000. This source also says that 1,268,000 "old" (i.e., pre-1949) cadres had retired, though the time period of these two changes may not have been identical.
33. *Lixiu* is short for *lizhi xiuyang* which means "leaving office to convalesce," implying an off-chance the cadre might return. Interviewees and *RMRB* references below provided the information.
34. This information is based partly on interviews.
35. For the odd 1979 rehabilitation rules, see Lynn White, "Thought Workers in Deng's Time," in Merle Goldman, Timothy Cheek, and Carol Lee Hamrin, eds., *China's Intellectuals and the State: In Search of a New Relationship* (Cambridge: Harvard, 1987), pp. 253-274.
36. *RMRB*, June 29, 1986. The five highest state levels are:
    1. province/ministry (*sheng/bu*),
    2. provincial commission/general bureau (*weiyuan-hui/zongju*),

3. prefecture (sometimes called "special district") or provincial department (*diqu or tingl ju*),
4. county/central division (*xian/chu*),
5. county department or central section (*ke*), and other names in other kinds of organizations or particular places.

For example, Beijing ministries are province-level, and all cadres in their "leadership groups" (*lingdao banzi*) are deemed at that level, though offices within them are mainly lower. Another example: urban districts in province-level cities (Beijing, Shanghai, and Tianjin) have county status. See the valuable table and discussion in Kenneth Lieberthal and Michel Oksenberg, *Bureaucratic Politics and Chinese Energy Development* (Washington: U.S. Government Printing Office for Department of Commerce, August 1986), pp. 123ff. An elaborate protocol system allows any cadre in China, even in organizations like hospitals, universities, companies, newspapers, and Army, or trade unions, to know his or her place in the official cosmos.

37. *RMRB*, June 29, 1986.
38. From a paper that will be published by Hong Yung Lee, who is doing the best current work on China's new leadership and thus becomes "new echelon" himself, this author has the impression that some third-echelon cadres who would be counted in these statistics have not yet been given leadership roles. It may be speculated that some lightly retired *lixiu* officials still perform important roles. "Adviser" (in Chinese, *guwen*) has long been an eminent role in East Asian settings. Even with this qualification, and even if some of the third echelon are more certified than intelligent, anything faintly resembling a 45 percent increase of educated cadres at these levels in China would represent a major change.
39. This assessment differs from others in works by Martin and Manion (see above) only because of recent evidence not available when they wrote.
40. *RMRB*, September 5, 1985. At the end of 1983, the average age of 27 provincial first Party secretaries, on whom age data were available, was 65.0 years; see Jurgen Domes, *The Government and Politics of the People's Republic of China* (Boulder: Westview, 1985), p. 72.
41. *RMRB*, September 14, 1985.
42. *RMRB*, February 9, 1986.

43. *RMRB*, October 22, 1986.
44. *Ibid. RMRB*, August 4, 1985, also reports that ten percent of PRC residents of Taiwan-origin had been favored with cadre positions. This is five times the frequency of cadres among the general population, though it may not be much greater than their incidence among people born in other areas of East China.
45. These and figures until the next note are summarized and rounded from tables in Li Cheng and Lynn White, "The Thirteenth Central Committee of the Chinese Communist Party: From Mobilizers to Managers," *Asian Survey* 28:4 (March 1988), 371-99.
46. Li Cheng with Lynn White, "Technical Elites...."
47. Reported in *Christian Science Monitor* [hereafter *CSM*], July 21, 1983, p. 13.
48. See *Hongqi* (Red Flag) [hereafter *HQ*] 1984:23, reprinted in *Xinhua wenjai* (New China Digest) [hereafter *XHWJ*], January 1985, pp. 10-12; and Lynn White, "Thought Workers in Deng's Time," noted above.
49. *Ibid.*
50. *Ibid.*
51. *RMRB*, September 25, 1985. The article also reports that the 519,000 Young Communist League members who joined the party in 1984 were twice as many as two years earlier. The 8.25 million new YCL members in 1984 represented an increase of 1.2 m. over 1983.
52. *RMRB*, January 7, 1987.
53. See Lynn White with Li Cheng, "The Diversification of China's Intellectuals" (forthcoming).
54. *RMRB*, December 9, 1986.
55. See Alfred Cobban, *The Social Interpretation....*, above.
56. *RMRB*, November 14, 1986.
57. *RMRB*, March 10, 1986. There is nothing quite like quantitative research, as these eight teeth show. (A passion for numbers is evident in all the sources used for this chapter. Whether that reflects modernity or tradition is debatable. It does not reflect revolutionary enthusiasm.)
58. June Teufel Dreyer, "The Chinese People's Liberation Army: Demobilization and its Effects," a superb draft that does not prohibit citation but is being revised, for a conference organized by Prof. Leng Shao-chuan at the University of Virginia, June 13, 1987.
59. *RMRB*, October 28, 1985. The four removed regions had headquarters at Urumqi, Fuzhou, Wuhan, and Kunming. The seven

remaining regions center in Beijing, Shenyang, Lanzhou, Jinan, Nanjing, Guangzhou, and Chengdu.

60. Li Cheng and Lynn White, "The Thirteenth...," p. 388. The text here combines information from *RMRB*, October 28, 1985, and July 6, 1987.

61. *RMRB*, December 16, 1986. An interviewee reports that a military "cadre" is any *paizhang* or above.

62. See three assaults on this particular hill: Paul Godwin, ed., *The Chinese Defense Establishment: Continuity and Change in the 1980s*; Monte Bullard, *China's Political-Military Evolution: The Party and the Military in the PRC, 1960-84*; and Charles D. Lovejoy, Jr., and Bruce W. Watson, eds., *China's Military Reforms: International and Domestic Implications* (all Boulder: Westview, 1983, 1985, and 1986 respectively).

63. Calculated from various other numbers in *RMRB*, July 5, 1986.

64. William L. Parish, "Destratification in China," in James L. Watson, ed., *Class and Social Stratification in Post-Revolution China* (Cambridge: Cambridge University Press, 1984), pp. 84-120.

65. Anita Chan, Richard Madsen, and Jonathan Unger, *Chen Village: The Recent History of a Peasant Community in Mao's China* (Berkeley: University of California Press, 1984), pp. 266-67 and *passim* gives the richest available description of such change in the early 1980s, locally symbolized by the victory of a nearly traditional cadre named Qingfa over a more radical one named Longyong. This is all put in terms of peasants' rational choice among Geertzian types in Madsen's *Morality and Power in a Chinese Village* (Berkeley: University of California Press, 1984).

66. *RMRB*, March 12, 1986.

67. Etienne Balazs, *Chinese Civilization and Bureaucracy*, tr. Hope M. Wright (New Haven: Yale University Press, 1964), p. 10.

68. *RMRB*, July 27, 1986. The last quoted expression is: *Zhangxia dajiang gege dou shi zidi bing*.

69. Few scholars pay enough attention to the mass political importance of housing shortage and household registration or to the symbolic importance of the Chinese state's claims on families; but an exception is the Australian Michael Dutton. See his "Policing the Chinese Household: A Comparison of Modern and Ancient Forms," *Economy and Society* 17:2 (May 1988), pp. 195-224; and "Classical Past, Socialist Past, or Reformist Future: The Household Registration System in the People's Republic of China," *Chinese Economic Studies* (forthcoming 1988).

70. *RMRB*, August 5, 1986.
71. Li Cheng and Lynn White, "The Thirteenth...," p. 376. (Most percentages in the text are rounded for presentational reasons; but it is worth noting that the decimal figures are 5.7, 8.0, and 11.2 percents.) The portions of non-Hans on the three previous CCs, in 1956, 1969, and 1973, were all lower; and their average was 5.1 percent.
72. *RMRB*, January 9, 1986.
73. *RMRB*, October 9, 1985, emphasized the Hong Kong-like qualities of Guangzhou's only woman deputy mayor, Chen Qiqi. *RMRB*, February 15, 1986, reports the election of Xie Lijun, an Overseas Chinese woman surgeon and member of the "democratic" (non-Communist) Jiusan Society, as a deputy mayor in Shanghai.
74. Li Cheng and Lynn White, "The Thirteenth...," p. 375. The 1956 CC was only 4 percent women (in both full and alternate categories). But the 1969 and 1973 full-member ratios were higher: respectively 8 and 10 percent. These ratios may be compared not only with each other, but also with the portion of China's people who are women.
75. *XHWJ*, July 1984, p. 7. The portion in Japan is 23 percent, not a model for women's liberation.
76. See Ezra Suleiman, *Elites in French Society*; and Moshe Lewin, *The Gorbachev Phenomenon*.
77. *XHWJ*, July 1984, p. 7.
78. *RMRB*, November 12, 1985.
79. See Franz Shurmann, *Ideology and Organization in Communist China* (Berkeley: University of California Press, 1966).
80. These differences are further explored in Lynn White with Li Cheng, "The Diversification of China's Intellectuals."
81. *XHWJ*, July 1984, p. 6.
82. Interviewees refer to the *"kuadiao de yidai"* or *"miwang de yidai,"* the Cultural Revolution generation.
83. For more on this, see Lynn White with Li Cheng, "The Diversification of China's Intellectuals."
84. *Beijing qingnian bao* (Beijing Youth News), May 22, 1984, tr. *Chinese Education* 17:4 (Winter, 1984-85), pp. 72-73.
85. From *Huangshi shiyuan xuebao* (Yellow Rock Teacher's College Journal) 2:1983, reprinted in *XHWJ*, October 1983, pp. 201-04. Whether these numbers are accurate or not, the politics of publishing them at this time is important.

86. These figures, from *XHWJ*, July 1984, p. 7, are close to, but not identical with, others compiled in Suzanne Pepper, *China's Universities* (Ann Arbor: University of Michigan Center for Chinese Studies, 1983), p. 125. The minor differences are less important than the reassurance provided in the extent to which they confirm, and for 1982-86 update the earlier compilation.
87. See *RMRB*, July 10, 1986, and Pepper, *China's Universities*, p. 125.
88. Calculated from figures in *RMRB*, March 20, 1986.
89. Interview information.
90. *RMRB*, October 8, 1986, and interviews.
91. *RMRB*, July 6, 1986.
92. From *Shehui* (Society), No. 2 (May 1982), tr. in David S.K. Chu, ed., *Sociology and Society in Contemporary China*, special issue of *Chinese Sociology and Anthropology* XVI:1-2 (Fall-Winter, 1983-84), p. 164. This survey, which is better than the more recent one noted above, is not tabulated in the text only because it is already available in English. On the independence that technical training can give employees, see the classic by Michel Crozier, *The Bureaucratic Phenomenon: An Examinination of Bureaucracy in Modern Organizations and its Cultural Setting in France* (Chicago: University of Chicago Press, 1964).
93. *Wenhui bao* (Literary New) [hereafter WHB], December 22, 1985.
94. For more on the reform period's relative toleration for new groups and ethical sensitivities, see Lynn White, "Changing Concepts of Corruption in Communist China: Early 1950s vs. Early 1980s," *Changes and Continuities in Chinese Communism*, Yu-ming Shaw, ed. (Boulder, Co.: Westview Press, 1988), pp. 316-53.
95. *RMRB*, February 6, 1986.
96. See *CSM*, August 6, 1985.
97. *RMRB*, February 7, 1986. Some ways for officials' families to make money were probably not illegal in the PRC only because the activities were outside China. An interviewee said the son-in-law of Gen. Yang Shangkun of the Central Military Commission ran a company in Macau whose capital came from the U.S., but whose profits were remitted.
98. *Guangming ribao* (Bright Daily), July 12, 1982.
99. Interviewees report the following members of "Li Peng's group" who have children abroad: Chen Yun sent his daughter Weili to Berkeley and may also have a son in America. Yang Shangkun's daughter came to Princeton (and the author's seminar). A later visiting scholar was probably also the daughter of another well-

known official, though in this and many other cases, the reports are unconfirmed.

100. Comparisons of the United States with the two different subjects in *The Modernization of Japan and Russia* by Cyril E.Black et al. (New York: Free Press, 1975) certainly shows this. Predictions in Gilbert Rozman, ed., *The Modernization of China* (New York: Free Press, 1981) are more open-ended and unsure than some critics say. Even the Chinese government is not wrong to claim that modernization "exists" in an analytic sense.

101. *RMRB*, February 19, 1986. This Westerner suggests a reading of Job ("Now I see you with my own eyes...."), which is like Incarnation or Isaiah but from the human side. One aspect of many religions apparently relates to revolutionary enthusiams, but Confucius as Kuang Yaming describes him (or Job) is in the opposite, more sober mood, "seeing" sharply but after enthusiasm. Compare also the *Bhagavad Gita* to the less contemplative rest of the *Mahabharata*.

102. Clifford Geertz's famous "Notes on the Balinese Cockfight," in *The Interpretation of Cultures* (New York: Basic Books, 1973), p. 452, denies functionalism but mentions the possibility of writing another essay about the Brahmana ordination ceremony, which is "like" Bali in its different situation of quiet. This other symbol is for other seasons.

103. *RMRB*, October 5, 1986.

104. See *XHWJ*, February 1984, pp. 137-38. See also Dai Houying, *Stones of the Wall* (New York: St. Martin's, 1985) and other contemporary Chinese literature.

105. Quoted in Brantly Womack, "Modernization and Democratic Reform in China," *Journal of Asian Studies* XLIII:3 (May 1984), p. 433.

106. Julian Baum, "China Youths' Rising Self-interest," *CSM*, November 3, 1986.

107. See Lynn White, "Thought Workers...," pp. 271-72. Also, Merle Goldman, "Culture," in Stephen M. Goldstein, ed., *China Briefing, 1984* (Boulder: Westview, 1985), p. 22.

108. *Pipan zichan jieji ziyouhua sichao.*

109. Interview and *RMRB*, January 13, 1987. The president had to be announced by the CAS Deputy Chair, Zhou Guangzhao, because Lu would not do it. Shades of Nixon's "Saturday Night Massacre."

110. This information has not been confirmed, but it comes from a person who traveled from China several months after this meeting and reported conversations with others who had attended.
111. *RMRB*, January 31, 1987.
112. Of course, this is not completely new. See Andrew J. Nathan, *Chinese Democracy* (New York: Knopf, 1985).
113. "Shao Ding," interviewed in *ZM*, August 1986, 36-37.
114. *Dang de shenghuo* (Party Life), 1981, No. 5, tr. John P. Burns and Stanley Rosen, eds., *Policy Conflicts in Post-Mao China* (Armonk: Sharpe, 1986), pp. 265-66.
115. See Li Cheng and Lynn White, "The Thirteenth Central Committee...."
116. See the papers at a New England China Seminar, May 1987, which will appear in *New Perspectives on the Cultural Revolution*, William Joseph, Christine Wong, and David Zweig, eds., (Cambridge: Harvard University Press, 1989), as well as a forthcoming book by Andrew G. Walder, and also Lynn White, *Policies of Chaos: The Organizational Causes of Violence in China's Cultural Revolution* (Princeton: Princeton University Press, 1989).

PART III

INSTITUTIONS IN FLUX

FIVE

THE CHANGING NATURE OF ELITE CONFLICT
IN POST-MAO CHINA

Parris H. Chang

In an interview with Edgar Snow in 1960, the late Premier Zhou Enlai disclosed that Communist China had been governed since 1949 by a group of approximately 800 key party and military leaders who had helped Mao Zedong seize power. Zhou predicted that they would run China for many more years to come.[1] Most of these "800," including Zhou, Mao, Liu Shaoqi, Zhu De, and Lin Biao are dead, or in some instances, in political disgrace. But 150 members of this elite group have survived although they are very old, and many are in poor health. It is striking that this "Old Guard," which includes Deng Xiaoping, Chen Yun, Li Xiannian, Peng Zhen, Yang Shangkun, and Wang Zhen, still have the final say over the regime's policy priorities, despite the fact that most of them are no longer members of the CCP Politburo or Central Committee (CC), and in spite of a highly publicized drive to promote talented younger cadres to the leadership.

The political longevity of the revolutionary elite notwithstanding, the CCP leadership and political system have undergone far-reaching changes in the wake of Chairman Mao's death. A different breed of leader is taking over and emphasizing economic growth, rather than revolutionary change. This chapter intends to analyze the changing nature of elite conflict, changes in the path to power, elite composition, sources of leadership power, and the norms of leadership.

THE HUA GUO-FENG INTERLUDE

On October 6, 1976, barely four weeks after CCP chairman Mao Zedong died, his wife Jiang Qing and three other radical disciples, who have since been labelled the "Gang of Four," were arrested and abruptly removed from power in a lightning coup in Beijing. The coup marked not only the "victorious close" of the Great Proletarian Cultural Revolution (GPCR) launched by the late chairman, but it also thrust a key organizer of the coup, Premier Hua Guo-feng into political prominence. At an enlarged Politburo session convened shortly thereafter, Hua was elected Chairman of both the party's Central Committee and its Military Affairs Committee (MAC), succeeding to Mao's mantle.

At age 56, Hua could not boast of a distinguished revolutionary career before 1949, nor did he possess the stature of a great national leader. But his political career had been aided considerably by fortuitous circumstances. Hua's good luck began in early February 1976 when he was unexpectedly designated acting Premier by Mao in the wake of Premier Zhou's death. Hua received the appointment not because of his seniority (he became a member of the Politburo only in 1973 and was only the sixth ranking Vice-Premier in the State Council), nor because of any exceptional talents or administrative experience but rather because he was least objectionable to the rival political groups in the leadership (the Gang of Four and the conservative veteran officials) and was not regarded as a threat to them. The fact that Hua was designated only "acting

Premier" also strongly suggests the tentative nature of his appointment.[2]

However, the riot in Beijing's Tienanmen Square in early April, 1976, a massive demonstration directed against Mao and his radical followers and in support of Vice-Premier Deng Xiaoping and the late Premier, greatly strengthened Hua's career prospect, for Mao had no choice but to forcefully confer confidence in Hua. Thus on April 7, at Mao's proposal, the Politburo resolved to dismiss Deng Xiaoping, from all leadership posts and elevate Hua Guo-feng to First Vice-Chairman of the party and Premier of the State Council, making Hua the number two leader in the regime. In so doing, Mao knowingly or unknowingly gave Hua heir-apparent status and completely wrecked an earlier plan he devised in 1973 to cultivate Wang Hongwen as his successor.

Although Hua concurrently occupied the three highest posts, in the party, government and the military after October 1976, he was unable to consolidate his leadership authority. The most difficult problem Hua faced was the outright challenge from the purge victims of the GPCR led by Deng, who had won his political rehabilitation in July 1977, over the objection of Hua and like-minded party and military officials. By the 3rd CC Plenum in December 1978, Deng and his allies (e.g., Chen Yun) had managed to neutralize Hua's influence and capture control over party councils.[3] Hua was allowed to retain his official titles for a few more years, but he was only in office and not really in power. In September 1980, he was forced to yield the post of Premier to Deng's protege Zhao Ziyang; and in June 1981, Hua formally stepped down as chairman of both the party and the MAC, and was replaced by Hu Yaobang and Deng Xiaoping, respectively. Seemingly as a consolation and certainly as a sign that political struggle has become more civilized, Hua was awarded the title of party Vice-Chairman during June 1981 September 1982.

Hua's predicament was that, despite his elevation to the party chairmanship under the political exigencies of 1976, he failed to prevail in the subsequent struggles and thereby prove that he deserved to be China's supreme leader. A number of factors account for Hua's difficulties. Because his training was limited and his leadership experience was confined largely to provincial politics prior to the 1970s, Hua was not equal to the tasks thrust upon him. Indeed, his performance as Party Chairman and Premier during 1976-80 had been highly undistinguished. Moreover, in a system like China's, where personal ties are the cement of political power, Hua simply lacked extensive networks of such links with China's power holders in the party and the PLA.

In retrospect, Hua appears to be a transitional and tragic figure. Although a Maoist, he nevertheless set in motion de-Maoization. He rose to political prominence on the waves of the GPCR and depended for support on the sacred aura of Mao's authority. With the wholesale restoration of "capitalist-roaders" and the growing repudiation of the Maoist legacy, however, he had increasingly become an anachronistic figure, a specter of the past to be exorcised.

FROM PERSONAL AUTOCRACY TO OLIGARCHY

The balance of power in the party leadership underwent a decisive shift at the landmark 3rd CC Plenum in December 1978, in which Deng Xiaoping and his allies wrested power from Chairman Hua, although they permitted him to keep his post for two more years. After that ouster, Deng who carried the titles of Party Vice-Chairman, Vice-Premier, and PLA Chief of staff, emerged as the strongman in the PRC and the chief architect of China's "open door" policy and reform programs. Moreover, his triumphant tour of the United States in January-February 1979 following the establishment of US-PRC diplomatic relations boosted his prestige enormously at home and abroad.

In the past ten years Deng has become the regime's paramount leader and the prime mover of its domestic and external policies. In his quest, Deng has relentlessly pursued three key objectives. The first is to institute economic and political reforms and fashion bold and pragmatic measures aimed at accelerating economic growth. The second is to remove officials opposed to his policies, and retire those he considers to be inept or too old. The third is to install a team of possible successors who are talented, like-minded, and in their "prime of life" to continue the modernization drive after Deng, now 83 years old, is gone.

The 12th CCP Congress held in September 1982 which Deng compared to the 7th CCP Congress of 1945 which officially legitimated Mao's leadership status, formally endorsed the Dengist policy line and put a stamp of approval on Deng's leadership. In addition, a large number of Dengists were elected to the central organs, including Hu Yaobang who was to head the party as General Secretary.

Deng and Hu had been close comrades in arms for four decades. After Deng was rehabilitated in July 1977, Hu held in succession such key posts as Director of the party Organization Department, of the Propaganda Department and Secretary-General, and when Hua Guo-feng was ousted in June 1981, the post of party Chairman. Hu was Deng's most important "brain-truster," campaign manager, and apparent successor. How, then, are we to explain China's leadership upheaval and Hu's sudden ouster in early 1987? Many Western analysts were surprised by this turn of events because they subscribed to the "Deng in Command" model of Chinese politics, and erroneously assumed that he possessed virtually absolute power. Such a model does not accurately reflect China's political realities, for Deng has never really enjoyed unrivaled authority, however prominent he has been politically. When Mao was still alive, Western writers were apt to apply the same analytical framework, i.e., "Mao in command." Even then the approach was found to be too simplistic and inadequate to explain China's major political developments.

Obviously Deng does not exercise the same great personal authority and enormous political power that Mao used to wield. The late chairman governed like an emperor, but Deng is only *primus inter pares* and has had to share a leadership role with a number of "senior statesmen" inside the party. Moreover, most Chinese leaders had suffered from Mao's autocratic rule and would never have let Deng become China's latest emperor even had he aspired to such a role. Besides, Deng was driven out of office twice in 10 years during the GPCR and had to make self-criticisms and other compromises to return. He thus bears too many political scars.

In fact, the post-Mao leadership structure has undergone far-reaching changes. It has ceased to be a system of one-man rule and has evolved into a complex mixture of oligarchy and gerontocracy, combining both the elements of collegial rule and fragmentation of power. Three points need to be emphasized. One, the CCP leadership system is based on the rule of man, in which politics is highly personalized and weakly institutionalized; hence the power or influence of a leader depends more on who he is and his *Guanxi* (networks of personal connections) than on his official position. Although General Secretary Zhao Ziyang is the head of the party hierarchy now, he does not make policy. The fact that he found it necessary to obtain Deng's approval of a plan to develop the coastal regions before it was submitted to the Politburo in 1988 is a clear indication of who has the ultimate authority in Beijing.[4] Likewise, Acting Premier Li Peng's visit with Chen Yun in mid-February 1988, which was well publicized in the *People's Daily*, indicates that Chen remains highly influential and his "advice" is sought even though he, like Deng, has stepped down from the Politburo and CC.

Second, the system is highly gerontocratic, in that the elders dominate and exercise greater influence than younger leaders regardless of what titles they may hold. The formula "one man, one vote" does not apply in senior policy councils. Many veteran party and military officials see themselves as the custodians of the Communist revolution and like Marshal Ye Jianying have asserted their unalienable right to "serve until the last moment of life."[5] Thus, on January 16, 1987, 17 retired officials, came out of their political retirement to decide on Hu's dismissal and Zhao's appointment as acting party General Secretary.[6]

Third, and this may be most consequential, inasmuch as Deng does not enjoy unrivaled authority and has to contend with a number of co-equals, the leadership system partakes of the attributes of collective leadership. When Mao was alive, he was in a class of his own; he was both the ruler and the "high priest"—performing such major leadership roles as legitimization of policy, initiation of policy, conflict resolution, political integration, and fulfilling the paramount function of the "law giver." In the post-Mao leadership, a number of patriarchal figures are Deng's peers; moreover, there is no "thought of Deng Xiaoping" as Deng has never been an established ideologist, and is not capable of combining all the key leadership roles. Collective rule inevitably leads to dispersion and fragmentation of power, which tends to generate leadership disunity. To maintain a viable coalition, Deng has had to rely on a mix of persuasion, cajolery, compromise, and threat. Often he has been forced to make concessions. This was the case with the forced resignation of Hu Yaobang in January 1987, and so was the leadership reshuffle at the 13th Party Congress in October 1987 and the NPC session in March 1988.

STRUGGLE OVER POWER AND POLICY

Many analysts believe that various CCP leaders agree on main objectives (e.g., modernization, reforms, etc.), and differ only on the tactics and means to accomplish such goals. However, as Hu's forced departure and the subsequent campaign against bourgeois liberalization have shown, there have been sharp conflicts at the top, not only over methods, but also over power, policy, and personality.

Chen Yun and Deng were political allies at the crucial party gathering during November-December 1978 as they joined forces to defeat Hua Guo-feng and the Maoists. After that historic meeting, they assumed key responsibilities in the leadership and became two of the leaders most responsible for shaping the regime's economic policy.[7] Their policy differences have become discernible since the mid-1980s, as Chen Yun is in favor of a more orthodox planned economy and has questioned the wisdom of Deng's open-door policies. For example, at the party's national conference in December 1985, Chen was outspoken in his criticism of Deng's reform measures, including what he viewed as a lack of central planning and excessive reliance on the market mechanism in the economy and "the worship of money" and its corrosive influence on the party's work habits and social mores. Without naming names, but unmistakably with Deng in mind, Chen urged that all major policy decisions be made collectively after full consultation and declared emphatically, "No one should try to have the final say."[8]

Another Deng critic is Peng Chen, a politburo member until November 1987 and chairman of the National People's Congress (NPC) until April, 1988. Peng is regarded by some Chinese as a "restorationist," preferring to return to the orthodox 1950s system of the "command economy" albeit with some adjustments.[9] Since Peng has been highly critical of efforts at structural reforms and the use of capitalist measures, the NPC held up the passage of an enterprise law and a bankruptcy law, much to the anguish of the Deng camp. The ideas of Chen and Peng remain surprisingly popular in the bureaucracy because many cadres have become accustomed to a system of party control and bureaucratic planning, and they naturally resist changes which threaten to undercut their power.

Many People's Liberation Army (PLA) cadres are highly ambivalent toward Deng's reform. It is no secret that many military leaders detest the regime's *laissez-faire* rural policy. In their view, the policy has undermined the ability of the PLA to recruit and to retain soldiers. Young people, they say, have been lured away by economic opportunities at home and are no longer attracted to the rigorous barrack life.

In theory, the PLA should welcome Deng's modernization drive because it would stand to benefit from the modernization of national defense. In reality, however, military modernization has been given low priority and defense spending has been cut for a number of years. The policy to retire old cadres and promote younger and better-educated ones, a major plank in Deng's platform, threatens the jobs and perks of veteran officers. Likewise the PLA has had serious misgivings on Deng's decision to cut PLA troops by one million and dragged their feet on it.

Moreover, many PLA leaders, antagonistic toward Hu Yaobang, successfully blocked Deng's plan to groom his hand-picked successor for the chairmanship of the party Military Affairs committee. Hu antagonized the PLA because of his stinging attack on Mao's past and his defense of intellectuals, including a playwright named Bai Hua who was denounced by the army paper for "uglifying socialist motherland, blackening the image of the party and the country, and defaming the people's army" in his movie script "Bitter Love."[10] Hu's excessive zeal in pushing the old cadres to retire has offended many of them. When the PLA held an enlarged conference on political work during December 11-25, 1986, Hu is said to have come under harsh criticism for, among other things, having neglected ideological work and for the decline in military spending.[11]

Although Deng's modernization drive and daring reforms have achieved remarkable results, they have not been an unqualified success. The "open-port" cities that were established to attract foreign capital and technology were such failures that 10 out of 14 of them had to be "closed" in June 1985. Notwithstanding marked improvements in living conditions in the rural areas of China's coastal provinces, most urban residents are suffering from soaring prices and annual double-digit inflation.[12]

Furthermore, because of policies that encourage people to get rich, corruption has become rife among cadres, and the gap is widening between the haves and have nots, and between resource-rich and resource-poor communities. Beijing's promises of economic modernization and a better life have aroused the material desires of average Chinese, but their unfulfilled expectations have turned into discontent and alienation. Moreover, the regime's open-door policy has fostered "bourgeois tendencies" in Chinese society and undermined people's faith in the regime's ideological teachings.

All of these problems have provided Deng's critics with heavy political ammunition. The critics mounted a campaign against "spiritual pollution" in 1983-84 and used it as a weapon to constrain Deng's open-door policy and reform programs. Although the campaign was short-lived, and Deng Liqun, a conservative ideologue who masterminded the campaign and gave it a big push was dismissed by Hu from the post of CCP Propaganda Department, the conflict between the reformers and their critics continued.

In the fall of 1985, the conservatives strongly reasserted themselves at the party's national conference.[13] They wanted the party to devote special attention to ideological education and "socialist ethics." Moreover, they scored a major victory in the following year when they blocked planned political reforms championed by the reform camp and, instead, pushed through the party CC Plenum in September 1986 a lengthy resolution that stressed "socialist spiritual civilization" to cope with the crisis of belief in China.

The intense leadership conflict that surfaced in early 1987 and Hu's forced resignation are best understood in the broad political context set out above. The student demonstrations that began in December 1986 and Hu's "mismanagement" of them only brought a simmering crisis to a head. There is no question that the conservatives and many more cadres with vested interests were not happy with Deng's programs and that the conservative upsurge had a distinct anti-Deng overtone. Then why was Hu singled out for attack? Was he made a fall guy?

As the party's chief executive and the "manager" of Deng's reform movement, Hu could not avoid the onus of the problems that have emerged. Although Deng ironically helped set up the pro-democracy movement last year by calling for political reforms he said were essential to economic reforms, in operational terms, Hu was on the front line. When student protest almost got out of hand, it was Hu who had to bear the blame. Worse, unlike Deng and other Chinese officials who regard democracy and the students as tools and as the means to other goals, Hu was seen by his colleagues as becoming "too soft"—defending students' constitutional rights in politburo meetings and speaking like an advocate of Western democracy and political freedoms. Even Deng is said to have been annoyed.

Besides, Hu had other political liabilities. Until his forced departure, he operated very much in the shadow of his mentor. Consequently his own leadership qualities remained largely unproven. Moreover, Hu's tendency to promote his former associates from the Communist Youth League (such as Hu Qili, Qiao Shi, Wu Xuequian, Hao Jianxiu, Wang Zhaoguo) had made him vulnerable to charges of factionalism and had alienated officials of other leadership factions.

Moreover, Hu made too many enemies. Many powerful people were alienated and provoked by two things Hu did in 1986, prompting them to join hands to have him toppled. First, Hu is said to have used the campaign against corruption, which was launched in January 1986 with immense publicity, as a political weapon against the conservatives and the critics of Deng's reforms. In a drive to strike at the "tigers," the big perpetrators, Hu reportedly approved the arrests of many high officials and their relatives, including Hu Shiying, a son of Politburo member Hu Qiaomu.[14] Second, in his eagerness to rejuvenate the policy-making councils, Hu Yaobang was too much of a threat to the veteran officials.

Thus, the student demonstrations provided a convenient pretext for Hu's critics. On December 27, 1986, according to sources inside China, Peng Zhen and six other conservative party and PLA leaders went to see Deng to make their case against Hu Yaobang.[15] They attacked the General Secretary for, among other things, poor leadership in ideological work, protecting writers who spread antiparty and antisocialist ideas, thereby creating conditions for the growth and dissemination of bourgeois liberalization, and asked for his dismissal.

It was a difficult choice for Deng. After all, Hu had been his close comrade-in-arms and hand-picked successor. Not long before, he had expressed confidence in Hu by telling foreign visitors that if the heavens were to collapse, Hu Yaobang and Zhao Ziyang could hold them up. To reverse himself and to sack Hu under the prevailing circumstances would not only reflect on his own poor judgment but would also expose his political weakness.

On the other hand, if Deng continued to back Hu, he would risk alienating large numbers of China's power-holders, and that could endanger both his leadership status and his modernization programs. Deng, a quintessential pragmatist throughout his political career, knew when to make a deal. In order to cut his losses, Deng decided to let Hu go, but replaced him with Zhao. In so doing, Deng sought to keep control of the situation and continue the course of reform and open-door policy at home, while projecting an image of leadership stability and continuity abroad.

On January 16, 1987, *Xinhua News Agency* formerly released the news that in an enlarged meeting of the CCP Politburo earlier that day, General Secretary Hu Yaobang had made a "self-criticism of his mistakes on major issues of political principles in violation of the party's principle of collective leadership" and resigned.[16] The enlarged Politburo meeting, added the news report, accepted Hu's resignation, appointed Zhao Ziyang acting General Secretary, and proposed to submit these two decisions to the "next plenary session of the Central Committee for confirmation."

According to the CCP charter, the party general secretary can be appointed and dismissed only by a CC Plenum; therefore the actions of the enlarged Politburo meeting were unconstitutional. Why did the CCP leaders choose not to convene a CC meeting to approve such important decisions? Is it possible that Hu commanded sufficient support in the CC to block or challenge the elders' decisions?

In any case, the fact that 17 leading members of the Central Advisory Commission, two leading members of the Central Commission for Discipline Inspection, and "other comrades" attended the enlarged Politburo session and joined the 18 members and 2 alternate members of the Politburo to decide on the dismissal and appointment of party general secretary sheds light on China's political life and illuminates who wields real influence. Clearly, the group of angry old men who were pushed into political retirement against their will have refused to "fade away" and engineered the ouster of party General Secretary Hu Yaobang. Moreover, they followed through in launching an intensive campaign to combat "bourgeois liberalization" throughout China.[17]

The campaign was short-lived, however. There is no question that such a political and ideological drive was very unpopular; ironically, the conservative upsurge turned Hu Yaobang into a national hero as many intellectuals came to like him and expressed support for the besieged former party head. More important, perhaps, was the adverse effect on the national economy generated by the campaign and the necessity felt by the reform forces to rein in the conservatives. Through the efforts of acting party General Secretary Zhao Ziyang and especially Deng's skillful maneuver, which I have treated elsewhere,[18] rival political forces compromised on leadership changes and policy issues and agreed to a temporary political truce.

LEADERSHIP CHANGES
SINCE THE 13TH CONGRESS

The end, when it finally came, was distinctly anticlimactic. To no one's surprise, the 13th CCP Congress, which met for two weeks during October-November 1987, approved the long-awaited leadership reshuffle and formally conferred the title of General Secretary on Zhao Ziyang who had served in that capacity since January 1987. To rejuvenate the leadership ranks, Deng himself had to set a personal example by leaving the Politburo and the CC. In so doing, he induced, if not compelled, more than 90 CC members, including such senior leaders as Chen Yun, Li Xiannian, and Peng Zhen who were also members of the Politburo, to do the same.[19] The exception was Yang Shangkun who, at the age of 80, was the only veteran official in Deng's peer group to remain in the Politburo. The fact that Yang would replace Li Xiannian as China's Head of State at the subsequent NPC session in April 1988 and, even more in the interim functioned as Deng's proxy, explains this exception.

At the first glance, the Deng camp seemed to have done remarkably well. The Dengists could draw satisfaction from three developments. One, Zhao was elected General Secretary and First Vice-Chairman of the MAC without a hitch. Two, virtually all the old soldiers and party officials left the Politburo and the CC at Deng's urging, while a large number of cadres in their "prime of life" were elevated to these organs.[20] Three, Hu Yaobang, who was forced to step down from the post of general secretary earlier in the year, and many of his former associates have remained in the CC and the Politburo. This indicates considerable political strength on the part of Hu's group, which constitutes part of the Deng coalition.

Several significant trends should be noted. When an established leader (a party general secretary, or a party chairman, i.e. Hua Guo-feng) is toppled and can still remain in the Politburo, that is a change from the practice during the GPCR when the fallen would be treated as an enemy of the people and would be totally disgraced. Now that the leadership conflict has become much less intense and violent, and not a matter of life or death, the rules of the game have become more "civilized."

Judging from the background and training of officials promoted during the Party Congress and at the NPC in April 1988, important changes are taking place with regard to the path to power and the character of a new generation of leaders. For example, five of the seven new Politburo members, and most of the new CC members have had a college education, and some even the experience of advanced technical training abroad. This is a clear indication that the importance of experts and the specialists is on the rise.[21] Li Peng, who studied engineering in Moscow, became a member of the Politburo Standing Committee, and was appointed Premier personifies the rise of the "technocrat" in the PRC. In the State Council a majority of the 45 ministers appointed in April 1988 are technical experts and at least 15 of them have studied in the USSR/East Europe. In the years to come, as the regime continues to emphasize modernization, knowledge will be converted increasingly to political power, and the cadres who possess expertise and master particular areas of bureaucratic activity will have better chances to advance to positions of leadership.

On the other hand, we should be attentive also to leadership cleavages and dissension. Although Zhao is now General Secretary, the functions of the CC Secretariat under him have been severely curtailed due to reorganization, and his stewardship is sure to be constrained and resisted by his colleagues. Take the Politburo Standing Committee, for example. Out of the five men who make up the regime's top policy council, only Zhao and Hu Qili can be identified as strong advocates of the open-door policy and bolder initiatives for economic development and structural reform. Premier Li Peng, senior Vice-Premier Yao Yi-lin, and Qiao Shi, who control the regime's intelligence/security apparatus tend to emphasize stability and the planned economy, and are cautious toward the market-oriented reforms promoted by Deng and Zhao.

Moreover, although the veteran leaders have left the Politburo, which has lost much power and prestige in any case, they have no intention to retire from politics. In order to secure their consent to retire from the Politburo and the CC, apparently Deng had to make deals with them and let them move to the NPC, and CCP Central Advisory Commission (CAC), or the Chinese People's Political Consultative Conference (CPPCC).[23] These organizations, are the bastions of the conservatives, especially the CAC which had been headed by Chen Yun since November, 1987. Deng's effort to rejuvenate the leadership ranks still has a long way to go because these old men will continue to intervene in the political process and exert influence on policy and the selection of future leaders.

Even Deng himself has stayed on as Chairman of the MAC and retained control over the armed forces, in spite of his repeated protestation that he wanted to retire. Is Deng, like Mao before him, a true believer of the dictum that political power grows from the barrel of a gun? Or, is it that Deng feels compelled to remain in the leadership hierarchy in order to prop up his political heir Zhao Ziyang? In any case, as long as Deng is there, he overshadows his protege and gives other senior leaders the pretext to remain in the political picture.

ZHAO'S CHALLENGE

Granted that Zhao is talented, a consummate pragmatist, and an accomplished administrator,[24] he has severe handicaps and faces difficult tasks ahead. First of all, the command of Communist ideology is not his forte, and he has not done much, if any, theoretical writing, qualifications which are important for the party general secretary.[25] Second, Zhao lacks impressive pre-1949 revolutionary credentials. He was too young to take part in the Long March and was not in a position to contribute to the Communist seizure of power. Third, he has yet to develop an extensive network of personal ties with the powerholders in the party and in the PLA.

In order to broaden his bases of power, Zhao must, first and foremost, garner the support of the military—something which his predecessor failed to do. It would be a challenge for Zhao who does not have much military experience to convince the military establishment that he can inherit Deng's mantle and perform the function of the supreme commander.

Equally important, Zhao will need great ability and political acumen to unite and preside over the 18-member Politburo, which is composed of several distinct leadership blocs, and divided on major issues. Hu Yaobang and his associates from the Communist Youth League are strongly represented in the Politburo (and in the CC) and will be a formidable political force to be reckoned with when Zhao seeks to forge a ruling coalition to promote reforms. Previously there were personal and policy frictions between Hu and Zhao, largely because of Hu's tendency to interfere in the affairs of Zhao's State Council. Henceforth, it will be up to Zhao to demonstrate his leadership skill to win over Hu and his supporters.

Zhao's most difficult task may well be handling premier Li Peng, a rising political star, and a rival, who undoubtedly aspires to take over the party leadership if and when Zhao falters. At 60, Li is favored by his relative youth and his technical education. In addition, Li is the foster son of the late Premier Zhou Enlai and has good family connections with most of the regime's veteran leaders. Furthermore, a considerable number of Soviet-bloc returned students have risen in the party and government hierarchy, and at least 15 of them are holding key ministerial posts in the State Council. Possibly these "technocrats" share Li's policy and political orientation.

As the experience of Hua Guo-feng and Hu Yaobang has shown, the party leader no longer has an "iron rice bowl" and is subject to removal. Chairman Mao was a towering leadership figure and, as the major architect of Communist revolution, possessed a great cult of personality and an aura of sacred authority. He did not have to account for his gross political and policy failures. The postrevolutionary elite, however, enjoys no such luxury; instead, they must deliver in concrete, contemporary terms, and prove to their elders and peers alike their claim to leadership. Zhao is giving a big push to his plan to develop coastal regions, apparently because he feels the political and psychological pressure to perform.

Lacking the leadership stature as well as the outstanding intellectual and personal qualities of the revolutionary generation, Zhao and other Chinese leaders may in the future find it much more difficult to consolidate their power. As they do not differ much in credentials, seniority, and career achievements, each will probably feel equally deserving and equally entitled to contend for the top leadership position. Coupled with the changes in the rules of the game in which the wages of defeat are demotion, and not physical liquidation, ambitious Chinese officials may not be easily deterred from joining the leadership sweepstakes.

NOTES

1. Edgar Snow, *The Other Side of the River: Red China Today* (New York: Random House, 1961), p. 331.
2. For an analysis of the leadership conflict in this period see Parris H. Chang, "Mao's Last Stand?" *Problems of Communism*, Vol. 25, No. 4 (July-August 1976), pp. 1-17.
3. See Parris H. Chang, "Chinese Politics: Deng's Turbulent Quest," *Problems of Communism*, Vol. 30, No. 1 (January-February 1981) pp. 10-11.
4. *Xinhua* (New China) News Agency (Peking), January 22, 1988, and *Renmin ribao* (People's Daily), March 21, 1988.
5. *Renmin ribao*, September 7, 1982, p. 2.
6. *Ibid.*, January 17, 1987, p. 1.
7. For an interesting political biography of Chen Yun, see David M. Bachman, *Chen Yun and the Chinese Political System* (Berkeley: Institute of East Asian Studies, University of California, 1985).
8. *Renmin ribao*, September 24, 1985.
9. Wang Jun-tao, "An Analysis of China's Past, Present and Future," *The Seventies* (Hong Kong) No. 134 (March 1981), p. 69.
10. During April 17-20, 1981, the PLA organ *Liberation Army Daily* published a series of attacks on Bai Hua, but *People's Daily* remained silent. Four months later, on August 18, the Party's organ felt compelled to print a self-criticism conceding the errors of not criticizing Bai Hua and other writers in good time.
11. Xiao Yi, "Why Has the Military Opposed Hu Yaobang," *Cheng Ming* (Hong Kong), No. 114f (April, 1987) pp. 20-21.
12. Such an assessment is reinforced by a CIA report to the Joint Economic Committee of the U.S. Congress in April 1988; for a summary of the report see *Washington Post*, May 1, 1988. p. 1.
13. See the Speeches of Chen Yun and Li Hsien-nien which were prominently published beside Deng's in the *People's Daily* on September 24, 1985.
14. According to sources inside China, Peng Zhen's daughter was also implicated in a bribe scandal and was investigated by police, but was set free later. Miss Ye Zhifong, an official at State Economic commission and daughter of Ye Fei, former commander of Navy, received seventeen years for accepting a bribe from a foreign company. The court declared Hu Shiying innocent in the wake of Hu Yaobang's resignation in January 1987.

15. Lu Keng. "The True Story Behind China's Political Shakeup," *Pai Shing* (Hong Kong), No. 141 (April 1, 1987), p. 3. These leaders were Yang Shangkun (Yu Qiuli), Wang Zhen, Bo Yi-bo, Hu Quiaomu, and Deng Liqun. Yang and Yu were members of the Politburo and also PLA leaders; Hu, a member of the Politburo and Deng, a member of the Secretariat, were two ranking conservative ideologues; Bo and Wang, formerly a PLA general, were Vice-Chairmen of the Central Advisory Commission.

16. *Renmin ribao*, January 17, 1987, p. 1.

17. Parris H. Chang, "China After Deng: Toward the 13th CCP Congress," *Problems of Communism*, Vol. 36, No. 3 (May-June 1987), pp. 36-37.

18. *Ibid.*, pp. 30-42.

19. Altogether 11 Politburo members were not reelected—they were Deng, Chen, Li who were members of the select Politburo Standing Committee, Peng Cheng, Yu Chiu-li, Yang Te-chih (Yang Dezhi), Hsi Chung-hsun (Xi Zhongxun), Hu Chiao-my, Fang Yi, Nee Chih-fu (Ni Zhifu), and Chen Mu-hua (Chen Muhua), who was an alternate member.

20. In the CC, 61 of the 175 members are new, while 59 of the 110 alternate members are new. Of these 285, 132 or 46.3 percent are under 55 years old; in contrast, only 93 or 26.8 percent of the 345 members and alternate members of the previous CC were under 55 years of age.

21. 209 or 73.3 percent of the 285 members of the 13th CC have college education; *Xinhua*, November 1, 1987.

22. Notable among them are Premier Li Peng, Li Tieh-ying (Li Tieying), Sung Chien (Song Jian), Tsou Chia-hua (Zhou Jiahua), and Li Kuei-hsien (Li Kueixian) who carry the title of National Councillor and head of key ministry/commission, Foreign Minister Chien Chi-Shun (Qian Qchen), and Ting Heng-Kao (Ting Henggao), Minister in charge of National Defense Industry and science commission.

23. Chen Yun has taken over the chairmanship of CAC, which was previously occupied by Deng Xiaoping. Li Xiannian, who yielded the post of Head of State to Yang Shangkun, has become chairman of the CPPCC. Three former Politburo members, Xi Zhongxun, Nizhifu, and Chen Mu-hua, have got new jobs as Vice-Chairman of the NPC. General Wang Zhen, at 80, has come out of retirement and become the Vice-Chairman of the Republic.

24. An excellent account of Zhao's career is found in David L. Shambaugh, *The Making of A Premier: Zhao Ziyang's Provincial Career* (Boulder, CO: Westview, 1984).
25. In this connection, Mikhail Gorbachev's new publication, *Perestroika and New Thinking for Our Country and the Whole World*, is highly instructive—to assert his leadership, Gorbachev apparently finds it necessary to project an image of a creative thinker with vision for the future, but also to present himself as a theoretician well-versed in the canon of communist ideology.

SIX

DISCIPLINARY PROBLEMS
AND THE CCP'S RECTIFICATION CAMPAIGN

Hsi-sheng Ch'i

The Chinese Communists have always believed that their party's ability to perform its revolutionary mission depends heavily on the quality of both its leaders and its members, as well as on a proper working relationship between these two groups. Minimally, all party members must possess special personal qualifications and strong revolutionary commitment. In addition, the leaders should be unified, far-sighted, and capable of following the correct ideological line in their policy-making, while the members should possess the ability to implement party policies faithfully, properly, and efficiently. Finally, the interrelationship between these two groups should conform to the principle of democratic centralism.

However, it has not always been possible for the party to attain these ideal conditions. When major deficiencies occur, the party has employed purges and rectifications to correct the problems. While these two terms are often used interchangeably in the Western press, the Chinese Communists have been careful to keep their distinctions.

Usually, a purge signifies the existence of an antagonistic relationship between the party and a clearly defined target.

The target usually involves a group of individuals, but always "a tiny minority" according to the party's account, who allegedly have committed serious political or ideological errors, or participated in plots to overthrow the established leadership. These targeted individuals are customarily branded as either antiparty elements, counterrevolutionaries, or conspirators and criminals. They are treated as a cancer of the party that must be isolated and removed to preserve the party's organizational purity. The means to achieve this goal can include not only dismissal, political exile, or disfranchisement, but also hard labor, imprisonment, and execution.

In contrast, rectification denotes the existence of certain problems within the party. The problems could be either of a specific or diffuse nature, and could affect either a minority or a majority of the party's members. However, even though the errant members' activities may pose a serious threat to the party, they are not viewed as opposing the party or its ideology by design, and therefore are not antagonistic in character. The object of rectification is not to eliminate people, but to eliminate erroneous styles, thoughts, and behavioral patterns.[1]

In reality, however, such distinctions are not always easily kept, and each method often contains some elements of the other. A purge may allow some repentant members to return to the party's fold, while a rectification may result in the expulsion or worse fate for a few recalcitrants. But the choice of either term by the party to characterize a campaign is an important indicator of the intent of the leaders and the means they plan to use.

Notwithstanding the more benign implications of rectification, the Communist party is still extremely reluctant to resort to it for several reasons. First, a Communist party's legitimacy to rule is predicated on its claim as the revolutionary vanguard. Ideological infallibility and behavioral rectitude are two putative attributes of a vanguard. In theory, Communists have always set high and exacting behavioral standards for themselves. As the Chinese have proudly asserted, "we Communists are made of special materials." Any time the Communists mount a rectification campaign, it is an embarrassing admission that something is amiss, and makes the party vulnerable to doubts about its fitness to rule.

Second, the Communist party is a fighting machine with twin missions. One mission is to protect the dictatorship of the proletariat (or, as the Chinese put it, "the people's democratic dictatorship") over the rest of society, and the other mission is to achieve socialist construction. When the party has to divert its attention to "house-cleaning," it reduces its "combat effectiveness," and may seriously hamper the pace of socialist construction.

Finally, comradeship and solidarity are more laboriously fostered within a Communist party than within most other political parties. Party membership is a life-long commitment. A rectification campaign could create intense emotional trauma when people bound by "fraternal love" are called upon to scrutinize their comrades' conduct, to criticize them, and even to struggle against them.

For these reasons, a rectification campaign is a major event for the Communist party and is launched only after much deliberation and procrastination. Such was the case when the CCP passed a Resolution in October 1983 to announce the start of a new rectification campaign. Once such a momentous decision was made, the leaders sought to solve all the major problems the party had experienced since the death of Mao.

In their view, the party's problems fell into four categories. First, it had suffered from ideological confusion caused both by the legacy of extreme leftism, and the contamination of capitalist thoughts. Second, its ranks were infested with a sizable number of members tainted by close ties with the Gang of Four and who were conspiring for a political comeback. Third, its members' conduct had deteriorated dangerously as manifested by their rampant bureaucratism and abuse of privileges. Finally, its internal operations were plagued by an autocratic style of leadership, factionalism, and disrespect of discipline which were directly attributable to the bad influence of the Cultural Revolution.

These gloomy assessments led the leaders to decide that the rectification campaign must solve all these problems simultaneously. As the Resolution declared, the rectification campaign was designed to unify thought, to purify organization, to rectify style, and to strengthen discipline.[2]

While the campaign's objectives were broadly defined, discipline remained a central concern throughout the entire campaign. The purpose of this chapter is to focus on the party's disciplinary problems and address three related issues. First, it will analyze the party's reasons for launching the rectification campaign. Second, it will highlight the campaign's main features. Finally, it will identify the factors affecting the campaign's accomplishments or failures and speculate on its long-range impact on Chinese politics.

THE DECISION TO LAUNCH
A RECTIFICATION CAMPAIGN

Discipline problems appeared within the CCP almost immediately after Mao's death. But in the first few years, top leaders were too preoccupied with the question of succession and their own positions within the new ruling hierarchy to pay much attention to the conduct of the rank and file. The intense power struggle reached a turning point in late 1978 to early 1979 when Deng finally edged Hua Guofeng from the top position.

Once in power, Deng's most pressing concern was to quickly bolster the legitimacy of his leadership. To accomplish this, he pursued two strategies simultaneously. The first strategy was to rebuild a ruling coalition among the party's national leadership by removing the most onerous policies of the Maoist era, and by soothing the wounds inflicted on leading party figures during the Cultural Revolution. Deng hoped that this would suffice to re-invigorate the party's organization and restore solidarity among its members. The upshot was the visible acceleration of the healing and rehabilitation process, culminating in the exoneration of Mr. Liu Shaoqi, the late president of the People's Republic of China.

Deng's second strategy was to inject a sense of mission by re-directing the nation's energy and attention to the task of the "four modernizations." The bold step he took in this connection was to launch the agricultural reform which expanded the private sector, legitimized material incentives, and increased the degree of personal autonomy among the rural population.

Hence, in the first two years after Deng's rebound to power, there was little evidence to suggest that he had developed any profound misgivings about the nature or the capability of the party, nor did he hint that massive and thorough party reform was to be a prerequisite of his other political programs.[3]

Meanwhile, party members' discipline continued its steep decline and simply became impossible to ignore. Many party organs ceased to perform such routine functions as collecting dues, conducting political study sessions, or holding regular meetings.[4] Instances of members refusing job assignments or bargaining for better treatment increased significantly.[5] Factional infighting also became more blatant, and the party organs in many places threatened to place themselves beyond the control from higher levels.[6]

Party secrets could no longer be protected. Not only did regular party members acquire the habit of talking openly and casually about the party's internal matters, but more serious was the tendency of leading cadres and their family members to peddle their privileged information. These people became the constant source of the so-called "side channel information" (*xiao-dao xiao-xi*) which gained wide circulation among the masses and often caused harm to the government's policies.[7]

The rehabilitated cadres, who were counted on to serve as the stalwarts of the party's tradition, hardly behaved any better. Many of them were profoundly affected by the realization of the transience of power. They assumed the cynical attitude that power must be exploited to its fullest extent while it lasted lest it disappear. Some also concluded that they had "pierced through" the fickleness of politics to take it seriously. While Deng counted on the rehabilitated cadres' support and experience to carry out his political programs, the latter were preoccupied with exploiting their privileged positions to advance personal interest.

Admittedly, the CCP had encountered the abuse of power by its members before, but there existed a significant qualitative difference between the situation in the late 1970s and earlier periods. During earlier periods, privileges were abused by a smaller number of people whose life-styles were carefully shielded from public view while the middle and lower ranks basically followed a frugal life-style. Starting in the late 1970s, abuse of privileges became more widespread, affecting cadres on every level of the party and government. Powerful cadres and their children boasted about their creature comforts and flaunted their newfangled gadgets in a manner that could only tempt the lesser cadres to emulate them with gusto. A clear trend existed for cadre misconduct to increase both in scope and in novelty.

When party leaders turned their attention to the deterioration of discipline in the late 1970s, they showed little sensitivity to the seriousness of the challenge. Initially, the party thought it would suffice merely to revive the old party structure and reestablish old organizational control mechanisms in a single package. Even Chen Yun who had always had a close personal interest in party discipline described the party's difficulties in 1977 as "temporary" in nature, and predicted a bright future for the party with its problems resolved "if our entire party could unify around the party's center, engage in collective consultation, and achieve unity of will."[8]

In late December 1978, during the CCP's 3rd Plenum, the problem of discipline was finally placed on the agenda and led to the creation of a Central Discipline Committee with Chen Yun appointed as its First Secretary. At the Committee's first meeting in January 1979, Chen emphasized the importance of restoring democratic centralism in handling intra-party affairs as an effective way to safeguard party rules and rectify party style.[9] Obviously, the leaders expected party unity to be restored once squabbles within the leadership were sorted out and resolved.

Party leaders initially took a complacent view of the methods needed to improve discipline. They assumed that it was only necessary to reactivate the party's former rules and procedures with renewed vigor. Thus a number of old rules discarded during the Cultural Revolution were re-issued (e.g., the 1951 "Provisional Regulations on Safeguarding National Secrets"). Several new rules were drafted to fill the gaps as required by the new circumstances (e.g., "Certain Rules and Principles Governing the CCP's Internal Political Life"). A network of party discipline organizations on national, provincial, and local levels was set up to enforce these rules.

Because the party leaders thought members' misconduct was possible only in the context of the breakdown of organizational control, they naturally assumed that once the organizational framework was resuscitated (e.g., the Central Party Secretariat), and once the theoretical and practical confusions plaguing the party were clarified, the party center would quickly reassert tight control over the rank and file. From this new basis of unity, the leaders could then guide the entire party to concentrate on achieving the four modernizations.

By February 1980, the major steps required by this assumption had been completed. They included the rejection of "sham democracy" (qua the "four freedoms"), the drafting of a new party constitution, and the historical evaluation of Mao and his legacy. At the CCP's 5th plenum, the party declared the time had come for members to leave the past behind them, and to concentrate on "looking forward."[10]

Events soon suggested, however, that the leaders' optimistic prognosis was unwarranted as discipline continued to deteriorate through the early 1980s. In November 1980, Chen Yun ominously declared that "the party style of the ruling party is a life or death issue for the party."[11] But, even at this point, the party was contemplating punishing only a tiny number of wrongdoers for demonstrative purposes.

Deng Xiaoping on the other hand showed serious concern with this issue only when it had begun to hamper his political and economic programs. Before 1982, Deng had thought that his modernization program could be implemented with minimal disruption of party organization. His major undertakings in 1980 and 1981 were bureaucratic streamlining and gradual transfer of power to younger cadres.[12] If successful, the undesirable leaders would have been eased out without risking a confrontation within the party.

By the spring of 1982, there was a marked increase of major economic crimes when perpetrators sometimes made off with loot exceeding a million Chinese yuan.[13] These instances could no longer be explained as the work of isolated errant individuals, but were the results of highly sophisticated and elaborate schemes that could only be orchestrated by leaders with considerable organizational resources at their disposal.

This trend led Deng to the reluctant conclusion that the party's organization was itself a major impediment to improving its members' discipline. In April 1982 Deng finally indicated the need to mount a "rectification campaign" to rid the party of its erroneous style and unhealthy organization.[14] Then, in his opening statement to the 12th Party Congress, Deng pointedly stated that in order to assure the successful implementation of the four modernizations program, it was necessary to "smash the criminal activities that are destructive of socialism in the economic and other realms."[15]

In the summer of 1982, the party center stiffened its position by initiating a nation-wide campaign to prosecute economic criminals. The party threatened to dismiss members from their jobs and expel them from the party whenever they were found guilty of economic crimes, and warned that no special consideration would be granted to offenders with long party history or high position. The party further indicated that lower level party organs with signs of serious ideological, political, or organizational deviations would be disbanded if they failed to shape up.[16]

When the party finally decided to launch a major rectification campaign in October 1983, it implied an admission that all previous attempts to treat undiscipline on a case by case basis had failed, and that in fact problems of undiscipline were interrelated and required a systematic solution.

MAJOR FEATURES OF THE
RECTIFICATION CAMPAIGN

According to the party's original plan, the rectification campaign would be implemented in three stages and completed in three years. During the first stage, only a small number of party organs on the national and provincial levels would undergo rectification.[17] This particular procedure had several obvious advantages.

First, it would allow the CCP to conduct the campaign in a measured pace allowing the leaders to learn the proper methods to conduct it, and to evolve certain models and operating procedures for later stages.

Second, the CCP had always put strong emphasis on the concept of "the initial phase of combat" (*chuzhan*). By picking a manageably small number of party organs within the center's effective reach to conduct the campaign, it had a better chance of scoring an impressive victory and creating momentum for subsequent stages.

Third, this phased approach meant that the entire party would not be gripped by a sense of urgency at the same time. A rectification of limited scope would allow the leaders to contain the anxiety level, and to fine-tune their methods to minimize potentially disruptive consequences, especially in the economic field.

That the campaign was plagued from the beginning was evidenced by the fact that the experimental stage took nearly fifteen months to run its course.[18] Even as the party redoubled its effort to combat undiscipline, the latter actually worsened. This can be seen by comparing the scope and nature of misconduct over time.

In the late 1970s, the downward spiral of discipline began when cadres embezzled small amounts of public funds, indulged in excessive eating and drinking, went on sight-seeing trips on the pretext of conducting official business, and vied for opportunities to travel abroad. The common feature of these acts was that the cadres took advantage of their official positions to gain sensual gratification.

By the early 1980s, the errant party members became more acquisitive and more interested in materialistic enrichment. The new wave of important misconduct included the unauthorized construction of residences, the embezzlement of large amounts of public funds, the confiscation or illegal sale and purchase of farmland for residential or commercial use, and the theft of public property for personal profit. Other forms of misconduct included the widespread misuse of personal connections for private gains such as favorable job assignments or transfers of domicile from countryside to urban areas.[19]

The expanded economic activities created new avenues for party members and cadres to indulge in corruption on a grander scale. Taking advantage of the new policy of opening to the west and allowing greater freedom in economic activities, numerous units in the party, the military, state bureaucracy, as well as members of powerful officials' families, rushed to engage in commercial activities.

According to incomplete accounting, more than 20,000 commercial enterprises were established between the fall of 1984 and the fall of 1985. Many of these enterprises quickly established liaisons with criminal elements or unscrupulous foreign businessmen, and their activities ranged from bribery and embezzlement, to smuggling, blackmailing, evasion of taxes and custom duties, manufacturing of counterfeit medicine and liquor, sale of pornographic materials, and prostitution.[20] By early 1986, nearly 90 percent of the major criminal activities investigated by the Party's Discipline Committee were economic in nature.[21]

The situation became so bad that the party convened a massive meeting attended by over 8,000 cadres in January 1986 where top leaders issued stern warnings that criminal deeds within the party would not be tolerated. Deng personally threatened to bring high ranking perpetrators to justice to deter other potential offenders.[22] The party also demanded that the national-level cadre and the cadre of the Beijing municipality serve as the model for the entire country in combatting illegal conduct.

But such repeated warnings fell on deaf ears. The cadres were neither persuaded nor intimidated. Even as the party stepped up its campaign of antieconomic crimes, and made occasional attempts to prosecute more visible and highly placed wrongdoers, the tide was not stemmed. Still the second stage of the rectification campaign on the provincial and district levels was terminated.

In late 1986, the campaign entered its third and last stage, in the rural areas. About half of the CCP's 42 million members as well as half of its 2.6 million basic level organs were located in the countryside where 80 percent of the Chinese population also resided. These factors should have given special importance to the rural stage of the rectification campaign. When the campaign's process is viewed as a whole, it appears that each successive stage affected a larger number of party members, but lasted a shorter time period. A logical explanation for this is that each stage of rectification probably benefitted from the preceding stage and therefore required less time to conduct.

Unfortunately, this was not the case. In fact, by the time the rectification reached the rural level, its momentum had been spent. There was simply not enough willpower or manpower to tackle the amount of disciplinary problems throughout the countryside. The socioeconomic changes in the countryside had greatly reduced the farmers' concern with politics, and brought a sharp decline to the power and prestige of party functionaries in their midst. For several years, the rural party had experienced difficulty in attracting young people to join. The rectification campaign only served as a fresh reminder to the rural masses that politics meant trouble and did little to arrest the party's organizational decline.

Discipline problems existed in nearly every party organ in the rural area. But most perpetrators remained unperturbed and unrepentant when they witnessed worse offenses occurring daily in high places. The smaller size of a rural party organ and the existence of more lasting personal ties among its members made it much harder for people to criticize their errant comrades. The situation was hardly improved when the county or township party organs dispatched cadres downward to supervise village level rectification. These agents had neither the dedication to the party's goals nor the intimate knowledge of the rural party's personnel and operations to perform their duty competently.

In December 1986 and January 1987, student unrest broke out in many major urban areas when the rural areas entered a critical juncture of their rectification campaign. The national party's vehement response caused the political atmosphere in the entire country to change overnight and quickly eclipsed the task of rural rectification. As a result, the party's rectification in the vast rural areas simply fizzled.

Possibly the most striking feature of the rectification campaign during 1983-1987 was the rapidly changing complexion of undiscipline. Often new forms of undiscipline emerged before the party could find effective ways to halt the old ones. The perpetrators always managed to stay one step ahead of the party's solutions, and were able to devise "counter-measures" to derail or deflect the party's policies. During these years, the party issued numerous injunctions against different types of misconduct, but they only provoked more ingenious ways of circumvention.[23] This created the impression that the party engaged in empty threats, but proved ineffective in stamping out erroneous behavior.

A major factor contributing to the party's ineffectiveness was the sluggish process of political communication and information flow in China. Without a free press or a genuine commitment to the mass line, most acts of wrongdoing by cadres were easily concealed from the national leaders until they became both excessive and extensive. By the time the national party noticed the problem and decided on a response, the more enterprising offenders had already exhausted the opportunities in a given area of criminal activity and were ready to move on to the next area. Thus, starting in the second half of 1984, a new trend emerged when many organs in the party, army, and state bureaucracy used their official status, backed by their leaders and often invoking the name of reform or the need to promote employees' benefits, to openly engage in large-scale illegal commercial activities.[24] Some of these enterprises conducted elaborate operations, often crossing bureaucratic boundaries and extending over large geographical areas. The diversification and increasing complexity of China's economy only presented more frontiers for the opportunists to conquer.

EXPLAINING THE CAMPAIGN'S FAILURES

What went wrong with the rectification? While many more factors contributed to the difficulties of the campaign than can be adequately analyzed in this chapter, several key factors deserve our critical attention.

First, the party's leaders were never able to achieve a consensus on the need for a rectification campaign. Leaders eager to accelerate the tempo of economic development were particularly wary about the disruptive potential of a political campaign. Others feared that rectification would revive the principle of letting "politics take command," and would drain people's energy and attention from productive activities.

Provincial and local-level cadres seemed particularly unenthusiastic about the rectification campaign as they were in direct charge of economic activities. They repeatedly admonished their subordinates not to allow rectification to interfere with their productive activities. Many believed that reform would lead inevitably to unconventional behavior and style. Some cadres actually argued for further relaxation of old rules governing party conduct by pointing to the positive effect resulting from relaxing old rules in the economic realm.

Factional considerations also colored party leaders' perceptions. A rectification campaign was strongly favored by those who professed alarm at the breakdown of discipline and at the prospects of a comeback by the remnants of the

Gang of Four to "settle old scores." These remnants (or "three types") caused genuine concern within the new ruling circle evolving around Deng and Chen Yun. But leaders of other factional affiliations were more suspicious of the intent of the rectification campaign and viewed it as a thinly veiled pretext by one faction to drive another out of power. Therefore, both policy differences and power calculations prevented the party from developing a unity of purpose and a sense of dedication to carry the campaign through.

Second, the campaign failed to inspire or energize the average party members out of their gloom and profound disillusionment. Having lived through the traumas of the Cultural Revolution, people had become wiser and more cynical than before. They had witnessed the utter futility and irrationality of political struggle, and the unpredictability of one's fortune as political winds shifted direction. Few were naive enough to take the party's pledges and promises at face value. Instead, a new mentality pervaded party members which counseled them to offend no one, to criticize no one, and to protect themselves by adopting a low profile in all stages of the rectification campaign.

Third, many leading cadres were themselves demoralized. They had played a critical role in the CCP's previous rectification campaigns by taking the initiative to push the campaign and to present themselves as models of exemplary conduct. But by the early 1980s, their enthusiasm had vanished. The concurrent implementation of a mandatory retirement program also produced a leadership vacuum in many places. Understandably, when cadres faced imminent retirement and the loss of power, they were in no mood or position to offend others who might later determine how generously their retirement years would be provided for. As both old and younger cadres became preoccupied with their own career mobility, the task of rectification was relegated to a low priority.

Fourth, to the extent that the campaign's success was contingent upon the methods of its implementation, the party offered nothing innovative or imaginative. The party adopted such standard practices as political study sessions, criticism and self-criticism, investigation by one's work unit, and final summation and organizational decision either to allow the individual to re-register, or be told to leave the party without prejudice, or, in the worst cases, be expelled. But the veteran party members had been through these trials numerous times before, knew exactly what to expect, and had honed their defense mechanisms to a high state of refinement. Most members made all the obligatory moves but never wavered from the principle of making no damaging remarks against either themselves or anyone else (or as they put it, "plant flowers, not thorns"), and aimed at gliding through the screening process to reregister at the end.

Finally, the top leaders lacked the uncompromising will to enforce discipline by all necessary means. Presumably, if the party's discipline had degenerated to such a point as to present a "life or death" threat to the party, then the party should have conducted the campaign with determination and persistence. But two additional factors hampered the party's work in this respect.

The first factor was the lack of organizational efficiency. Potentially, the party had several options to enforce discipline. One was to charge a special functional branch of the party (such as its security forces) with investigating errant party members and enforcing discipline on them. The other option was to pursue the mass line and to mobilize public opinion to expose members' wrongdoings from below. The CCP eschewed both options. It rejected the first option for fear that it might rekindle memories of the Cultural Revolution. It shunned the latter (even though excessive lip service was paid to the need for public input) for fear that the intensity of public discontent would become impossible to contain.

In the end, the party chose a safe path by designating a hierarchy of discipline committees from the national to the local levels to be the campaign's watchdog. These committees typically consisted of the personnel who led the party's regular organizations on the same levels, and were often themselves the perpetrators of misconduct. The existence of intertwining personal ties and interdependent organizational interests only made it easier for the perpetrators to form defensive alliances to sabotage the rectification campaign.

The other factor was the party leaders' excessive anxiety to avoid any resemblance to the Cultural Revolution. From the beginning, the leaders went out of their way to assure the party that harsh methods would not be used. Instead, they wanted the current rectification to be conducted in the manner of "gentle breeze and mild rain." In mid-1985, Hu Yaobang indicated that he expected the total number of people to be expelled from the party not to exceed 40,000.[25] This meant that the party planned to expel less than 0.1 percent of the CCP membership, a figure which would make the rectification campaign look like a totally inappropriate operational overkill, but which would also seem a woefully inadequate response to the massive wrongdoings by its members.

The above factors caused the rectification campaign to lose credibility early. When the party began to threaten severe punishment in the face of mounting undiscipline, its threats no longer had any deterrent power. Such threats also lost their moral authority when discipline was selectively enforced, penalizing lower level people for minor infractions but ignoring the serious offenses committed by high-level cadres and their family members.

The loss of faith in the party's commitment to rectification emboldened people to commit further crimes with impunity. In the end, the leaders' anxiety to minimize pain combined with the lower-level cadres' instinct for self-protection to produce a rectification campaign marked by sound and fury, but little substance as the vast majority of wrongdoers were allowed to sail unscathed through the campaign.

CONCLUSIONS

What conclusions can we draw concerning the CCP's rectification campaign insofar as discipline is concerned? To answer this question, it is necessary to note the subtle changes of the party leaders' perceptions of danger. There is no doubt that the post-Mao leaders were genuinely worried about the possibility of a comeback by the "Cultural Revolutionists." By instituting a policy of intensive "exposing, criticizing, and investigating" (jie, pi, cha) in 1978-79,[26] they had hoped to identify key figures with factional ties to the Gang of Four and remove them from leadership positions.

At the campaign's outset, party leaders concluded that it was not enough to remove a few ringleaders because more followers of the Gang of Four on middle and lower levels were purposefully trying to destroy the party's tradition. They further concluded that the most serious criminal deeds were committed by the so-called "three types" who gained political power by closely following the leftist ideology of the Gang of Four, and by resorting to ruthless beating, smashing and looting during the Cultural Revolution. These elements not only contributed to the breakdown of discipline but were believed to be actively conspiring to overthrow the present leadership and reverse its political agenda.[27]

The new leaders consciously rejected the recommendation of giving the "three types" an opportunity for reeducation on the grounds that the latter would never abandon their ultra-leftist views and practices, and would never truthfully accept the party's new policies.[28] The new leaders dismissed the argument that the "three types" were merely the blind and hapless followers of the Gang of Four who obeyed the Gang's script. Instead, they regarded the "three types" as the Cultural Revolution's main beneficiaries. Therefore, if the bad conduct associated with the Cultural Revolution were to be thoroughly repudiated, then the "three types" must also be resolutely cleansed from the party.[29] In their place, the party planned to install a new group of revolutionary successors to give organizational guarantee, continuity, and stability to the new programs.[30]

Consequently, flushing out the "three types" became a top priority in the first stage of the rectification campaign, and, in December 1984, Bo Yibo was able to report that about 50 percent of people who fitted the description of "three types" had been exposed up to date.[31] By mid-1985, Hu Yaobang indicated that about 3-5,000 members who belonged to the "three types" had been removed from their positions.[32] Their removal, coupled with a thorough and massive revamping of China's leadership on all levels, gradually eased the leadership's anxiety about the party's survival.

Once their sense of imminent danger subsided, the party leaders began to view the problem of indiscipline in a new light. Originally, the party's analysis of the decline of discipline cited two additional factors after placing primary responsibility on the Gang of Four. One factor was the suspension of rigorous admissions standards during the Cultural Revolution which permitted the influx of a large number of unqualified members. The other factor was the corrosive influence of capitalism which demoralized many party members with its "sugar-coated bullets."[33]

Each of these points carries different implications. Whereas the key remnants of the Gang of Four probably numbered only in the thousands and could be identified and isolated with relative ease, people who joined the CCP during the Cultural Revolution years (1966-1976) constituted nearly half of the party's membership in 1979-80.[34] Worse still, as China continued its course of economic reform, an even larger number of party members would continuously face the danger of exposure to capitalist contamination.

Therefore, although poor discipline was still regarded as a highly objectionable aspect of political life that should be corrected, leaders gradually conceded that it had become a way of life not amenable to quick solutions. Accordingly, the party began to revive its estimate on the length of time that rectification would require to show its effect. By 1986, the party began to characterize rectification as a sustained process, and hinted that rectification work must continue even after the campaign was formally concluded.[35]

Rectification also ceased to occupy the urgent and undivided attention of the party. Previously, it had been assumed that other reforms could not proceed without the prior rectification of the party's discipline problems. Now many leaders concluded that other reforms could go on even as undiscipline remained unresolved.

This transformation was reflected in a statement made by Mr. Xiang Nan, first party secretary of Fujian province when he asked in January 1986, "what is the objective of our conducting a party rectification? It is to facilitate our economic work, to realize modernizations, but not for rectification's own sake."[36] Mr. Xiang remarked further that his province as a whole had not made much effort to conduct the rectification campaign because it had given top priority to economic work.[37] Since Mr. Xiang Nan had a reputation as a progressive leader and was noted for many accomplishments and innovations in Fujian, his attitude was readily shared by many other provincial leaders.

With the above observation in mind, what statements can we make about the overall effect of rectification? Time will provide a better perspective, but several points already seem clear.

First, insofar as the campaign actually set out to rectify specific misconduct, it produced negligible effect. In the early 1980s, the rapid deterioration of discipline created a crisis of confidence among the Chinese people. Many doubted the qualifications of the Chinese Communist party as a vanguard party or as the enforcer and protector of the dictatorship of the proletariat.

If party leaders once genuinely thought that this crisis of confidence among the Chinese masses could pose a threat to the party from the outside, few would feel similar anxiety today. The crisis of confidence has certainly continued and has probably deepened, but the party has demonstrated that it still remains a highly effective machine to keep itself in power, no matter how ineffective it might have been in accomplishing constructive socioeconomic objectives. Furthermore, as long as the party continues to cope with undiscipline by conventional methods and strategies, the prospects for success will remain slim because the larger environment has changed so fundamentally as to render these methods and strategies irrelevant. Under prevailing conditions, the problems of discipline will not get better, but may get worse.

Second, insofar as the campaign aimed at the removal of politically dangerous elements from the party, it worked well. In the first two years of the campaign, the more conspicuous remnants of the Gang of Four who dared to defy the new leaders were dislodged from their bureaucratic strongholds. The lesser figures quickly abandoned hope to "alter the verdict." The party's deliberate and sustained effort to build up the third echelon of revolutionary successors has greatly enhanced its organizational control, and assured its political survival for years to come. Therefore, from the point of view of consolidating political power in the post-Mao era, the rectification campaign must be viewed as successful.

However, it is difficult to speculate whether this reconstructed leadership is better equipped to realize the party's modernization objectives. Two factors have to be taken into account. First, the new leaders' professional qualifications have definitely improved, especially when compared with those of the Maoist era. But the new leaders are basically technocrats serving at the pleasure of the senior leaders who set the political tone. For at least the next decade, the party's aging leaders will continue to shape its political orientations and demarcate the parameters within which the technocrats can safely operate.

The swift and decisive reaction of the party against the student demonstrations in early 1987 reminded us once again of the volatility of Chinese politics. The sudden resurgence of people with unmistakably "conservative" reputations who also enjoyed the military's backing clearly indicated the conservatives' strong staying power even as their ideology was losing its relevance. During the party's shakeup, the prominent new leaders of the third echelon remained quiet in spite of their expertise and convictions. In this sense, the higher professional qualifications of the new leaders provided a necessary but not sufficient condition for further political development.

Second, we should remember that even though the leadership change of the mid-1980s was massive and unprecedented by the CCP's own standards, its scope still paled by the enormity of the party's membership size as well as the nation's multivarious problems. This raises the question of the speed at which a small leadership core, however talented and well-educated, could drag a huge political machine composed of poorly educated, dogmatic, basically corrupt, and apathetic rank and file to mount an extremely ambitious modernization program.

This in turn raises the sensitive issue of the party's insistence on its exclusive domination over Chinese politics. There is no doubt that a rectified party is infinitely preferable to a corrupt and ineffectual party in its present form. However, China's political and economic development would accelerate only when fundamental normative, procedural, and institutional changes are introduced that, among other things, also redefine the role and functions of the party itself within the body politic.

Prior to the convening of the party's thirteenth Congress in October 1987, expectations were raised that it would strike a new political path for the party and the country. General Secretary Zhao Ziyang declared at the Congress that the party's central mission was to "accelerate and deepen the reforms."[38] However, his speech offered nothing new to combat poor party discipline. In fact, there was a reduction of the power to punish misbehaving members by the already ineffectual discipline committees without a corresponding increase of power through the legal and administrative processes.

The other features of the political reform outlined by Zhao at the Congress also contained little conceptual innovation. The division of labor between the party and the government, decentralization, and bureaucratic streamlining had all been cherished objectives of the party for many decades, and were only given obligatory reiteration.

While it is still too early to predict the outcome of the reforms outlined by Zhao, the developments since the Party Congress have not been encouraging. There are signs that the pace of reform has stagnated in recent years. It is entirely possible that the aging leaders like Deng Xiaoping and Chen Yun have already exhausted their intellectual resources and reached the limits of their vision for change. Yet, even in semiretirement, they in fact continue to set the parameters within which Chinese politics must operate. There is no doubt that their contribution to China's political change since the death of Mao has been enormous, but a more daring break from the past may have to wait until after their departure from the political stage.

NOTES

1. For a more comprehensive but slightly different treatment of the meanings and ramifications of purges and rectifications, see Frederick C. Teiwes's *Politics & Purges in China: Rectification and the Decline of Party Norms,* 1950-1965 (New York, M.E. Sharpe, Inc. 1979) pp. 3-12.
2. *Renmin ribao,* Editorial, October 14, 1983, p. 1.
3. *Deng Xiaoping wenxuan, 1975-1982,* [Hong Kong, 1983], pp. 144-350.
4. *Renmin ribao* June 7, 1982, p. 2; June 28, 1982, p. 3.
5. *Beijing ribao,* December 8, 1979, p. 2. The ultimate gesture of defiance and expression of displeasure with their job assignments was for party members to stay home and refuse to report to duty, an act which would have been unthinkable in earlier years. See also *Renmin ribao,* June 11, 1982, p. 3; *Beijing ribao,* May 14, 1980, p. 1.
6. *Beijing ribao,* April 25, 1980, p. 1.
7. *Beijing ribao,* April 11, 1980, p. 1.
8. *Chen Yun wenxuan, 1956-1985,* [Beijing, 1986] p. 207
9. *Chen Yun wenxuan, 1956-1985,* pp. 216-19.
10. *Yearbook on Chinese Communism, 1980* [Taipei, 1980], pp. 3:26-28.
11. *Chen Yun wenxuan, 1956-1985,* p. 245.
12. *Renmin ribao,* July 1, 1983, p. 3.
13. *Renmin ribao,* May 24, 1982, p. 4.
14. *Renmin ribao,* July 1, 1983, p. 3.
15. *Deng Xiaoping wenxuan, 1975-1982,* p. 372.
16. *Renmin ribao,* June 9, 1982, p. 3.
17. *Zhengdang yinian,* [Beijing, 1985], pp. 33-34. The rectification affected 390,000 party members in 159 party units.
18. *Zhengdang yinian,* p. 31.
19. *Hongqi,* 1986, No. 3, [February 1, 1986], pp. 5-7.
20. *Chen Yun wenxuan, 1956-1985,* pp. 309-10.
21. *Renmin ribao,* May 29, 1986, p. 1.
22. *Liaowang,* [Beijing], 1986, no. 14, [April 7, 1986] pp. 11-12.
23. Thus for instance, when the government forbade cadres to use public funds to build their own houses, they would then employ public funds to "subsidize" construction nominally being built by individual cadres, or use public funds to buy houses at higher cost and resell them for higher values and pocket the profit. See

Lilun yu shijian, [Shenyang], 1986, no. 6, [March 16, 1986] pp. 8-10.

24. *Hongqi*, 1986, no. 3, pp. 5-7.
25. Lu Keng, *An Interview with Hu Yaobang*, [New York, 1985] p. 35.
26. Basically the policy was implemented in 1977-1978, see *Renmin ribao*, Editorial, January 1, 1977, p. 1; Editorial, October 29, 1977, p. 1.
27. *Zhengdang yinian*, pp. 12-13.
28. *Renmin ribao*, Editorial, March 15, 1984, p. 1.
29. *Renmin ribao*, Commentator, August 4, 1984, p. 1.
30. *Zengdang yinian*, pp. 36-38.
31. *Zhengdang yinian*, p. 39.
32. Lu Keng, *An Interview with Hu Yaobang*, p. 34.
33. *Renmin ribao*, February 20, 1982, p. 1.; May 11, 1982, p. 1.
34. *Renmin ribao*, July 1, 1979, p. 1.
35. Hu Yaobang's speech as reported in *Renmin ribao*, January 11, 1986, p. 1.
36. *Zhibu shenghuo*, [Fuzhou], January 1986, pp. 3-4.
37. *Zhibu shenghuo*, January 1986, p. 3.
38. Report by General Secretary Zhao Ziyang at the CCP's 13th National Congress, October 25, 1987.

SEVEN

THE COMMUNIST PARTY OF CHINA
AS A POLITICAL INSTITUTION

Peter R. Moody, Jr.

In December, 1986, student demonstrations demanding freedom and democracy spread from Hefei, the capital of Anhui, to Shanghai and, thence, to Peking. The authorities waited until the winter vacation in January to begin a general crackdown. At the end of December the newspapers still claimed that no one had been arrested for participating in demonstrations or for putting up wall posters. Another story on the same page detailed the arrest of one Xue Deyun, unemployed, from Guizhou province. He had helped organize the Shanghai demonstrations and also those by students at Peking Normal University. His crime was an attempt to change the "one party dictatorship of the Communist party of China (CPC)."[1] The demonstrations climaxed a discussion begun in the spring on "political structural reform" which had focused upon the limits of political power, how to make power more responsible, and how to define the sphere of authority of the party. The repression of 1987 hit most directly those party members who had tried to find ways to make the party more responsive to society, and it raises the perennial question of how a vanguard revolutionary party adapts as ruler of a stable yet developing society.

During 1987 proponents of political reform gradually re-gained influence at the center. Political reform became a major theme of the Thirteenth Party Congress, held at the end of October of that year, with political reform described primarily as the separation of the party from the govern-ment implying at least a division of labor if not a separation of powers. If this division takes hold it may help resolve an enduring institutional weakness of the CPC, even if it does not lead to greater liberty for society. Given the context in which the proposed change is occurring, however, it is at least as likely to exacerbate the problem—the domination of the political system by the party and the domination of the party by an uninstitutionalized oligarchy.

In the 1960s Samuel Huntington brought a shock of fresh air to American theorizing about political development, suggesting that the general problem was less to nurture social and economic modernization than to build political institutions strong enough to withstand the contradictory and unreasonable demands resulting from increased political participation. Huntington argued that the political party was the institution best fit to meet the needs of modernization, its function being to mediate between state and society. Since the problem is to direct and channel demands, not to facilitate their competition, Dr. Huntington prescribed a single-party regime, with a special recom-mendation for the Leninist brand.[2]

At about the same time, other scholars were questioning whether parties were still the key political institutions they once had been. The postindustrial democracies were be-coming increasingly bureaucratized and political parties were less able to act as responsible representatives of specific social interests.[3] Immanuel Wallerstein found that the one-party state in Africa was becoming a no-party state: while parties continued to exist as membership lists, they lost their particular role as their functions and personnel were absorbed into the state machinery.[4] In the 1960s and

1970s military coups in Latin America produced bureaucratic authoritarian systems, ruled by soldiers, officials, and technocrats without the mediation of political parties. [5] East Asian regimes which are neither liberal nor communist tend toward bureaucratic authoritarianism, although their social base is not always the same as in Latin America. Where there are ruling parties they tend to be *ad hoc* combinations of politicians who have attached themselves to the regime. Where the single party does keep an independent identity, as on Taiwan (or perhaps Singapore), it seems that the party has a Leninist heritage and keeps a Leninist tinge.

Superficially, Leninist parties are exceptions to the general decline in the importance of party rule, and Leninist organization may counter forces eroding the party's autonomy from other political institutions. Here a distinction must be made. We often hear, for example, that Taiwan is ruled by a combination of the state bureaucracy, the military, the political police, and the Nationalist party (Kuomintang [Guomindang]: KMT). Clearly most, if not all, of the big bureaucrats, generals, and police are party members. But the addition of the party to the list is not superfluous. Also, we hear that the KMT is about 70 percent Taiwanese in composition. This should correct a picture of Taiwan politics as a stark confrontation of Taiwanese and mainlanders and nothing else, but it does not mean that the KMT is a Taiwanese institution. Rather, the party as the sum of its membership, as a club, should be distinguished from the party as a specific institution. In Taiwan the party as part of the structure of rule refers to the organization concerned with party work and the professional staff of the party organization. So, according to opposition sources, the KMT central organization remains very mainlander in atmosphere and hostile to hints of political slackness.[6]

The party machinery on Taiwan is one institutional interest among several. In a less adulterated Leninist system, such as the Soviet Union, the party organization is not part of an institutional oligarchy in competition for influence with other organizations, but, rather, dominates the other institutions. The party controls the staffing of other organizations and the head of the party organization, the General Secretary, has come to be generally acknowledged as the boss of the whole country.

It is still proper to ask, however, what the party does to maintain its dominance—does it perform some function in the system? Jerry Hough argues that the party organization at the regional level and above provides the coordination necessary for the working of a highly centralized administratively directed economic system.[7] But there is also plausible evidence that the centralized, planned system imposes economically unnecessary burdens in efficiency, welfare, and freedom on the rest of society, and one might hypothesize that just as the party allows the economy to function, the economy functions as it does to maintain the dominance of the party. It may be that the Leninist party performs those functions which allow it to dominate society, and structures society in such a way as to make its own domination necessary.

The CPC has also been thought to dominate Chinese society. In contrast to the Soviet and East European experience, however, none of the top Chinese leaders, Mao Zedong, Hua Guofeng, or Deng Xiaoping, attained his position through control of the party machinery[8] (although Deng at one time headed it), and the purges of early 1987 make one question whether the central party organization will be that strategic in the future. In the post-Mao period the leadership has acted to bolster and to rationalize the position of the party while simultaneously following policies which promise to make the party superfluous to the daily operation of the economy and government. Tensions between the party and society have thus become more evident in China than in the Soviet Union, although the Soviet comrades, if they continue to emulate the Chinese reforms, will no doubt experience similar problems.[9]

THE PARTY IN MAO'S DAY

For almost a generation before taking national power the CPC had controlled large areas of China, gaining experience in government and military affairs. After power had been achieved, however, this same experience stood in the way of developing an institutionalized party rule, with the party distinct from the government or army.

Mao's victory represented a triumph of the military and governmental branches of the party over those segments directly concerned with central party work. The Maoist coalition itself was heterogeneous, and the party may not have become truly cohesive and disciplined prior to the Rectification movement of 1942-1944. The inculcation of Leninist discipline on the party at this time was coupled with building Mao up as the party's supreme Leader and Thinker. The 1945 party charter which Mao's lieutenant, Liu Shaoqi, presented to the Seventh Party congress, incorporates the Thought of Mao, defined as the combination of the universal principles of Marxism-Leninism with the concrete practice of the Chinese revolution, as the party's guiding thought. Mao himself technically headed the party's central organization—he was then chairman of the Secretariat as well as chairman of the Central Committee—but he did not owe his position to his organizational role. Rather, he was acknowledged as leader because of his personal prestige, his skill in holding together a diverse coalition and giving it direction, and his reputation for having been right when his rivals had been wrong.

By the mid-1950s China seemed to be moving toward a Soviet system of institutionalized party rule. The central apparatus consisted in large part of persons recruited by Liu Shaoqi after he took charge of the party's Northern bureau in 1935. This organization had worked in the so-called white areas, operating underground in territory held by the Japanese or the KMT. Not all comrades were happy to see this group gaining influence. Gao Gang, an old Soviet areas leader and in the early 1950s boss of Manchuria, ranking high on the Politburo, is said to have asserted that the party was divided into a white areas party and the "red areas and military party." The party, Gao said, was created by the army and the red areas should predominate over the white.[10] The attack on Gao at that time accused him of waging an "unprincipled" power struggle, one involving no substantial question of doctrine or policy, and foreign analysts tend to agree. But Gao's "theory" at least had organizational and political consequences. Had he prevailed those party members in state and military work would have been even more prominent than they have been, and the cohesion of the party might have cracked earlier. The Cultural Revolution alliance of Mao Zedong, Lin Biao, and Zhou Enlai against Liu Shaoqi can be interpretated as a vindication of Gao Gang.

One consequence of the defeat of Gao was probably the reorganization and strengthening of the Central Secretariat around 1954. Unlike in the Soviet Union, however, the General Secretary did not hold the highest rank in the party. The central party apparatus remained one institutional interest among several. It is common to hear that before 1966 Liu Shaoqi controlled the party apparatus. The General Secretary, however, was not Liu or even one of his people. It was, rather, Deng Xiaoping, a red areas man, someone Gao Gang had thought might go along with him. Deng's selection may have helped make the increasing influence of the central party organization more palatable to those of the red areas tendency. It may also have helped counter any image of the apparatus as nothing more than Liu Shaoqi's system of personal connections.

During the late 1950s the party organization extended its functions to embrace much of the work of the state, while at the same time it became overshadowed at the national level by the personal rule of Mao Zedong. Overextension and personalism weakened the party as an institution, and both are organically connected with each other. When the tensions between the principles of party versus personal rule developed, the party organization was too weak to resist Mao's assaults upon it.

PERSONAL AND INSTITUTIONAL POWER

In the early 1940s Mao's Moscow-trained advisors, Liu Shaoqi and Chen Boda, began building up his personal image. They were conforming at least outwardly to the current Stalinist vision of the world communist movement, with each of the component parties headed by its own little Stalin. In fact, Mao's supremacy was also a symbol of the CPC's tactical independence from Moscow. Mao was being built up not only as a leader of the party but of the Chinese people, with his wonderfulness contrasted with the wretchedness of Chiang Kai-shek. Mao had established a position not only as head of the party but also as a leader apart from, if not independent of or above, the party.

Robert Tucker, trying to differentiate among totalitarian or "movement" regimes, distinguishes what he calls the Bolshevist type, characterized by party rule, from fuhrerist parties dominated by a leader.[11] Tucker considers Stalin's Russia to have been fuhrerist instead of Bolshevist, which suggests that rather than identifying two different types of regime he has shown different stages of the same type. Lenin's pre-Revolution left-wing critics predicted that his organizational principles would ultimately subordinate the party to its leader, and bourgeois academics find this to be a general tendency of totalitarian movements, whether fascist or communist.[12] Franz Schurmann identifies a general political conflict between bureaucracies and chief executives. Bureaucracies want things reduced to routine, shrinking the function of leadership. Executives, to carry out their functions, shake things up, disrupt routine, and trample bureaucratic interests.[13] However general this conflict may be, it is especially acute in a totalitarian movement claiming a monopoly of power to achieve the total transformation of society.

The party does not like to see itself as a bureaucracy. It is the vanguard of the proletariat exercising political, not bureaucratic, leadership over the state in the name of the working class or laboring masses. But the party is still a large organization and tends like other large organizations to become bureaucratic. Institutionalized party rule becomes rule by or through the party bureaucracy. Bureaucratism and institutionalization may not necessarily be synonyms, but they will be presented as such by those whose interests are damaged by institutionalization.

The bureaucraticization of the CPC became a theme of comment by the mid-1950s. The young writer Wang Meng complained of the party's loss of revolutionary vitality as it became buried in daily routine.[14] Institutionalized party dominance was as distasteful to leaders as to idealists. After the purge and suicide of Gao Gang, as the central apparatus consolidated its position, Mao was moving into the "second line." He was not, however, content to stay there. The 1956 party charter removed special reference to the Thought of Mao, Deng Xiaoping explaining that the 1945 formulation was out of date. At the same time, the 1956 party charter contained a provision for the election of an honorary chairman, a hint, perhaps, that the Thinker himself had seen better times. Liu Shaoqi announced that the storm of revolution had passed; now is the time for peaceful construction. Mao Zedong did not have much to say at this Eighth Party congress, except briefly to intimate that the comrades had fallen too deeply into sectarianism, dogmatism, and bureaucratism.[15]

Mao's assault on the party's bureaucratic complacency was also a reassertion of his own leadership. His method, a call for a hundred flowers to bloom, for outside criticism of the party organization from the general public, is not a part of Leninist norms. The criticism was more severe than Mao had expected (and perhaps vindicated the apparent skepticism of Liu Shaoqi and Deng Xiaoping), and the liberal atmosphere of 1956 gave way to harsh repression in 1957, which in turn fed the overheated radicalism of the 1958 Great Leap Forward.

Administratively the Leap resolved the tension between Mao and the party organization. The cult of Mao was taken to unprecedented heights, with the radical policies carried out in his name. Chen Boda revived the Thought of Mao, connecting it with the notion of the imminent transition to Communism. At the same time the slogan "politics takes command" implied not only that technical decisions should be made by political criteria but also that party cadres would be making them. The party organizations took over functions previously performed by local governments, the prosaic reality behind the talk of the withering away of the state.

Problems with the Leap became evident almost immediately. Given Mao's commitment to the Leap, however, an open repudiation of it became impossible as long as Mao had influence. The failure of the 1960 harvest finally forced a radical economic reform, but the new policies could be legitimated only as temporary expedients, to be abandoned as soon as things improved. Given the enlargement of the scope of the power of the party, the party leadership inevitably was involved in the formation and implementation of the new policies. The identification of Mao and the party leadership with different policy lines brought the institutional conflict between party and leader to a head. As a political curiosity, the state leaders, such as Zhou Enlai or Li Xiannian, who had more conservative records than the party leaders, could continue to side with Mao in this conflict despite the policy disagreement, although their position was always precarious. This is perhaps a consequence of the position of leader and party as alternative sources of legitimacy. Those at the top of institutions other than the party organization would tend to have greater freedom of action in a personalized system, while the great leader requires influential support to counter the potential power of the party organization.

While the civilian party was finding fault with Mao and the Leap and the civilian state leaders were keeping a cautious silence, Lin Biao, the new head of the army, was using the party machinery in the military strongly to affirm both. Mao, reasserting himself, told the comrades in 1962: Never forget class struggle. The Leap had failed not because the policies were misguided but because the class enemy remained strong enough to sabotage them and the party and the people were insufficiently committed to proletarian thought.

From 1963 through 1965 the post-Leap policies remained in place but the propaganda line became increasingly radical. "Class struggle"—attacks on "bourgeois thought"—was pushed in schools and the countryside. In early summer, 1966, a socialist cultural revolution was announced, and students were encouraged to make revolution against the bourgeois reactionary line. An alarmed Liu Shaoqi sent work teams, party-led groups from outside the affected units, to take over the revolution in the schools. In August Mao ordered the work teams withdrawn. The "masses," first the students, who were forming themselves into Red Guard groups, were told that to rebel is justified. The should make revolution against persons in power within the party walking the capitalist road. As in the hundred flowers period Mao was mobilizing mass discontent directly against the party, although this time the masses were encouraged to use violence and had the backing of the army. The two main capitalist roaders were Liu Shaoqi and Deng Xiaoping. There is no indication that they formed anything like a faction. Rather, their pairing was institutional: Liu was the godfather of the civilian apparatus, while Deng was its official head.

Mao's supporters were not limited to Red Guards. With him at the center was his personal entourage or inner court (his wife, his secretary, and various clients of each) allied with the political police; Lin Biao, the head of the army; and Zhou Enlai, the head of the government. Viewed as a power struggle among the elite, the Cultural Revolution was not a division between pragmatists and radicals. By 1966 the non-Maoists—Liu, Peng Zhen, Deng—had certainly become pragmatic enough, while Mao himself and the inner court were rather radical; in retrospect Lin Biao's principles can only be described as flexible, but in 1966 they were certainly radical; Zhou Enlai, however, had always been at least as pragmatic as anyone in the non-Maoist camp, and more consistently so. The Maoist coalition included those who in a more established Communist system find themselves subordinated to the party apparatus. Tao Zhu, the able head of the Guangdong party committee and of the Central South region, probably an ally of Lin Biao, seemed slated to replace Deng as head of the Secretariat. It is probably no accident that he was the first in the Maoist camp to fall victim to the purge as the coalition disintegrated.

The party organizations at all levels (except, probably, in the army) were disrupted by the Cultural Revolution. The provincial party committees began to rebuild in 1970, and those at lower levels a little later. The central party organization remained fragmented. Politics after 1968 degenerated into palace intrigue with everyone waiting (some with less patience than others) for the old man to die.

Hua Guofeng, who succeeded Mao, had previously succeeded Zhou Enlai as head of government, probably because among the possible contenders for that position he aroused the fewest negative passions. His institutional base in 1976 was the police, and he owed his succession to the party leadership to his supposed personal selection by Mao and his leading role in the coup against the Gang of Four, Mao's wife and her friends. Deng Xiaoping had been rescued from oblivion by Zhou Enlai in 1973. In 1975, as Zhou lay dying, Deng attempted a power play of his own against the inner court radicals and failed. He was purged again in 1976 as an unrepentant capitalist roader. He was brought back in 1977 because of his prestige among the surviving elite (enhanced by his having been the final object of hate by the hated Gang of Four) and also, we might assume, because not everyone in the surviving elite was enchanted with Hua's attempts to build himself into a little Mao, complete with cult.

Deng consolidated his position by campaigning against the Cultural Revolution. He put in new policies and built new institutions. One was a revived Secretariat, on paper more important than it had been when he had headed it. In a noble effort to stress the authority of the institution rather than the man, Deng did not become General Secretary himself. He refused, in fact, to take any position of direct leadership in either the party or the government (except for the army, where his personal authority was needed to keep the soldiers in line). But he did remain as boss behind the scenes, and his power continued to be personal rather than institutional.

THE PARTY'S SCOPE OF AUTHORITY

With the Great Leap Forward the Soviet system of one-man management (a term the Chinese may have interpreted more literally than the Soviets) in factories was abandoned. Factories came to be run in effect by their party committees. There was a general devolution of power from the center to the local levels, especially over economic decisions. The central planning system was disrupted, as were the functions of the central economic ministries. In rural areas the lowest level of local government, the township (*xiang*), was abolished, replaced by the commune, a collective rather than state organization. Decisions on the commune level were made by its party committee.

Over the long run, however, this did not strengthen the party. At the Eighth Congress in 1956 Deng Xiaoping had complained of a "dangerous deviation" whereby comrades in state organizations claim their work is so special that they don't have to obey party leadership. "They try to turn their sections into independent countries."[16] The Leap, paradoxically, gave the comrades a firmer basis for their claims to autonomy. Li Xiannian, one of the top economic bureaucrats, a man not at all enthusiastic about the Leap, noted that party leadership at the local level meant leadership by party members. Township personnel would be absorbed by the commune party committee and would continue to perform the same functions as before.[17] State functionaries also infiltrated the party organization at the top, with the addition of ranking bureaucrats and Politburo members Li Xiannian and Li Fuchun to the Secretariat in 1958.

Putting state functions under party jurisdiction diluted party control over those functions. In early 1961, in an attempt to reassert some central control and rationalization, the Central Committee set up six regional bureaus, each embracing several provinces.[18] These may have helped only to build more independent kingdoms. Three of the bureaus were headed by powerful provincial first secretaries. Two others were headed by men from the central Secretariat, and one suspects this either further weakened the Secretariat or was a reflection of its already weakened condition, since running the regional bureaus was probably a full-time job. There were no moves to reconstitute the state equivalents of the regional organizations which had been abolished in 1954, perhaps an indication of how unimportant the state organization below the central level had become.

Lin Biao was able to establish his own autonomy by politicizing the army, asserting himself through the party organization in the army. He was minister of defense, but the Defense Ministry in China concerns itself mainly with military administration. Operational control over troops is vested in the General Staff. Lin exerted his control through his position as first vice chairman (under Mao Zedong) of the Military Affairs Committee (MAC). In his rhetoric if not in practice he stressed ideological indoctrination of the army over military training, and he strongly articulated the cult of Mao. The mechanism for party control of the army was the General Political department (GPD), nominally subordinate to the Secretariat but probably in fact more responsive to the MAC. The head of the GPD was simultaneously in charge of the MAC's own secretariat.

In 1965 the army abolished all distinctions of rank. NCO ranks had been eliminated in 1961, with appointment to NCO functions made by the relevant party committee with the approval of the unit commander.[19] By analogy appointments to higher command positions after 1965 must have been in the hands of the military party organization, removed from the general staff, then unsympathetic to Lin. Lin also carried his battle to the civilian party, offering to staff local party committees, reviving, without attribution, Gao Gang's thesis: "Historically, our army has been the school of our party cadres...In fact, the army is able to train cadres for the localities...our party has grown out of the barrel of the gun."[20]

Lin's maneuvers resulted not in increased party control over the army but in increased power for Lin. In 1964 the people were summoned to learn from the People's Liberation army: the propaganda status of the army was elevated above that of the party itself. The state bureaucrats Zhou Enlai, Li Xiannian, and Bo Yibo showed that they, at least, were not too proud to learn. They set up political departments in economic and financial agencies, modeled after similar institutions in the army. Franz Schurmann believes that these allowed the central ministries to recover some of the functions they had earlier lost in the local party committees.[21] The chain of command, however, ran not through the government structures as such but through the party organizations within the government structures. In the meantime, major decision-making in this period passed from the regular institutions like the Central Committee, the Politburo, the Secretariat, or the State Council to *ad hoc* work conferences whose membership varied with the desires of those convening them.[22]

During the 1961-1962 retrenchment the party center tried to find a better definition of party leadership:

> The party...cannot take the place of all other organizations. The development of the functions of all other organizations under the united leadership of the party does not weaken the nuclear leadership function of the party but strengthens it. We must not mix together the party organization and all other kinds of organizations.[23]

The pragmatists of the early 1960s, like those 20 years later, wanted a "separation of party and state" precisely to improve party control. Franz Schurmann argues that in the early 1960s "It may be an exaggeration to say so, but in effect these 17,000,000 party members had nothing to do except what they had to do otherwise in their practical roles (for example, as factory directors)."[24] This may be, as Schurmann thinks, a result of a lack of ideological direction. It may also come from the enlargement of the scope of party activities during the Leap, which meant that by becoming everything, the party as such had not become much of anything. The central party organization provided neither cohesion nor coordination and, thus, was vulnerable to attack in 1966.

The Cultural Revolution disrupted all organization, not just that of the party; but it disrupted the army least of all.

The revolutionary Committees, the new organs of state power, tended to be headed by soldiers, as did the new party committees which took over leadership of and almost immediately effectively displaced the Revolutionary committees. The old fusion of functions was intensified: typically the commander of troops stationed in a province also headed the province's party and revolutionary committees, reflecting the then dominant position of the army (for there does not seem to be a case in which a civilian party functionary took over direct command of troops).

The army lost prestige with the failure of Lin Biao's 1971 attempt to overthrow Mao. A reorganization of the military regions in 1973 eliminated what danger there may have been of revived warlordism. By 1975 military and party functions were again becoming separate. The party organizations in localities, firms, and state offices resumed their "normal" functions, in effect, running the entire show. During Mao's day what central party organization there was seems to have been run by the Gang of Four: but throughout the 1970s the central party organization remained weak.

THE PARTY IN REFORM

By the 1980s the Chinese media were full of complaints about crises of faith and confidence. The Cultural Revolution was said to have damaged the prestige of the party. But the Cultural Revolution is itself evidence of a preexisting crisis in the party, and its effect was to extend the crisis to the entire system. The new rulers tried a radical reform of both the economic and political structures, including reform of the party.

The reform process has been caught up in political expedients, so the rebuilding of the party institutions has been conditioned by politics. One reason for the unprecedented emphasis on the Secretariat has been that since that institution had to be remade from the ground up it was relatively easy for the reformers to get control of it (although they could not monopolize it). In 1978 the party set up a Discipline Inspection Committee, headed by the economic theorist Chen Yun. A revival of the old Control Commission, its job is to chase down misbehavior in the party. Its earlier targets were the old economic bureaucracy who, because the economy was so much under political control, had been able to convert political position to private economic advantage. As Chen Yun became disenchanted with reform he began to find corruption instead among those who wheel and deal in the liberalized economy. To curb Chen's influence, in 1986 responsibility for rectification was shifted from the Discipline Inspection committee to an *ad hoc* Rectification Guidance committee, responsible to the Secretariat.

The larger problem is the structure of reform itself. All but the most radical reformers within the party are determined to keep the party's supremacy over society and one goal of reform is to rationalize party control and revitalize the party organization. Another aim has been to depoliticize the economy and society, a policy which threatens to make the party superfluous.

REBUILDING THE PARTY ORGANIZATION

After the purge of the Gang of Four, one of their crimes was said to be a desire to "kick out the party committee and make revolution." The old party organization was something the radical Maoists wanted to make revolution against. The radical line has at least affinities with the Yugoslav dissident Milovan Djilas's critique of party rule as the dominance of a "new class."[25] Radicals denounced the central Leninist principle of democratic centralism (the minority obeys the majority, and the like) as "slavism."[26] In the 1970s the Maoists detailed how the political order spontaneously generated "new bourgeois elements," and even implied the need for a new revolution.

Both the Hua Guofeng and Deng Xiaoping regimes determined to restore the orderly functioning of the party organization. Certainly at first this was seen by most people as benign. The Gang's attacks on authority had not meant liberty and justice for all but, rather, no law and no heaven, an utterly irresponsible and capricious use of power. The restoration of party routine meant at least order and predictability.

The rebuilt central party organization became Deng Xiaoping's main instrument for putting through the reforms. He also courted support for his policies in society, and, indeed, one motive for reform was the need to restore social morale, especially among intellectuals. Intellectuals, while finding little appeal in the Gang or their positive program (such as it was) did sometimes respond to the radical criticism of the regime's structure of power and privilege. Especially during the Hua Guofeng period the attack on the Gang often seemed a reassertion of the power of a closed elite over everyone else. The Deng reforms were directed as much against this as against radicalism. But to the extent that implementation of reform required strengthened party control, there was the danger of alienating reform from its social base among intellectuals. "Conservatives" or "leftists" (in Deng's time the terms were synonyms) are opposed to reform anyway, but gain strength from the more radical reformers' protests against the authority of the party establishment.

Deng reorganized the party to remove his opponents from positions of influence and to create positions of influence for his friends. In 1980 there had been talk within the party of establishing an Advisor's Committee, a kind of party senate, as a way of decentralizing power within the party. The organization no longer had this function when it was finally established in 1982: by that time the consensus was to keep to the conventions of democratic centralism. The covert function of the Advisors' Committee was to provide a graceful withdrawal from politics for the older, more conservative cadres. In the event, old cadres who still had any clout chose not to join the new committee except for Deng Xiaoping, who became its chairman: he had to join because it had been his idea. The more prominent members tended to be older cadres in at least semi-disgrace, persons without much influence in 1982 but whose membership in the committee gave at least the potential for revived influence.

The other major organizational reform was the restructuring of the party along the more familiar lines of the Communist party of the Soviet Union. In 1981 Hua Guofeng was replaced as party chairman by Hu Yaobang, a client of Deng Xiaoping's. In February, 1980, Hu had become head of a revived Secretariat. In 1982 the position of Chairman was abolished and the General Secretary (still Hu Yaobang) became the head of the party. By 1984, A. Doak Barnett reports, the Secretariat had become China's major decision-making institution.[27] In retrospect one is inclined to believe this showed less the strength of an institution than of a faction.

PARTY, STATE, AND SOCIETY

Another thrust of reform was to separate the functions of the party and the government. This would in principle allow improved party control over policy, relieving it of responsibilities for direct implementation. Also, the responsibility system in industry and agriculture depoliticize economic decision-making, encouraging economic rationality. A reassertion of the proper functions of the state would subject both party members and the party organization to rule through law.

One effect of reform has been to decrease the power and prestige of lower-level party secretaries. The economic reforms threaten to deprive the party organization of control not only over decisions but also over personnel placement, the party's major lever of political power. Prior to the thirteenth Congress the National People's Congress had refused to pass into law the more far-reaching proposals for limiting the power of party committees in business firms. The cost, presumably, is the loss of the increased economic efficiency which the reforms would have brought.

A story from Hunan shows one kind of change the reformers had in mind. There were complaints at a meeting of the county People's Congress (the lowest state legislative organ) about the shortage of oil and gasoline. One delegate had exploded: The Communist party is worse than the feudal dynasties. The county party secretary then ordered the local Discipline Inspection committee to investigate, and the committee ordered the head of the county congress to turn over the records. The congress head refused and was upheld by the central authorities, who asserted the principle of legislative immunity: the party has no authority over what elected representatives of the people say while in session.[28]

The responsibility system in agriculture puts decisions in the hands of farm households, removing them from the jurisdiction of the commune cadres. The reforms were resisted by cadres, who lost status along with control.[29] Later cadres realized that they can use their political influence to get the best lands allocated to themselves, their families, or their clients.[30] The impression is that rural cadres have become reconciled to reform partly through corruption. Political scientists are sometimes nostalgically sentimental about old-style machine politics, and patronage can sometimes be a way to develop a strong political party. In China, however, patron-client connections are apt to do more for the particular patrons than for the Communist party, and the use of political power for personal profit discredits the reforms. The struggle against bourgeois liberalization, it is interesting to note, was not carried out in the countryside. One may wonder to what degree the apparent stability of the new agrarian policies reflects the interest of a new party gentry.

A long-discussed urban reform, similar in principle to that in the countryside, began to be implemented on a large scale in 1984, with mixed results. Firm managers, urged to enrich themselves, issued bonuses and raised wages without regard to productivity in order to "stimulate workers' activism." They used state money for speculative ventures and, in general, pursued the quick buck. Also, greater play for market forces put pressure on prices which had long been kept artificially low. The consequence in the spring of 1985 was a frightening inflation and some questioning of the direction of reform among the general public as well as among the more rigid party cadres.

Urban reform entailed both separation of party and state functions and also the separation of economics from administration. This implies a radical redefinition of the role of the party in day-to-day affairs, although a detailed survey of the implementation of the policy suggest that actual changes were rather less far-reaching than a perusal of the general directions from the center would lead one to think.[31] The manager responsibility system places authority for decisions on production and personnel with the factory manager, freeing him from much of the earlier need to coordinate with the party committee or, in practice, the firm's party secretary. The manager is supposed to make his decisions in accord with economic rationality—that is, at least within bounds he is supposed to maximize profits— rather than administrative orders (although the national plan continues to provide "macroscopic guidance" and there has been no intention of completely abolishing administrative direction). Rather than receiving funds from the relevant ministry and returning profits to that ministry, the firm would pay a tax on its profits and otherwise use them as prudence dictates. The reform at its purest cuts not only into the role of the firm secretary but also into the functions of party and state cadres at the local level, according to Jerry Hough's "Soviet Prefects." The "downward transfer of the firm" (*xiafang qiye*), unlike the decentralization of the Great Leap Forward, is not supposed to mean that the central ministry transfers its jurisdiction to the local government or party, a system called in 1986 a change of mothers-in-law. Rather, the firm is supposed to be on its own, allowed to cultivate "horizontal relations" with other firms, making its own deals on purchases and sales rather than working through higher administrative organs. Economic coordination would be provided by the market and through contracts enforced, if necessary by the courts, rather than through political direction.[32]

The reforms not only affect party control over policy but also reach into the key area of personnel. In a 1986 model, "party control is a principle that must be strictly adhered to."

At the same time, the principle of party control of cadres cannot be used as a rationalization for direct party appointment of cadres. Party control of cadres first of all indicates a guarantee of the party's political leadership of the cadres; that the cadres must conform to the standards formulated by the party; that they must carry out their work in the light of the party's demands; that they must earnestly and thoroughly implement party policy.

Mundanely, however, the party committee's function would be limited to checking out the manager's choices, with the manager both proposing candidates and making the actual appointment.[33]

There are occasional suggestions that factory party secretaries be appointed to serve as plant managers and that managers take positions as party secretaries (presumably not in their original work units). But the typical party secretary may not have the training now required of managers. University students find the idea of political work loathsome and the best technical students will have ample scope for their talents elsewhere.

Rather than running the firm, the party is to concentrate all the more on political and thought education. No one is clear about what this is supposed to mean. Sometimes it amounts to social work, visiting workers when they are sick, helping them with family problems, and the like. More recently it has come to imply the indoctrination of people concerning the rectitude of the money-grubbing ways appropriate to a "socialist commodity economy," convincing them that all they had previously been told about socialism was wrong, a task the regular political thought workers may not find congenial. There will be, one suspects, pressures or temptations for party secretaries to nose out instances of "thought problems," to become the scourges of spiritual pollution and bourgeois liberalization.[34]

The reform has been associated with corruption, but corruption in the party clearly predates reform and concern for corruption was, in fact, a motive for reform. Reform may give new opportunities for corruption, for while the economy has been liberalized, access to political position remains a major economic resource. The logic of reform cuts against the old definition of party functions. The party remains central to the overall structure of power, but there is no clear notion of what its functions should be. The structural reform of the economy would seem to require political structural reform as well.

POLITICAL STRUCTURAL REFORM

The efficient cause of the revival of political structural reform in 1986 was probably the evolving play of politics within the party. It was also a controversial topic: the Central Committee plenum of September confined its public comments to the matter of spiritual civilization when political reform was obviously the hot issue. Deng Xiaoping had become cagey in his comments about political reform, in 1986 using the term but not meaning much beyond administrative changes. In 1980, however, he had complained of overly centralized and concentrated power in both party and state.³⁵ The 1980 discussion of political reform was overwhelmed by reaction in 1981. Its call for decentralization was tacitly anti-Leninist and it also posed an ideological danger, a Cultural Revolution-type implication that the ruling structure itself constituted a new dominant exploiting class. This was also the implication of the later thesis about alienation in socialist society, the idea that political power under socialism is a form of external domination, a notion condemned as the heart of spiritual pollution.

The more radical reformers were perhaps reconciled to the political supremacy of the Communist party. Their more evident concern was to ameliorate political control over the economy, culture, and daily life, breaking the hold of a single orthodox ideological line. For the party leftists or conservatives, however, this ideological orthodoxy guaranteed party supremacy. The reformers, on their part, became aware of the futility of personnel and ideological changes that left untouched the basic structure of the system.³⁶

By early 1986 the balance had shifted to reformers, a result, it seems, of personal misfortunes and tactical blunders by the conservatives and the ability of the reformers, through their control of the Secretariat, to determine the policy agenda and make the key appointments in the Propaganda Department and the Ministry of Culture. Political reform became a theme of a series of unpublicized meetings beginning in April and continuing into early summer. An early manifestation of the change was a new discussion of Mao's old principle of letting a hundred flowers bloom, a hundred schools contend. The reformers differed over how this should be taken. The older reformers, for example, Lu Dingyi (the propaganda boss who first detailed the policy in 1956) and Yu Guangyuan asserted, in effect, that the policy had been intended to protect scientific research and cultural creativity from political intrusion. Mao and the radicals politicized the slogan, turning it into a tool to destroy intellectual freedom.[37] The more radical reformers concluded that if the policy means anything it guarantees not only intellectual liberty but political democracy also; it requires that all behavior which does not explicitly violate the laws and constitution be protected (presumably from party functionaries) by the law.[38]

Yet even the radical reformers had a rather passive view of democracy. They conceived it less as a way of asserting their own will upon society than as a check on the arbitrary exercise of political power. There was particular interest in the "tripartite division of power," the American system of separation of powers and checks and balances.[39] The general consensus was that this system, however useful it might be under capitalism, does not apply to a socialist society (the discussants either ignorant of or deliberately ignoring the extent to which in the contemporary world the system is specifically American, and that even "bourgeois" parliamentary systems tend toward the fusion of powers). But there was also extensive agreement that something analogous to separation of powers and checks and balances would do China no harm.

An otherwise intelligent discussion of limits on state power notes, perhaps with a straight face, that checks and balances are not necessary under socialism since the Communist party directs and supervises the state.[40] Even the most radical argument took care to genuflect: political reform can be carried out only under the leadership of the Communist party (and even Deng Xiaoping would add: but the party must be good at leadership). Any real limitation of power, however, would require restrictions on the scope of the party. The reformers were hardly unaware that the major problem was not the state form but the position of the party in the party-state system. Party leadership is necessary, one comment runs, but the party leaders are men, not gods. We respect party leadership when it is correct, not when it is in error, and some Communist party leadership has been a "negative experience."[41] The overseas edition of the *People's Daily* reproduced some comments from a pro-Peking Chinese-language paper in New York: Cadres get their authority from the party, not from society. Power over society comes from the party, not from the laws or from elections. The big problem is the lack of responsibility of party cadres to the people.[42]

The discussion of political reform was the background to the student demonstrations in November and December and these provided the occasion for the repression of January, with its strident reassertion of party supremacy. General Secretary Hu Yaobang was blamed for having let things get out of hand and for being too liberal himself. The repression brought home several lessons, notably how little difference in the real locus of power the talk of reform had made. Fang Lizhi, the maverick scientist from the University of Science and Technology, was fired from his university position at the behest of the university and provincial party committees and then, a few days later, was thrown out of the party: so much for the separation of party and state. Zhao Ziyang, the premier, kept his government job while acting as Hu's replacement as head of the party. The repression showed up the institutional weakness of the Deng Xiaoping system. Deng operated behind the scenes, working through Hu in the party and Zhao in the state. But while Hu and Zhao were in basic (or even complete) policy agreement (differing, however, in style), the system made them natural rivals, and a triumphant Zhao began to bad-mouth poor Hu while desperately attempting to contain the damage to reform.

The repression highlighted the institutional weakness of the Secretariat or at least of the office of General Secretary.

Hu's dismissal might be taken as a healthy sign, showing that the party bureaucracy does not dominate what are supposed to be the policy-making organs such as the Central Committee or Politburo: rather, it is subordinate and responsible to them. This would, however, be an optimistic interpretation. Hu was purged at an *enlarged* Politburo meeting, one including outsiders. Attending were Politburo members, 18 persons; alternate Politburo members, 2 persons; Secretariat, 4 persons; Advisors' committee, 17 persons; Discipline Inspection committee, 2 persons; plus "other concerned comrades"[43] not one who would reveal his name. The balance, one assumes, was provided by the conservative old men on the Advisors' committee. The institutional structure still means less than the informal establishment, and the party at its top ranks looks as much as ever like a club, even a secret society.

The party also seems isolated from the larger society it dominates. It thunders against the dissidents: to be sure, the party has made mistakes in the past, but the glory of the party is that it has always been able to correct its mistakes by itself. But the organization seems devoid of any constructive ideas of its own, willfully deaf to any from outside, and determined to rid itself of anyone who might have any.

CALLING IT A DAY

Deng Xiaoping says: "The core of bourgeois liberalization is opposition to party leadership."[44] It is difficult to believe that, whatever opposition there may be, Deng and the rest are afraid they will be overthrown. The party is secure in power, but it is also in crisis. It is separated from the rest of society, a huge but closed club, and is in danger of becoming parasitic.

The party need not, of course, worry about lack of members, even if quality should become a concern. It will remain what some call a tool of life, and membership will continue to give one a more-than-even shot at power and privilege.

The danger, without more radical reforms, is that membership will be taken more even than it is now, both by members and nonmembers, as transparent opportunism.

The paradox of the repression is that its effect may be to make the party more of a club, and less of an institution. The theme of the repression was the strengthening of the party leadership, and the more hostile one had been to reform the more one talked of party leadership. Yet the manner of repression hit the main institution for strengthened leadership, the Secretariat, presumably since the Secretariat had been the institution most consistently at the forefront of reform.

Yet there are subtleties. General Secretary Hu Yaobang was purged for being soft on liberalism. But, as Hong Kong gossips point out, Hu alone among the big reformers in 1986 did not allow the words political structural reform to pass his lips. Political reform meant restricting the scope of the party, and the Hong Kong observers speculate that the issue was an occasion for a power struggle between Premier Zhao and Secretary Hu.[45]

There is more. Another theme of reform was to elevate the legislative assemblies above their rubber stamp status, giving them real power and autonomy. To this end the 1982 state constitution created a Standing Committee of the National People's Congress, to supervise the State Council when the NPC is not in session. Under the leadership of Peng Zhen the Standing Committee in fact exercised a measure of autonomy, usually to hinder reform. In 1986 it delayed passage of, and caused amendments to, a bankruptcy law desired by the State Council and Secretariat, necessary if state firms are to be put under a responsibility system. In 1987 (although, of course, the whole political atmosphere was different) the Standing Committee refused to send to the Congress a bill which would further restrict the managerial functions of factory party secretaries.

Throughout 1987 there was a shift in power back to the reformist camp. One speculates that Deng Xiaoping regretted the degree to which he had earlier given in to the conservatives. This shift, however, is perhaps as much a reflection of objective problems as it is of changes in power relations in the Central South Lake. During the summer Deng announced that "political reform"—that great slogan of a year earlier—would be "on the agenda" of the Thirteenth Congress. The themes stressed at that Congress were indeed reformist. The party took an official position that China was now in the early stage of socialism in which the main task of all political work should be to strengthen the forces of production—attempting to provide reform with a heretofore lacking ideological justification, thus hindering attempts to label it a return to capitalism or some such thing (although whether the notion of the early stage of socialism will be any more effective than previous attempts, such as practice being the criterion of truth, is still in doubt). Zhao Ziyang's political report also demanded political structural reform, defined primarily in terms of the separation of functions between party and state. The party was to confine itself to political thought work and not attempt to manage directly either government offices or economic firms. The amended party charter[46] permitted the party to form its own small groups within other institutions, but this was no longer mandatory. In both governmental and party elections there were to be more candidates than positions open.[47] The Discipline Inspection Committee announced that from now on (as it was supposed to have been doing all along) it would concern itself with violations of party discipline by party members and would no longer investigate violations of the laws of the state.[48] While in 1986 the demand for separation of party and state had become material for an as-it-were mass movement calling for greater political democracy, in 1987 the main result of the separation was supposed to be improved efficiency. If the change does take hold, the party will gain greater institutional integrity while its weight will rest more lightly on society and the long-term effects may well be liberalizing and even democratizing.

In November Zhao Ziyang finally submitted his resignation as premier (as the separation of party and government implies he ought), and Li Peng provisionally took his place. In the spring of 1988 Li was formally designated premier. Peking spokesmen indignantly deny there are "factions" at the central level, but in the spring of 1988 the official media spoke of the formation of the "Li Peng cabinet," a brand new way of putting things. This may be open acknowledgment that a certain tendency predominates in the top state organ which is not the tendency in control of the party Secretariat.

Zhao remains head of the Secretariat, with the number one rank in the party hierarchy. His institution has been weakened even more, however. The Secretariat is now designated by the Politburo Standing Committee, and according to the description of its functions it is to remain a kind of clerical office for the Politburo. Its membership has been reduced to five people and one alternate. Of these only Zhao himself, Hu Qili (who probably agrees with Zhao on most things, but who is politically closer to Zhao's old rival, Hu Yaobang), and the problematical Qiao Shi have yet demonstrated any weight. By the end of 1987 the reform line seemed about as strong as ever, but its institutional basis was severely weakened.

This weakening, however, may simply mean that the potential power of the Secretariat has been curbed. The dispersal of power throughout the party and its leading organs is not necessarily a bad thing for reform. There is a partial basis for at least an institutional pluralism in the party, and this may be the grounds for a genuine political pluralism. In the Soviet Union the supremacy of the Secretariat has hardly been the foundation of a liberal social order, and in

China it is accidental (if explicable) that the Secretariat has been the main institutional promoter of reform. To a degree, power in China may be devolving to the institutions less hospitable to reform (the Politburo, the Advisors' Committee[49], the State Council, the National People's Congress's Standing Committee). But this means that the opposition to reform itself comes to have the strongest interest in limiting the power of the party organization, in political decentralization and democratization.

This is an optimistic forecast, probably much too optimistic. The ideology continues to call for the unquestioned primacy of party leadership, even when conditions do not allow the party to lead in a coherent way. No institution within the party exercises political leadership, and party membership is spread throughout all institutions. In the future there may not even be the kind of personal leadership held by Chairman Mao or Chairman Deng (for it is unlikely that his peers will give Secretary Zhao unquestioned deference). The place of the party in the Chinese political system may even prevent the emergence of political leadership, condemning that system to drift.

NOTES

1. *Renmin ribao* (People's Daily), overseas edition (PD(O), December 31, 1986.
2. Samuel P. Huntington, *Political Order in Changing Society* (Yale University Press, 1968), Ch. 1.
3. Otto Kirchheimer, "The Transformation of European Party Systems," in *Political Parties and Political Development,* edited by Joseph La Palombara and Myron Weiner (Princeton University Press, 1966), pp. 177-200; William J. Crotty, Gary C. Jacobson, *American Parties in Decline* (Boston, 1980).
4. Immanuel Wallerstein, "The Decline of the Party in Single-Party African States," in *Political Parties and Political Development,* pp. 201-214.
5. Guillermo O'Donnell, *Modernization and Bureaucratic Authoritarianism: Studies in South American Politics* (Institute of International Studies, University of California, Berkeley, 1979).
6. Sima Wenwu, *Chuanli Douchangshang di Zhengzhi Renwu* (Political Personages on the Battlefield of Power) (Taipei, 1986), p. 233.
7. Jerry Hough, *The Soviet Prefects: Local Party Organs in Industrial Decision-Making* (Harvard University Press, 1969).
8. In a perverse way Zhao Ziyang might be said to have achieved his top position through the party machinery, although he gained control of the party machinery through his position in the government and his connections with Deng. It is still too early to say whether he will be a "top party leader" in the sense the others were.
9. In the Soviet Union those who attain top positions, say, the level of the Politburo or the Council of Ministers, typically spend most of their early careers in the party organization. It would take a systematic comparative study to test the proposition, but the impressionistic evidence suggests that this is not typical of China. The older members of the Politburo come from a variety of sources. Among the newer members, the 1985 "third echelon" cohort, Qiao Shi and Li Peng are technocrats, while Tian Jiyun's earlier work was in local government. Wu Xueqian and Hu Qili worked not in the party apparatus proper, but in that of the Youth League. All seem to owe their promotions more to personal and family connections than to their earlier work.
10. On the Gao Gang affairs, see Frederick C. Teiwes, *Politics and Purges in China: Rectification and the Decline of Party Norms, 1950-*

1965 (White Plains, 1979), pp. 167-169. Deng Xiaoping includes a short memoir in his *Wen Xuan* (selected Works) (Peking, 1983). Gao's term red areas and military should probably not be considered redundant: guerrilla fighters behind enemy lines would be part of the tendency he approved.

11. Robert C. Tucker, "Toward a Comparative Politics of Movement Regimes," *American Political Science Review*, XLIII (April, 1968), pp. 435-451.

12. Joseph Nyomarkay, *Charisma and Factionalism in the Nazi Party* (University of Minnesota Press, 1967); Leonard Shapiro and John Wilson Lewis, "The Role of the Monolithic Party Under the Totalitarian Leader," in *Party Leadership and Revolutionary Power in China*, edited by John Wilson Lewis (Cambridge University Press, 1970), pp. 114-147.

13. Franz Schurmann, *The Logic of World Power* (New York, 1974), pp. 28-29.

14. Wang Meng, "The Young Newcomer in the Organization Department," *Renmin Wenxue*, September, 1956, pp. 29-43. Wang's articulate discontent got him 20 years of prison and exile. He returned in the late 1970s to become a major literary figure and, in 1986, Minister of Culture, an old man in the organization department, critics sometimes gibe.

15. For the documents see *Zhongguo Gongchandang di-ba-ci Chuanguo Daibiao Dahui* (Eighth National Congress of the Communist Party of China) (Peking, 1956).

16. *Jen-min Shou-ts'e, 1957*, p. 32.

17. Li Xiannian, "How to Look at the Reform of the Management System of Finance and Trade in the Rural Areas," *PD*, January 17, 1959.

18. Huang T'ien-chien, *Fei-wei Zhengchuan Shi-ba-nian* (Eighteen Years of the Bogus Bandit Regime) (Taipei, 1969), p. 419.

19. *Gongzo Tong-xun*, August 26, 1961.

20. *Ibid.*, May 19, 1961, p. 4.

21. Franz Schurmann, *Ideology and Organization in Communist China* (University of California Press, 1966), p. 304.

22. Parris H. Chang, "Changing Loci of Decision in the CCP," *China Quarterly, 44* (October-December, 1970), pp. 169-194.

23. Xu Bing-i, "Develop Even Better the Nuclear Leading Function of Basic-Level Party Organizations in the Countryside," *Hongqi*, October 16, 1961, pp. 21-25, p. 24.

24. Franz Schurmann, "The Attack of the Cultural Revolution on Ideology and Organization," *China in Crisis*, Vol. I, edited by Ping-ti Ho and Tang Tsou (University of Chicago Press, 1968), pp. 525-564, p. 543. One thing a party member could still do, if he chose, was to lord it over nonparty persons in his unit.

25. Milovan Djilas, *The New Class: An Analysis of the Communist System* (New York, 1957).

26. Lin Jie, "Down with Slavism: Strictly Obey Proletarian Revolutionary Discipline," PD, June 16, 1967.

27. A. Doak Barnett, *The Making of Foreign Policy in China: Structure and Process* (Boulder, 1985), Ch. 4.

28. *PD(O)*, November 7, 1986. Things are rarely simple. The hidden meaning of this is probably an attempt by Deng Xiaoping and Hu Yaobang to rein in Chen Yun.

29. David Zweig, "Opposition to Change in Rural China: The System of Responsibility and the People's Communes," *Asian Survey*, XXIII, 7 (July, 1983), pp. 879-900.

30. Compare Jean C. Oi, "Communes and Clientelism: Rural Politics in China," *World Politics*, XXXVIII, 2 (January, 1985), pp. 238-266.

31. This discussion draws on Shuhfan Ding, "The Party-State Relationship in the People's Republic of China Since 1978," PhD dissertation, University of Notre Dame, 1987.

32. *PD(O)*, August 9, 1986. Deng's evidence indicates that local party organizations did in fact continue to play a prefectural role, in that they were the institutions which decided what the ambiguous central directives really meant and thus brought consistency to local policy.

33. *Dang de Jiao-yu*, 7, 1986, in *Inside China Mainland*, November, 1986, pp. 16-17.

34. In fiction political thought work generally means malevolent, envious snooping into other people's business. See, for example, Ran Rong, "A Present of a Blooming Nightshade," *Hua Cheng*, 1, 1987, in *Xin Hua Wenzhai*, April, 1987, pp. 97-116. A 1988 Politburo decision asserts that political thought work will itself fall under the jurisdiction of the factory manager, with the party committee only supervising how it is done. *PD*, August 30, 1988. If this is how things are developing, the party secretary may really be becoming superfluous.

35. *Chan Wang*, April 1981, in *FBIS/CHI*, April 26, 1981, pp. W1-W14. For his 1986 position, see his comments to Prime Minister Nakasone, *PD(O)*, November 10, 1986.

36. Li Kejing, "China's Political Restructuring and the Development of Political Science," *Social Sciences in China*, VII, 3 (1986), pp. 9-24.

37. *PD(O)*, May 9, 1986; *PD(O)*, May 16, 1986.

38. *PD(O)*, May 30, 1986.

39. Xi Jing, "Discussing China's Political Structural Reform (Interview with Yen Chia-ch'i)," *Guangming Daily*, June 30, 1986, in *Xin Hua Wenzhai*, September, 1986, pp. 9-11.

40. Hu Kelong, Zheng Pin, Li Yongfeng, "Comparative Study of Limits on State Power," *Journal of the graduate School of the Chinese Academy of Social Sciences*, 3, 1986, in *Xin Hua Wenzhai*, August, 1986, pp. 8-15, pp. 12-13.

41. *PD(O)*, November 28, 1986.

42. *PD(O)*, November 16, 1986.

43. *PD(O)*, January 17, 1987. The numbers given for the Secretariat and other organizations presumably means members who were not also on the Politburo already.

44. *PD(O)*, January 20, 1987

45. *Jiushi Niandai*, February, 1987.

46. The Thirteenth Congress was the first since at least the Sixth which did not completely rewrite the party charter. Unlike at the time of the earlier congresses, the line in 1987 was neither that the Chinese revolution was entering an entirely new phase nor that the previous party line had been grievously mistaken. In this respect, at least, the party may be building itself as an institution.

47. See *PD(O)*, November 2, 1987, for a list of amendments to the party constitution and for a discussion of the general themes of the congress. For Zhao's speech see *PD(O)*, November 4, 1987.

48. *PD(O)*, November 5, 1987.

49. The Advisors' Committee describes itself, however, as a transitional organization, so it may not be around for long. *PD(O)*, November 5, 1987. If it does endure, it may develop into a kind of party House of Lords, resulting in a formal break with the party's Leninist structure.

PART IV
LAW AND POLITICS

EIGHT

LEGAL REFORM IN POST-MAO CHINA
A TENTATIVE ASSESSMENT

Shao-chuan Leng

Among recent changes instituted in post-Mao China, legal reform appears to have been making considerable progress. In contrast with the scarcity of information on Chinese law under Mao Zedong, barely a single day passes now without the appearance of new legal materials in the PRC news media and other publications.

This chapter attempts to make a tentative assessment of the current Chinese leadership's effort to build a stable legal order and a regular judicial system. It will begin with a brief discussion of the legacy of past legal experience, including Chinese tradition, Soviet influence, and Mao's personal impact. Then it will proceed to examine the reasons for the post-Mao legal reform, the measures undertaken, and the changes brought about. The limits of the reform and the relevance of Chinese tradition will be discussed in connection with the so-called "socialist legality with Chinese characteristics."

LEGACY OF THE PAST

The legal system of the People's Republic of China was described by Dong Biwu as a product of many years of experiment through selective assimilation of Chinese and foreign experiences and particularly creative application of

Communist doctrine and the Soviet model to the concrete conditions of China.[1] As is generally known, as *Fa* (positive law) played only a supplementary role to *Li* (moral code) in traditional China as a regulator of human behavior and social order. Despite the promulgation of some impressive codes by the imperial dynasties of China, Confucian elites insisted that the rule of *Li* or the rule of man (benevolent and virtuous rulers) through moral example and persuasion was superior to the rule of *Fa* through rigid, impersonal codes, and severe punishment. With good reason, the Chinese traditionally preferred to stay away from the court of law and to have large areas of offenses and disputes handled by extrajudicial organs and procedures. In line with the spirit of social harmony and compromise, the informal means of mediation and conciliation became the prevailing forms of dispute resolution in old China.[2]

Intentionally or not Mao and his comrades seemed to have assimilated through the years certain traditional Chinese attitudes toward law, such as subordination of law to a dominant political philosophy and preference for informality in settling disputes and imposing sanctions. Also, from Marxist-Leninist ideology and the Soviet model they drew basic concepts to develop a system of revolutionary legality and class justice during the pre-1949 and post-1949 years. Mao once said:

> Such state apparatus as the army, the policy, and the courts are instruments with which one class oppresses another. As far as the hostile classes are concerned these are instruments of oppression. They are violent and certainly not, "benevolent things."[3]

Because of his antibureaucratic bias and mass orientation, Mao preferred informality and flexibility in handling political-legal issues. While recognizing the need for a legal system in a society, he nevertheless considered law merely as a tool useful to achieving political ends and would not let formal rules and procedures hinder the interest of the revolution. "Proper limits have to be exceeded," he contended "in order to right a wrong, or else the wrong cannot be righted."[4]

What emerged in the People's Republic of China under Mao was the competitive coexistence of jural (formal) and societal (informal) models of law, as in the case of *Fa* and *Li* in traditional China, to regulate human behavior and social order. The jural model stood for formal, elaborate, and codified rules enforced by a centralized and institutionalized bureaucracy, while the societal model focused on socially approved norms and values inculcated by political socialization and enforced by extrajudicial apparatuses consisting of administrative agencies and social organizations.[5]

Overall, the entire legal experience of Mao's China bore a strong imprint of the Chairman with a clear emphasis on class justice, mass tactics, the party's dominant role, and the societal model of law over the jural model.[6] There was a short period during 1954-1957 when the PRC was moving in the direction of legal stability and codification, marked by the adoption of a constitution, organic legislation for the court and procuracy, and a series of substantive and procedural laws and regulations. However, this move came to an abrupt end in 1957 as the Anti-Rightist campaign was launched by Mao and his associates. The formal legal structure suffered even more serious damage from the Cultural Revolution during the second half of the 1960s. Gong-Jian-Fa (Police, Procuracy, and Courts) were among the main targets of attack by the Red Guards. In an editorial titled "In Praise of Lawlessness," the *People's Daily* called for the complete destruction of the "bourgeois" law so that the proletarian legal order could be established.[7] A Red Guards' document also quoted Mao Zedong as saying: "Depend on the rule of man, not the rule of law."[8]

There is little question that the decade immediately preceding Mao's death and the arrest of the Gang of Four was the most regressive period of China's legal life. Excesses and abuses in the administration of justice are reported to have occurred easily and frequently. Tens of thousands of innocent people are said to have been cruelly tortured and persecuted. The "ten years of great catastrophe" was a nightmare that the Chinese would not want to happen again.

REASONS FOR LAW REFORM
IN POST-MAO CHINA

Since the ouster of the Gang of Four and the emergence of Deng Xiaoping's leadership, the PRC has taken steps to institute law reform and to develop a "socialist legality with Chinese characteristics." Undoubtedly, the resurgence of PRC's current interest in law is closely linked to the commitment of this post-Mao leadership to the four modernizations. After the bitter experience of the recent past, China badly needs a regular legal order to ensure stability, unity, and an orderly environment essential to the successful development of its economy. Chinese writers have described the new socialist legal system as a "sharp weapon" for safeguarding the four modernizations because it maintains and strengthens the stability and unity of the socialist order.[9]

The post-Mao leadership must also have realized that in order to get the population in general and intellectuals in particular enthusiastically involved in the program of modernization, it is imperative to have a system of law to help create an atmosphere of security and to overcome the "disease of lingering fear" referred to by former President Jiang Hua of the Supreme People's Court.[10] After all, not only the common people but many top officials including Deng Xiaoping, were victims of arbitrary treatment and lawless cruelty during the Cultural Revolution.

Moreover, the PRC has reason to expect a growing demand for economic legislation with the progress of its modernization program. For one thing, there is a need for various economic statutes, decrees, and rules to regulate production processes and the relationships among production units. For another, a formal legal system is a prerequisite for China to secure international cooperation and support for its four modernizations. In order to expand external trade, import advanced technology, and attract foreign investment the PRC must project itself as a stable and orderly society with relevant laws to protect the interests and rights of foreigners in areas of patents, trademark, joint ventures, etc.[11] To this end, as shown in the following section, China has been adapting and drafting a number of economic laws and regulations, especially concerning economic cooperation and technological exchange with foreign countries. The close linkage between Beijing's legal reform and its four modernizations is clearly underscored by the frequently quoted statement made by Deng Xiaoping in early 1986: "We must use two hands to carry on the four modernizations: grasping construction with one hand and grasping the legal system with the other."[12]

MAJOR MEASURES IN LAW REFORM

Since 1978 the new Chinese leadership has undertaken a series of measures to develop the legal system. One key step is the reestablishment of a constitutional order. In 1978 a third constitution was enacted to replace the Maoist constitution of 1975, which supplanted the "liberal" document of 1954.[13] The current constitution, enacted in 1982, is the PRC's fourth state constitution, upon which the new legal system is built.

To be sure, the 1982 constitution affirms in its preamble adherence to the four basic principles, namely, socialism, the People's Democratic Dictatorship, Marxism-Leninism and Mao Zedong Thought, and the leadership of the CCP. Nevertheless, it does attempt to make a clear distinction between the functions of the state and those of the party. In particular, it makes a serious effort to institutionalize the rule of law. Article 5 requires all organs of state, all political parties, and all organizations and institutions to abide by the constitution and the law. In the judicial field, it provides that people's courts and people's procuratorates exercise their respective authority independently according to law and are not subject to interference by administrative organs, public organizations, or individuals (Articles 126 and 131). The present constitution also puts more emphasis on individual rights with twenty-four articles on the "fundamental rights and duties of citizens," including equality before the law.[14]

The question of implementing constitutional provisions is a matter for future discussion. Now we can turn our attention to other measures of law reform.

INSTITUTIONAL REVITALIZATION

One major aspect of post-Mao China's law reform is to restructure formal legal institutions seriously damaged by the Cultural Revolution. While public security organs (police) and other extrajudicial apparatus continue to play important roles in the administration of justice and exercise of social control, one cannot but be impressed by such steps taken by the present Chinese leaders as the reorganization and expansion of the court structure, restoration of the procuracy, revival of the Ministry of Justice, and the resurrection of the lawyer system.

Court

In accordance with the Organic Law of the People's Courts in 1979 and its revision in 1983, the courts have been reorganized and strengthened. The court system is composed of the Supreme People's Court, local people's courts (higher, intermediate, and basic courts), and special people's courts. With minor modification, the current organic law reiterates the provisions of the 1954 law concerning judicial independence, equality before the law, public (open) trials, the right to defense, people's assessors, the collegiate system, adjudication (judicial) committees, and the two-trial (one appeal) system.[15] One significant change in the new law is to make the court accountable only to the People's Congress and free the court from direct supervision by local governments (Articles 35-36). Another important feature of the 1979 Court Law is to provide the Supreme People's Court with the power to give "explanations on questions concerning specific applications of laws and decrees in judicial procedure" in addition to its adjudication functions (Articles 32-33).

The people's courts at all levels have a criminal division and a civil division. In addition, economic, communications, and transportation divisions of the courts have also been established. In recent years the courts have continued the clamp down on major crimes while handling increasing numbers of civil cases, especially economic disputes. According to President Zhang Tianxiang of the Supreme People's Court, crime rate in China has remained about 5 per 10,000 persons for four years (1984-1987), compared to 7.4 per 10,000 in the early 1980s. However, the number of serious economic offenses has continued to be large. As in 1986, the courts handled nearly 300,000 cases of economic crimes and sentenced 350,000 persons in 1987. At the same time, there were 1.2 million civil cases and 365,000 economic disputes handled by the courts in 1987, representing substantial increases over the 1986 figures of 989,000 and 320,000, which, in turn, constituted 16.9 percent and 42.11 percent respectively over 1985. Among the civil cases, those involving debt, marriages, and alimony have been on the rise, while the overwhelming majority of the economic disputes have been those concerning economic contracts, many involving foreigners as well as people from Hong Kong and Macao.[16] It should be noted that in line with the traditional Chinese preference for informal dispute resolution, a large majority of civil cases have been settled through mediation. In this regard, the courts have been helped particularly by the following two organs: people's tribunals and mediation committees.

Different from the feared people's tribunals which used to carry out mass campaigns during the early years of the PRC,[17] the present people's tribunals are the agency of the basic people's courts to handle many ordinary civil cases, uncomplicated economic disputes, and minor criminal cases. While there are over 3,400 regular courts in China, the number of people's tribunals is now over 14,500 operating in 90,000 villages and towns.[18] Below the judiciary structure there are more than 900,000 mediation committees with nearly six million mediators.[19] Along with other extrajudicial organs, these committees perform the functions of settling civil disputes and disposing of minor criminal cases at the grassroots level. Up to 90 percent of the civil cases in China are reported to have been resolved through mediation in the past few years, and the work of the mediation committees has received rave comments from former U.S. Chief Justice Warren Burger and other foreign lawyers.[20]

Procuracy

The procuracy was the victim of the Cultural Revolution. However, the 1978 organic law of the People's Procuratorates reinstituted the procuracy with a hierarchy parallel to that of the courts, namely, the Supreme People's Procuratorates, three-level local people's procuratorates, and special people's procuratorates. Under the principle of dual leadership, Article 10 of the Organic Law makes the procuratorate at each level accountable to the People's Congress and its standing committee at the same level and also to the next higher level procuratorate. The 1983 revision of the Organic Law of the procuratorates appears to enhance the power of the procuracy. Greater freedom is given to local procuratorates to establish departments to handle their work (revised Article 20), and only the appointment and removal of chief procurators, not all other officials, at local levels must be approved by the standing committees for the next higher-level people's congresses (revised Articles 22 and 23).[21]

Among the functions of the procuracy are investigating criminal cases, supervising the police, instituting prosecution, scrutinizing trial procedures, and overseeing the execution of judgments and operations of prisons (Article 5). Article 9 of the Organic Law provides that "People's Procuratorates shall exercise their procuratorial authority independently in accordance with the law and shall not be subject to interference by other administrative organs, organizations, or individuals." In recent years the procuratorates have increased their activities against abuses of official power and corruption, bribery, and other economic crimes. As reported by Procurator General Yang Yichen, procuratorial organs handled in 1986 more than 32,000 cases regarding infringements on the people's democratic rights and dereliction of duty. Most of these cases involved extortion of confessions by torture, illegal detention and imprisonment, illegal search, the bending of the law for personal gains, and major accidents due to negligence. In 1986 the Procurators also handled 82,591 economic cases and recovered captured illicit money and goods worth 800 million yuan. The number of economic cases dealt with in 1986 was said to have increased 54 percent over the previous year. Among these cases, 13,888 were major, 4.3 times the number for 1985. More than 700 cases of economic crimes involved leading officials at the county level and above, and 137 cases involved officials in central government departments.[22]

Ministry of Justice

Abolished in 1959, the Ministry of Justice was reestablished in 1979 as a means to strengthen the legal system under the guidance of the State Council. The Ministry of Justice carries on its judicial administrative work with the support of provincial level judicial departments, county level judicial bureaus, and grassroots level judicial assistants.

The main tasks of the Ministry of Justice are to handle the judicial administration of the people's courts, manage and train judicial cadres, supervise and expand political-legal institutions. The Ministry also publicizes the law and educates the people in the legal system, supervises the work of the lawyers' and notaries' organizations, and exercises leadership over the organization and work of mediation committees. Furthermore, it compiles collections of laws and decrees, conducts legal research in cooperation with scholarly institutions, and engages in or coordinates the publication of law books and periodicals.[23]

Lawyers

The system of people's lawyers established in the mid-1950s practically ceased to exist after the Anti-Rightist Campaign of 1957-1958.[24] Resurrection of the Chinese bar is another important aspect of law reform in post-Mao China. According to the 1980 Provisional Act on Lawyers, China's lawyers are "state's legal workers" and have the duty to "safeguard the interests of the state, the collectives and the legitimate rights and interests of citizens" (Article 1). One prerequisite for law practice in China is Chinese citizenship. It is for the provincial level judicial department to evaluate, approve, and issue the lawyer's certificates to those candidates who have met the cultural and/or practical experience requirements and register such certificates with the Ministry of Justice. In September 1986 China held its first national examinations for new lawyers with more than 15,000 applicants.[24a]

Legal advisers offices (law firms) are the work organs of people's lawyers in China. Each office oversees the professional activities of the lawyers, collects fees from its clients, and distributes work to its members. In addition, under the guidance of the Ministry, Chinese Lawyers Associations have been organized at the national, provincial, municipal, and autonomous regional level, "to protect the legitimate rights and interests of lawyers, to exchange work experience, and to promote lawyers' work and contacts between legal workers both at home and abroad."[25]

Although burdened with a heavy workload, Chinese lawyers receive rather low wages, with starting salaries of about $20 a month. Lately, some law offices have become responsible for their profits and losses, by retaining 55 percent of the profits for developing the company, 20 percent for employee benefits, and 25 percent for bonuses.[26] Despite the heavy workload, the low income, and the low status associated with the legal profession because of the Chinese prejudice against those "defending criminals," there is hope that things will improve as more people appreciate the importance of the rule of law.

In 1981 there were 4,800 lawyers and 1,300 legal advisers offices in China. Now there are about 30,000 full-time and part-time lawyers and 3,300 legal advisers offices.[27] China is said to plan to increase the number of lawyers to 50,000 by 1990. In Beijing, the number of lawyers has increased from 40 in 1979 to the present 1,300.[28] The Ministry of Justice has, since 1984, set up 20,000 legal service organs with more than 50,000 workers, to assist rural enterprises and handle civil disputes. Under the guidance of legal advisers offices, these legal service organs reportedly had settled at the end of 1986 over 110,000 business disputes and saved rural enterprises from losses of 187 million yuan.[29]

LEGISLATIVE ACTIVITY

According to the constitution, the PRC's supreme organs of legislative authority are the National People's Congress and its standing committee (Articles 62 and 69). When bills are submitted for consideration, they are first reviewed by the Legal Affairs Commission of the NPC Standing

Committee (composed of standing committee members and outside legal scholars) and the Law Committee of the NPC (composed of NPC deputies only).[30] Then they are given to all local authorities and departments of the central government for examination before the NPC or its Standing Committee formally deliberates these bills. Technically, all people have the freedom to voice their views.[31]

In regard to its legislative output, post-Mao China has proceeded with surprising speed to enact new codes and revise old laws or affirm their validity. Since 1979 the NPC and its standing committee have promulgated 58 important laws and made 52 decisions revising, supplementing, or implementing the laws. At the same time, the State Council has issued 400 administrative statutes and regulations and the people's congresses and their standing committees at the provincial level have also enacted over 800 local decrees.[32] Among the major enactments in 1979 were Organic Laws of Courts and Procuratorates, Criminal Law, and Criminal Procedure Law. The latter two were the first criminal codes enacted in the PRC's history, defining punishable acts and penalties and regularizing the sanctioning procedure. Together they prescribe appropriate standards to guide judicial work and the framework for "due process" to protect the individual. The Civil Procedure Law was adopted in 1982 and the Civil Law General Principles in 1986. China's Civil Code is yet to be enacted, although there are a number of separate laws related to civil affairs including laws on economic contracts, patents, trademarks, marriage, and inheritance.

In an effort to invigorate the domestic economy and to implement the open-door policy, the PRC has quickened the pace of economic legislation. The NPC and its standing committee and the State Council have promulgated 200 economic laws and regulations in recent years. There are in China more than 160 laws and regulations governing its foreign economic relations and trade. Prominent among them are those concerning joint ventures, taxation, foreign economic contracts, technology imports, trademarks, patent rights, and exclusively foreign-owned enterprises.[33] In April 1987 the State Council announced a five-year program to draft 30 new laws and 300 administrative regulations. One purpose of the plan is to continue the reform of China's foreign trade system, improve the country's investment environment for foreign business, and accelerate the development of the special economic zones.[34]

LEGAL EDUCATION

One significant aspect of China's legal reform in the post-Mao era is the restoration and expansion of legal education. There are in the PRC today 35 departments of law at universities, one political-legal university (China Political-Legal University), and four political-legal institutes with a total enrollment of over 25,000.[35] In addition, the Ministry of Justice has established 28 judicial schools, 27 political-legal cadre schools, and other *ad hoc* short-term institutes for judicial personnel. Each year over 20,000 cadres have been given basic legal education.[36]

Besides formal legal education, the PRC has used mass propaganda campaigns to educate the public about socialist legality. In November, 1985, for instance, the NPC standing committee adopted a five-year program for 1986-1990 to popularize legal knowledge among Chinese citizens. With cadres at all levels and young people as its major targets, this educational drive has set out to publicize the Constitution, Criminal Law, Criminal Procedure Law, Civil Procedure Law, Marriage Law, Law on Economic Contracts, and other basic laws. Colleges, middle schools, primary schools, as well as other schools have incorporated legal studies in their curricula. Newspapers, magazines, radio and TV broadcasts have launched legal columns or programs. According to Minister of Justice Zou Yu, nearly 300 million Chinese citizens studied China's laws in 1986.

More than 90 percent of central government officials, 90 percent of provincial and municipal leaders, 84 percent of cadres at the prefectural and city levels, and 81 percent of the cadres at the county levels also participated in the studies.[37]

EMERGENCE OF "SOCIALIST LEGALITY WITH CHINESE CHARACTERISTICS"

What has emerged from the law reform in post-Mao China is "socialist legality with Chinese characteristics." This phase is not clearly defined and just as ambiguous as "socialism with Chinese characteristics" leaving plenty of room for broad interpretations.

First of all, socialist legality is viewed by the Chinese as legally compatible with the needs of socialism and with the will and interests of the proletariat and the entire people.[38] Second, the Communist party plays a leading role in formulating socialist laws, which are the finalization and codification of the party's policies through the state's legislative process. Once such laws are adopted, their enforcement is insured by the compulsory power of the state. They enjoy full authority and must be conformed to by all people including party members.[39]

In developing their legal system, the Chinese have obviously borrowed experiences from the Soviet Union and other countries. However, as stated by Chinese leaders and legal experts, their socialist laws must be based on the contemporary and historical realities of China. So by proceeding from the actual conditions of China and acting according to the principles of socialist legality the PRC is establishing a "Chinese-style socialist legal system."[40]

Fully in line with the Chinese Li-Fa tradition, Beijing now gives due attention to both jural and societal models of law. Parallel to the restructured judicial system, there are in China public security organs and other extrajudicial apparatus that continue to play important roles in maintaining law and order, imposing administrative sanctions, and set-tling civil disputes.[41] In criminal legislation, Chinese laws, while reflecting strong Soviet influence, are considered to be "much more simple, much more general, much more programmatic, and more moralistic in their syntax and style."[42] The frequent use of "circumstances," without any specific listing, in determining penalties in China's Crimi-nal Law, the practice of combining punishment with education in its penal policy including the suspension of the death sentences for two years, and the right of the people's court and the people's procuracy to bring up for readjudica-tion a case where a legally effective judgment contains actual error are a few examples marked with pronounced Chinese characteristics.[43]

The General Principles of Civil Law promulgated in 1986 has some features peculiar to China's socialist economy in that they protect the property rights of the state, collectives, and individuals and that they give support to Deng's open-door policy to the world. For instance, Chapter 2 of The General Principles allows the existence and operation of the private sector of the economy, namely, individual in-dustrial-commercial households, rural contract-manage-ment households, and partnerships between individuals, and Chapter 5 contains provisions on the right of contracted management for collectives as well as individuals. Chapter 3 stipulates the status of entrepreneurial legal persons to in-clude Chinese foreign equity joint ventures, cooperative ventures, and wholly foreign-owned enterprises in China. It also reorganizes and encourages the establishment of economic associations between enterprises and between en-terprises and institutions, thus making China's control over economic activities less rigorous than is exercised in some other Communist countries. Finally, the General Principles devotes a full chapter, Chapter 8, to civil relations involv-ing foreign matters to underscore the PRC's concern with international business transactions.[44]

Dispute resolution through mediation has had a long history in China, and this traditional preference for informal means to handle civil matters is manifested both in law and practice in the current Chinese approach to domestic civic disputes and to disputes involving foreign economic and trade activities. Article 6 of the Civil Procedure Law stipulates "in trying civil cases, the people's court shall stress mediation." There is a special section for mediation in the Civil Procedure Law (Articles 97-102) and the spirit of stressing mediation and provisions concerning mediation are found in each stage of hearing and trying procedure. When mediation fails, the Civil Procedure Law also provides that a court decision will be promptly made.[45] According to the Economic Contract Law of the PRC, when a contract dispute arises, the parties concerned should try to reach a settlement through negotiation and mutual accommodation. If the negotiation fails, either party can apply for mediation or arbitration to the agency designated by the state for contract management or file a lawsuit directly with the people's court.[46] Although the mediation process must follow the principle of voluntary participation, it is considered by the Chinese as the most effective and commonly used method to settle economic contract disputes.[47]

By the same token, in handling disputes arising from international business transactions, the Chinese generally prefer informal negotiation between the parties and third-party conciliation (mediation). If it becomes necessary to resort to a formal dispute resolution mechanism, the Chinese show a strong preference for arbitration rather than court adjudication.

Article VIII of the U.S.-PRC trade agreement of 1979 encourages the prompt and equitable settlement of any disputes through "friendly consultations, conciliation, or other mutually acceptable means." If unsuccessful, it further provides, the parties to the dispute may submit the matter to arbitration conducted by an arbitration institution in the PRC, the United States, or a third country.[48]

Similar patterns concerning dispute resolution can also be found in China's economic and trade agreements with other foreign countries and in its legislation on joint ventures, joint exploitation of petroleum resources, and foreign economic contracts. Parties to a dispute are usually expected to seek its settlement through the following three successive stages: (1) Friendly consultation (direct negotiation), (2) Conciliation, and (3) Arbitration. Consistent with its traditional preference for mediation, China has in recent years adopted joint conciliation as a means to settle disputes between its citizens and those of another country, especially the United States. Under this arrangement between the China Foreign Trade Arbitration Commission and the American Arbitration Association, each organization appoints a conciliator and the two work jointly to help the parties to find a solution to their problem.[49]

The evolving legal system in China retains some characteristics distinctly Chinese and at the same time innovates changes to meet the requirements of the time. One key constraint on its development, nevertheless is the so-called Four Basic Principles (socialism, the People's Democratic Dictatorship, Marxism-Leninism and Mao Zedong Thought, and the leadership of the CCP), within which the legal system is expected to operate. In the name of upholding the Four Basic Principles, Beijing has taken actions against movements for democracy and human rights, i.e., against the Democracy Wall and political dissents in the late 1970s and against student demonstrations and "bourgeois liberalism" in early 1987. Unless the policy of upholding the Four Basic Principles is modified or diluted in the future, the PRC's legal system is unlikely to function too differently from its counterpart in the Soviet Union. No principle, however normatively stated in the constitution or law, is permitted to conflict with the policy needs of the Communist Party, though in normal situations, the legal system can operate generally in a reasonable and predictable manner.[50]

PROBLEMS AND OBSTACLES
FOR CHINA'S LAW REFORM

Under Deng's leadership, considerable progress has been made in building a new, stable legal order in the PRC. However, much remains to be done in the implementation of the reform measures. Some problems are practical ones, and others are more basic and political in nature. A survey of them is in order for our overall assessment of the reform effort.

First of all, there is an acute shortage of trained personnel in the legal field despite recent improvement in coping with this glaring weakness. According to the information of the Ministry of Justice, China has trained in recent years almost 250,000 judicial personnel and plans to double this figure by 1990 at the rate of 20,000 per year.[51] As for the number of lawyers, it is now over 20,000 and expected to reach 50,000 by 1990.[52] Nevertheless, the combined present or future numbers of Chinese judicial cadres and lawyers fall short of the minimum figure of one million trained legal personnel set for China by Deng Xiaoping in 1980.[53]

Low salaries, low status, and social prejudice have contributed to the serious shortage of qualified lawyers in China. With the growth of economic activities, some 4 million enterprises would like to have legal advisers of their own, but many of them have to share one lawyer.[54] Shanghai has 26 law offices with more than 1,000 full-time and part-time lawyers. With a population of 12 million, the city practically has one lawyer per 10,000 persons.[55] As pointed out by a Vice Minister of Justice, of nearly one million cases handled by China's courts annually, only 6 percent have been represented by lawyers, and of several hundred thousand criminal cases, only 20 percent by lawyers.[56] Judicial work in Jilin Province, where one-third of its lawyers have quit since 1984 because of poor treatment, has been particularly hampered. In 1985, only 8.6 percent of criminal trials in the province were conducted with lawyers present, and the percentage for civil cases was 8.1.[57]

Second, both the populace and bureaucracy tend to have an indifferent and skeptical attitude toward law, as "legal ignorance." And these old beliefs cannot be overcome overnight. Harassment of lawyers is a case in point. Many people consider lawyers as "those who speak for criminals." Some officials regard arguments from lawyers as challenges to their authority. Not only has lawyers' work been obstructed by state and party cadres, but they themselves have been expelled from the courtroom, arrested, and persecuted, as reported by the press.[58] Such publicity led the authorities in Hebei Province to deal with a judge who had a lawyer handcuffed to a tree for 80 minutes.[59] More importantly, President Zhang Tianxiang of the Supreme People's Court has recently urged the courts to genuinely protect lawyers in exercising their rights during adjudication proceedings.[60]

The problem confronting China today, Jurist Zhang Youyu noted, is not the lack of laws but the failure to implement them.[61] Official abuses of power have continued to occur in illegal arrests, unlawful detention, and interference with judicial work. According to Chief Procurator Yang Yichen, Chinese procuratorates in 1986 handled more than 32,000 cases concerning infringement on the people's rights and dereliction of duty, most of which involved extortion of confessions by torture, illegal detention and imprisonment, illegal search, and the bending of the law for personal gains.[62] President Zheng Tianxing also pointed out the tendency of some officials to interfere in the work of the courts and to use the "word of those in positions to substitute for the law" and to use "the authority to overpower the law."[63] The unfamiliarity with legal concepts and strong attachment to personal and familial relations account for those cadres who are inclined to ignore or break the law and to apply "disciplinary measures instead of legal sanctions" in criminal cases.[64]

In a report issued in September 1987, Amnesty International said that the unprecedented publicity given by official statements and press reports over the past two years showed that "torture and ill-treatment of prisoners is a persistent and widespread problem in China," where suspects are reported to have been beaten, whipped, and brutally assaulted with electric batons in order to extract confessions. While pointing out those statements and reports as evidence of the Chinese government's concern about the problem, Amnesty International nevertheless, maintained that at the same time they "have highlighted the difficulties encountered in educating the general public and law enforcers about the need to respect the law, and in trying to investigate and redress cases of abuse. They also show that abuses often occur because Chinese law does not include sufficient safeguards for detainees' rights."[64a]

By the same token, Chinese bureaucracy and its attitude toward legal issues have given rise to concerns by foreign lawyers and investors in China. For one thing, they complain about the frustrating red tape of Chinese bureaucracy. Political support and personal relations are crucial to getting things done in the PRC.[65] For another, among major difficulties facing foreign investors in China are the vagueness and inadequacy of Chinese laws and the constant recourse by the Chinese to internal rules that should be held in strict confidence from foreigners. There is also the question of legal enforceability of contracts signed with Chinese entities, as government agencies sometimes directly interfere with the performance of the contract by imposing new rules or conditions.[66]

Finally, the fundamental problem confronting the PRC's current law reform remains the relationship between the party and the legal system. Technically, the party and its members must all work within the confines of the Constitution and the law.[67] In practice, party officials too often let political consideration prevail over legal requirements.

Take for example the principle of judicial independence guaranteed by the Constitution and the law.[68] Although the practice of party Committee secretaries reviewing and approving cases in Mao's China has been discontinued, the people's court still has to seek guidance from the party Committee on broad policy matters and on important or complex cases. In the early 1980s the Political-legal Committee of the CCP Central Committee launched a nationwide anticrime drive, in which the prominent influence of the party's political-legal committees at all levels of legal affairs appears to have limited the degree of independence allowed to the judiciary. In an effort to strike a swift and severe blow at serious criminal activities, the Chinese authorities resorted to such harsh measures as mass arrests, publicized executions, expansion of the list of capital crimes, and removal of procedural guarantees for certain felons, steps that evoked criticisms from sympathetic observers.[69]

While there has been an obvious drop in the number of violent crimes in the last few years, economic offenses in China have been on the rise. According to President Zhang Tianxiang of the Supreme People's Court, in 1986 the courts handled 78,133 cases, an increase of 55.52 percent over the previous year. And cases involving speculation, embezzlement, tax evasion, bribery and fraud to obtain public property were more than double the 1985 figure.[70]

Since offenders are often party and government officials and their relatives, Beijing has made fighting economic crime a top priority. In January 1986 the Secretariat of the CCP Central Committee set up a leading group, headed by Qiao Shi, to take charge of the "rectification of party style." At a national conference on political and legal work convened by the Political-Legal Committee of the CCP Central Committee in March 1986, it was stressed:

> Whoever is involved in economic criminal activities, whoever breaks the law, will be dealt with according to law. We should strive to...prosecute those who break the law, making everyone equal before the law. Economic punishment should not be substituted for criminal punishment for those who are criminally responsible; party and administrative disciplinary actions should not be substitutes for legal punishment; verified economic crimes should not be handled as unhealthy practices; verified power abuses should not be treated as bureaucratism.[71]

The above quotation underscores the concern about the persistent practice of favoring people of power, influence, and connections without regard to the principle of equality before the law.[72] In the view of some observers, the PRC's drive against corruption and other economic crimes has "only struck flies but not tigers."[73] Thus far only mid-rank cadres have been punished; no high officials have ever been criminally prosecuted and sentenced for their wrongdoing.

In early 1986 two sons of senior cadres of Shanghai were sentenced to death and a former Vice Major of Beijing was said to be under investigation for economic problems. This prompted the commentator of the *People's Daily* to title his article: "All Are Equal before the Law," although Deng Xiaoping's intervention was reported elsewhere as responsible for the court action.[74] An even more publicized case in 1986 was that of Yeh Zhifeng. Yeh, deputy chief of a department in the Export-Import Bureau of the State Economic Commission, was convicted of selling state secrets to foreigners. Daughter of General Yeh Fei (Vice Chairman of the NPC Standing Committee), she was the principle offender in the case and was sentenced to 17 years imprisonment, while her accomplice received the death penalty. This case has not only provoked critical reactions but also called into question the credibility of China's new legal system with respect to the principles of judicial independence and equality before the law.[75]

CONCLUSION

As seen in the preceding pages, a host of difficult problems confront China in implementing its law reform program. Most obstacles however, appear to be surmountable and need not block continued and sustained advances to a sound legal order given a firm commitment to the current reform on the part of the Chinese leadership. Already the PRC has come a long way from the Maoist era to develop a Chinese-style socialist legal system that contains elements of both continuity and change.

On the one hand, progress in instituting a formal and normalized system of law is in evidence. For the first time in the PRC's history there is now in place a regular, stable legal structure along with impressive legislative output on substantive and procedural matters. On the other hand, principles and practices deeply rooted in China's traditional political culture can also be found in its new legal order. The use of informal mechanisms to handle disputes and minor offenses and the stress on the role of education in the legal process have made positive impressions on foreign observers. But the revival of the police's power to apply a wide range of "administrative" sanctions, including reeducation through labor, can hardly brighten the prospects for legality. Similarly, the traditional emphasis on personal relations and respect for the rule of man continue to complicate law enforcement in China today. Ironically, the PRC still relies upon a strong leader like Deng Xiaoping to push forward the novel idea of the rule of law.

One sign of hope for the future is that the various problems facing the legal reform are openly discussed in the PRC. Furthermore, Chinese leaders appear to be aware and are making conscientious efforts to alleviate them. For example, in 1986 Beijing launched a five-year program of

American lawyers, whose criticism of Chinese systems is cited elsewhere in this paper, also commend the substantial progress made by the PRC in creating an attractive investment environment: "By enacting a large body of business legislation, approving many bilateral and multilateral economic treaties, and strengthening domestic legal institutions, the People's Republic of China has established many of the infrastructures such cooperation requires." They further note that "a successful investment process requires efforts not only by the host country but also by investor countries and their companies."[77]

Even on the touchy issue of subordination of law to political dictates, hope for change and moderation is not beyond the realm of possibility. Lately in Chinese legal circles, the classic legal concepts of Marx have been openly challenged. Writing in *Jurisprudence*, Zhang Zonghou rejects the traditional Marxist-Leninist view on the class nature of law by maintaining that law cannot be considered a product of class struggle nor as peculiar to class society.

In this jurist's opinion, law can be distinguished from other social phenomena only when examined from the perspectives of its social character, coercive character, and character as rules.[78]

Understandably, his position has been criticized by those who follow the orthodoxy.[79] Others tend to be more ambivalent. Zhang Youyu, the distinguished jurist, contends that the class nature of law exists, although it may be strongly or weakly expressed. In *Studying Legal Systems*, he says, "we should be opposed to the dogmatism of Marxism and even more to the dogmatism of the capitalist class."[80] Another legal writer takes a middle-ground approach that in essence disputes Marx's orthodox theory. In an article in *Studies in Law*, Yin Yong suggests that law has a clear class character but also an undeniable supraclass character because it reflects not only the will and interest of the ruling class but also the general interest and wish of human society.[81]

Of course, prospects for the further development of the legal system are closely tied to the PRC's political stability and the outcome of Deng's overall reforms. Despite setbacks and problems, the program of reforms pushed by Deng and Zhao Ziyang appears to command a broad mass support of the Chinese people and has a built-in momentum of its own. Affirmed by the CCP's 13th Party Congress, it calls for, among other things, political reform that would separate functions of the party from those of the government.[82] If carried out successfully, the overall reforms would further strengthen the legal system and vice versa. In his report to the 13th Party Congress, Zhao linked the socialist legal system with socialist democracy:

> We must attend to legislation and to economic development and reform at the same time. During the whole process of reform we must go on building our legal system. On the other hand, we should improve legislation and the procedures for law enforcement, enable the judicial organs to exercise independent authority, as prescribed by law, and enhance citizens' awareness of law; on the other hand, we should see to it that legislation guarantees good order in economic development and reform and consolidates achievements scored in reform.... In short, through reform we should gradually establish a legal framework for our socialist democracy and institutionalize it.[83]

Since the conclusion of the 13th Party Congress, there have been several encouraging signs regarding China's legal development. For one thing, the NPC seems to be playing an increasingly assertive role as the PRC's supreme legislative body. It is currently undertaking the task of drafting, examining, and revising over the next five years 117 laws covering economic reform, protection of citizen's rights and freedoms, social welfare, military and national defense, reform of government institutions, civil and criminal jurisdiction, etc.[84] Also Ren Jianxin, a man with lengthy legal experience, has been chosen as President of the Supreme People's Court. The new chief judge stresses openness in court work and his commitment to improve the system of public trial, respect lawyers' rights, protect the right of citizens to litigation, and bring the trial process into the open for greater public scrutiny.[85]

Still, it would be unrealistic to expect the rule of law to take root in China in the foreseeable future. What appears possible is a regularized socialist legal system with sufficient functional autonomy and professional competency to help institutionalize the fruits of the reforms and to provide the Chinese with a stable, orderly, and secure environment. Considerable time may be needed before the following Chinese goals for legal reform announced in 1978 can attain some measure of realization: "There must be laws for people to follow, these laws must be observed, their enforcement must be strict, and law breakers must be dealt with."[86]

NOTES

1. Dong Biwu, *Lun Shehui Zhuyi Minzhu Yu Fazhi* (On Socialist Democracy and the Legal System) (Beijing: People's Press, 1979), pp. 130-131.
2. For a detailed examination of law in traditional China, see Derk Bodde and Clarence Morris, *Law in Imperial China* (Cambridge, Mass: Harvard University Press, 1967); Chu Tung-tsu, *Law and Society in Traditional China* (Paris, Mouton 1961), Sybille van der Sprenkle, *Legal Institutions in Manchu China* (London: The Athlone Press, 1962).
3. Mao Tse-tung, *On People's Democratic Dictatorship* (Peking: Foreign Languages Press, 1951), pp. 16-17.
4. "Report on the Investigation of the Peasant Movement," *Selected Works of Mao Tse-tung* (Peking: Foreign Languages Press, 1967), Vol. I, p. 27.
5. Although using different terms, most authors seem to agree on the existence of two models of law in the PRC. See, e.g., Jerome A. Cohen, *The Criminal Process in the People's Republic of China, 1949-1963: An Introduction* (Cambridge, Mass: Harvard University Press, 1968); Shao-chuan Leng, *Justice in Communist China* (Dobbs Ferry, NY: Oceana, 1967); Victor Li, "The Role of Law in Communist China," *The China Quarterly*, No. 44, October-December 1970, pp. 66-111; Stanley Lubman, "Form and Function in the Chinese Criminal Process," *Columbia Law Review Vol. 69*, No. 4, April 1969, pp. 535-575.
6. For a detailed discussion, see Shao-chuan Leng, "The Role of Law in the People's Republic of China as Reflecting Mao Tse-tung's Influence," *Journal of Criminal Law and Criminology, Vol. 68*, No. 3, 1977, pp. 356-73.
7. For this and other aspects of China's legal experience under Mao, consult *ibid.*, citations in note 5, and Chapter 2 in Shao-chuan Leng with Hungdah Chiu, *Criminal Justice in Post-Mao China* (Albany: State University of New York Press, 1985).
8. Canton, *Fan Peng-Lo Heixian* (Anti-Peng and Lo's Black Line), No. 1, July 1968; English translation in *Selections from China Mainland Magazine* (Hong Kong: U.S. Consulate-General), No. 625, September 3, 1968, pp. 23. It should be noted here that according to a Chinese author in a more recent publication, there was a debate in 1958 in China's legal circles concerning the following authoritative view: "We want the rule of man, not the rule of law; we

don't rely on civil and criminal laws to maintain order, but rather rely on our use of public meetings and mass movements." Wang Guiwu, "A Brief Discussion of the Integration of the Rule of Man and the Rule of Law," *Fazhi Yu Renzhi Wenti Taolun Ji* (Collection of Essays Discussing the Problems Concerning the Rule of Law and the Rule of Man) (Beijing: Mass Publishing House, 1981), p. 256.

9. Liu Guangming, "The Socialist Legal System Is a Sharp Weapon for Building a Modern and Strong State," *Liaoning Daxue Xuebao* (Journal of Liaoning University), No. 3, 1978, p. 37; Wu Lei, "A Sharp Weapon for Defending the Four Modernizations," *Guangming ribao* (Enlightenment Daily), July 14, 1979, p. 3. Chen Weidian and Zhou Xinming, "Strengthen the Legal System, Ensure Stability and Unity," *Faxue Yanjiu* (Studies in Law), No. 1, 1980, pp. 35-36.

10. *Renmin ribao* (People's Daily), Oct. 21, 1978, p. 1.

11. Fox Butterfield, "Peking Issues Rules to Lure Investment," *New York Times*, July 9, 1979, p. Al; Masao Sakuru, "Investing in China: The Legal Framework," *JETRO China Newsletter*, No. 37, 1982, pp. 7-12, 32.

12. Deng's statement, for example is quoted in Commentator, "The Legal System and Construction," *Liaowang* (Outlook), February 17, 1986, p. 4 and Zhang Zhongfu, "Democracy, the Legal System, and High-Level Civilization," *Renmin ribao*, April 21, 1986, p. 2. Deng is said to have made this statement at a meeting of the Standing Committee of the Politburo on January 17, 1986. See "Reforms to Promote Economic Development; The Legal System to Combat Evil Trends," *Zhong bao* (Center Daily News), March 15, 1986, p. 6.

13. The English text of the 1978 constitution is in *The Constitution of the People's Republic of China* (Peking: Foreign Languages Press, 1978); For the 1954 and 1975 constitutions, see Michael Lindsay, ed., *The New Constitution of Communist China* (Taipei: Institute of International Relations, 1976), pp. 291-311 and 328-336 respectively.

14. For the English text of the 1982 constitution, see "Constitution of the People's Republic of China," *Beijing Review*, Vol. 25, No. 52, December 27, 1982, pp. 10-29.

15. Articles 4-12 of the 1979 Organic Law, whose text is in *Zhonghua Renmin Gongheguo Fagui Huibian, 1979-1984* (Collection of Laws and Regulations of the People's Republic of China, 1979-1984)

(Beijing: People's Press, 1985), pp. 81-89. Text of the 1983 revised law is in *ibid.*, pp. 480-489. For a discussion of the courts under the 1954 Organic Law, see Leng, *Justice in Communist China*, pp. 77-101.

16. "Report on the Work of the Supreme People's Court, April 6, 1987," *Zhongguo Fazhi bao* (China's Legal System Paper), April 16, 1987, p. 2; Work Report of the Supreme Court, April, 1988," *Renmin ribao*, April 18, 1988, pp. 2,3.

17. For a discussion of the people's tribunals in 1950-52, see Leng, *Justice in Communist China*, pp. 35-39.

18. *Zhongguo Fazhi bao*, February 23, 1987, p. 1.

19. *Zhongguo Baike Nianjian, 1984* (Chinese Encyclopedia Year Book, 1984) (Beijing: Chinese Encyclopedia Press, 1984), p. 246.

20. Leng and Chiu, *Criminal Justice in Post-Mao China*, p. 68; *Zhongguo Fazhi bao*, February 19, 1987, p. 3.

21. Text of the 1979 Organic Law of the People's Procuratorates is in *Fagui Huibian, 1979-1984*, pp. 91-97; text of the 1983 revised law in *ibid.*, pp. 492-498.

22. See "Work Report of the Supreme People's Procuratorates, April 6, 1987," *Zhongguo Fazhi bao*, April 6, 1987, p. 3.

23. *Zhongguo Fazhi bao*, for example, is published by the Ministry of Justice.

24. As told to the author in 1982 by Ma Ronju, editor of *Faxue Yanju*, after the Anti-Rightist campaign, only 4 lawyers were allowed to function in China, Ma being one of the four.

24a. *Renmin ribao*, September 28, 1986, p. 4.

25. *Zhongguo Fazhi bao*, July 8, 1986, p. 1; August 6, 1986, p. 3.

26. Vigor Fung, "China's Lawyers Suffer from Low Status," *The Asian Wall Street Journal*, April 13, 1987, pp. 1, 6.

27. *China Daily*, October 8, 1985, p. 1; August 2, 1988, p. 1.

28. Fung, "China Lawyers," p. 6.

29. *Renmin ribao*, May 13, 1987, p. 4; *Zhongguo Fazhi bao*, May 13, 1987, p. 1.

30. Taotai Hsia and Constance A. Johnson, *Law Making in the People's Republic of China* (Washington, D.C.: Library of Congress, 1986) p. 6. Hsia uses "Legal Work Commission" instead of "Legal Affairs Commission."

31. "NPC to Improve Lawmaking, Nationwide Legal Work," *FBIS, Daily Report: China*, March 27, 1987, p. K7; "New Legal Rules Promise to Guard Reform" *China Daily*, April 8, p. 1.

32. *Xinhua*, Beijing, March 27, 1987.

33. *Renmin ribao*, August 13, 1986, p. 1; *Beijing Review*, Vol. 29, No. 22, June 2, 1986, pp. 4-5; *ibid.*, vol. 30, No. 7, Feb. 6, 1987, pp. 14-16.
34. *FBIS, Daily Report: China*, April 27, 1987, pp. K6-K7.
35. *Xinhua*, September 13, 1986; also interviews with visiting Chinese lawyers in July 1987.
36. *People's Republic of China Year Book, 1986* (Beijing: Xinhua Publishing House, 1986, pp. 186-187; *Zhongguo Fazhi bao*, Dec. 25, 1985. p. 1.
37. "Justice Minister Gives Report," *FBIS, Daily Report: China*, March 11, 1987, pp. K2-K3; also "Resolution on Education," *ibid.*, Nov. 26, 1985, pp. K8-K9.
38. Chen Chunlong, et al, *Falu Zhishi Wenda* (Questions and Answers in Legal Knowledge) (Beijing: Beijing Publishing House, 1979), p. 18.
39. Li Buyun "On the Scientific Character of the Concept of Rule of Law", *Faxue Yanjiu* (Studies in Laws), No. 1, 1982, p. 9; Yi Jianging, "Closing Address," *Main Documents of the Second Session of the 5th NPC of the PRC* (Beijing: Foreign Languages Press, 1979), pp. 224-225.
40. "Gist of Peng Zhen 1981 Speech on Civil Code," *FBIS, Daily Report: China*, May 29, 1985, pp. K12-K13; Xiang Chunyi, et al, "Make Effort to Establish a Chinese-style Socialist Legal System," *Hongqi* (Red Flag), No. 3, 1984, pp. 8-12, 18.
41. See Leng and Chiu, *Criminal Justice in Post-Mao China*, pp. 76-79.
42. Harold Berman, et al, "A Comparison of Chinese and Soviet Codes of Criminal Law and Procedure," *Journal of Criminal Law and Criminology*, Vol. 73, No. 1, 1982, p. 257.
43. "Concepts of Law in the Chinese Anti-Crime Campaign," *Harvard Law Review*, Vol. 98, No. 8, June 1985, pp. 1901-1902; Leng and Chiu, *Criminal Justice in Post-Mao China*, pp. 127-128, pp. 142-143; Xu Yichu, "On the Establishment of Procedure with Chinese characteristics for Adjudication Supervision," *Faxue Yanjiu*, No. 4, 1986, pp. 75-76.
44. Text of the General Principles of Civil Law is in *Zhonghua Renmin Gongheguo Guowuyuan Gongbao* (Gazette of the State Council of the PRC) No. 12, 1986, pp. 371-393. For explanations or comments, see Wang Hanbin's statement made on April 2, 1986 at the Sixth NPC, *ibid*, pp. 393-399; Xiang Chunyi, "The Chinese Characteristics of the Civil Generalities," *Zhongguo Faxue* (Law of China), No. 3, 1986, pp. 3-9; Jerome A. Cohen, "China Adopts

Civil Law Principles," *The Chinese Business Review,* September-October, 1986, pp. 48-50; "The 'Civil Law's General Rules,'" *China News Analysis,* No. 1312, June 15, 1986, pp. 1-9.

45. Text of the Civil Procedure Law, adopted for trial implementation in 1982, is in *Fagui Huibian, 1979-1984,* pp. 283-324. In commenting on the Law, Chang Youyu, the noted Chinese jurist, said that "up to 90 percent of the civil cases have been resolved through mediation in the past few years." *Xinhua,* March 8, 1982.

46. The relevant articles are Articles 48-50. Text of the Economic Contract Law is in *Fagui Huibian, 1979-1984,* pp. 239-259.

47. See Pitman Potter, "The Economic Contract Law of the People's Republic of China," *Chinese Law and Government,* Vol. 18, No. 1, Spring 1985, pp. 25, 91, 97-98.

48. Jerome A. Cohen, "The Role of Arbitration in Economic Cooperation with China," in Michael J. Mosher (ed.) *Foreign Trade, Investment and the Law in the People's Republic of China* (Hong Kong: Oxford University Press, 1984), pp. 299-300.

49. *Ibid.,* pp. 303-304 and Yang Xiaobing, "Laws Back Foreign Economic Activities," *Beijing Review,* Vol. 30, No. 7, February 16, 1987. For other related issues, consult Cohen's entire Chapter (Mosher, pp. 296-318); also Charles Pettit, "Dispute Resolution in the People's Republic of China," *Arbitration Journal,* Vol. 39, No. 1, March 1984, pp. 3-13.

50. A good discussion of Soviet concepts of socialist legality and socialist democracy is in Bernard Reamundo, *The Soviet System, A Primer* (Chicago: American Bar Association, 1971), pp. 27-28.

51. *Zhongguo Fazhi bao,* December 25, 1985, p. 1.

52. *Renmin ribao,* July 7, 1986, p. 4.

53. *FBIS, Daily Report: China,* August 10, 1983, p. K22.

54. *Renmin ribao,* July 11, 1986, p. 4.

55. *China Daily,* June 6, 1986, p. 4.

56. *Renmin ribao,* July 11, 1986, p. 4.

57. *China Daily,* November 29, 1986, p. 3.

58. Fung, "China's Lawyers Suffer from Low Status," p. 1; "On China's Lawyers," *Zhongbao,* February 8, 1986, p. 16; "How Can You Say That 'Lawyers Only Speak for Criminal Element?'" *Renmin ribao,* September 25, 1986, p. 4.

59. *Renmin ribao,* August 27, 1986, p. 4.

60. *Zhongguo Fazhi bao,* June 9, 1987, p. 1.

61. *Beijing ribao,* February 14, 1986, p. 1.

62. *Zhongguo Fazhi bao,* April 16, 1987, p. 2.

63. *Ibid.*

64. Su Ting, "Party and Government Disciplinary Sanctions Cannot Substitute for Criminal Sanctions," *Renmin ribao,* August 30, 1986, p. 4; "Law Enforcement Discussed," *FBIS, Daily Report: China,* pp. K13-14; Wu Gasoheng, "Oppose using Disciplinary Sanctions for Criminal Sanctions: Insist on the Faithful Enforcement of Law," *Minzhu Yu Fazhi* (Democracy and Legal Systems), No. 4, 1985, pp. 17-18; "China Cracks Down on Illegal Detention," *China Daily,* September 19, 1986, p. 3.

64a. Amnesty International, *China: Torture and Ill-treatment of Prisoners* (London: Amnesty International Publications, September 1987), p. 44. In response, a Chinese spokesman accused Amnesty International of bias against China. Instead of attacking China, the spokesman said that Amnesty should have praised it for having publicized illegal behavior. *South China Morning Post,* September 17, 1987, p. 8.

65. Julia Leung, "Success in China Means Following Rules," *Asian Wall Street Journal,* June 16, 1986, pp. 1, 11. See also James Sterba, "U.S. Report Faults China Venture Rules," *ibid,* June 12, 1986, pp. 1,9.

66. Edward A. Gargan, "Investing in China: Still Hard, *"New York Times,* July 16, 1987. This article summarizes a report by Jerome A. Cohen and Stuart J. Valentine. Also consult Stanley Lubman and Clark Randt, "Taking the Mystery Out of Investing in China," *Asian Wall Street Journal,* April 24, 1986, p. 12.

67. Peng Chen, head of the Standing Committee of The National People's Congress, said in 1986 that they should but he did not give an unequivocal answer to the question: "Which is Superior, the Law or the Party?" *Shi-chieh Jih-pao* (World Daily) (Editorial), April 22, 1986, p. 2.

68. For a discussion of this issue, see Leng and Chiu, Criminal Justice in Post-Mao China, pp. 98-104; Hsia Tao-tai, Judicial Independence (Unpublished paper, 1986), pp. 1-23.

69. Chou Hui, "Beijing is in the Process of 'Big Sweep', *Cheng Ming* (contending), no. 10, 1983, pp. 11-13; Hsu Hsing "Mass Arrests and Rule of Law," *ibid,* pp. 14-16.

70. *Zhongguo Fazhi bao,* April 16, 1986, p. 2.

71. "National Conference on Political Legal Work Held," *FBIS, Daily Report:China,* March 10, 1986, p. 7.

72. Commentator, "Those Who Commit Crimes Should be Punished Under the Law," *Zhongguo Fazhi Bao,* January 20, 1986, p. 1.

73. Wen Lie, "Determination, Trust, and Hope," *Faxue* (Jurisprudence); no. 3, 1986, p. 30.
74. *Renmin ribao*, February 20, 1986, p. 1; *World Daily*, April 22, 1986, p. 2.
75. "Cheng Ming Details Crimes of CPC Cadre Families," *FBIS, Daily Report: China*, May 14, 1986, pp. W3-W5; *Zhongbao*, May 13, 1986, p. 9.
76. On July 3, 1986 Chinese elites led by Hu Yaobang, Hu Qili, Qiao Shi, Li Peng, and other members of the Secretariat of the CCP Central Committee attend a two hour lecture course on legal knowledge. *Zhongguo Fazhi Bao*, July 4, 1986, p. 1; *Liaowang* (Outlook), No. 29, July 21, 1986, pp. 9-11.
77. Jerome A. Cohen and Stuart J. Valentine, "Hurdles to Investing in China Are Being Toppled," *New York Times*, June 25, 1987. p. A26. For their other comments, see *supra* note 66.
78. Zhang Zonghou, "Query About the Three Basic Concepts of Law," *Faxue*, No. 1, 1986, pp. 2-7.
79. Chen Haoran, "Query about the 'Query'," *ibid.*, pp. 8-0; Sun Guohua, "Law Cannot Be Understood in Isolation," *Guangming ribao* (Enlightenment Daily), Dec. 28, 1986. p. 3.
80. Zhang Youyu, "A Problem that Has to be Researched and Explored Seriously," *Zhongguo Faxue*, No. 2, 1987, pp.6-8.
81. Yin Yong, "On the Supra-Class Nature of Law," *Faxue Yanjiu*, No. 4, 1986, pp. 18-25.
82. See Zhao Ziyang's report "Advance Along the Road of Socialism with Chinese Characteristics" delivered at and approved by the 13th CCP Party Congress in late October 1987 in *Beijing Review*, Vol. 30, No. 45, Nov. 9-15, 1987, pp. 37-39.
83. *Ibid.*, p. 43.
84. "NPC Faces Heavy Task of Legislation," *China Daily*, August 1,1988, p. 3.
85. *Renmin ribao*, April 36, p.1; *China Daily*, May 12, 1988, p. 1.
86. Ironically, these goals were first set by the communique of the 11th Central Committee of the CCP in December 1978. Leng and Chiu, *Criminal Justice in Post-Mao China*, pp. 3-4.

NINE

CHINESE ATTITUDES TOWARD INTERNATIONAL LAW OF HUMAN RIGHTS

IN THE POST-MAO ERA

Hungdah Chiu

Despite the gross violation of human rights in the People's Republic of China (PRC) after the Chinese Communist Party (CCP) came into power in late 1949 until the late 1970s, there have been few extensive studies on the human rights situation in China.[1] This is especially true for the period of the so-called "Great Cultural Revolution" (1966-76), when most Western visitors and scholars made favorable reports on the human rights situation.[2] Ironically, Chinese leaders and people now consider this period ten years of "disaster" and the worst period that has ever occurred in Chinese history.[3] In March 1977, for the first time since the CCP established control over China, a letter was sent to the *Far Eastern Economic Review* in Hong Kong with a request that it be forwarded to President Carter.[4] In this letter, a self-described Shanghai intellectual characterized China as an "enslaved" society and called upon President Jimmy Carter of the United States to take measures to safeguard the human rights of the Chinese people. In the letter, the writer states:

In the world today there is a country, enslaved to an even more miserable degree than the feudal states, which enslaves its people even more miserably than the serfs were enslaved in tsarist Russia. The people there have completely lost their human rights. They are the 800 million people of our Chinese mainland.

The thousands and thousands of people who in their bid to survive either attempt to cross the border, escape from small farming villages, or to secure freedom and the enjoyment of human rights, are locked up by the Communists in prisons or labor reform camps, with the result that their lot becomes even more painful. On the mainland there are tens of thousands of prisons and labor reform camps.

If you make one wrong statement, while you won't be beheaded, you can be locked up for many years. The people on the mainland have lost all their human rights, shivering [with] fear night and day. The more one thinks about it, the more one wants to cry, straining one's eyes to wish for human rights.[5]

The last part of the letter is an emotion-charged appeal to U.S. President Carter stating that "on the basis of the founding spirit of the United States and your own career in righteously defending human rights, do not forget the suffering of the 800 million people on the Chinese mainland who have lost their human rights, and support us with the same commitment you [have given] to the Soviet human rights leaders, thus enabling us to hope for the restoration of our human rights one day."[6]

Whether by coincidence or prompted by this letter, thereafter Western reporters and scholars began to devote attention to the human rights situation in China. In October 1977, a series of articles on human rights in China, written by Ross H. Munro, which first appeared in the *Toronto Globe & Mail* and were then reprinted in *The Washington Post*, vividly described the gross violations of human rights in China.[7] In November 1978, Amnesty International, which published many reports criticizing human rights in many non-Communist countries but not China, finally released a comprehensive study entitled *Political Imprisonment in the People's Republic of China*.[8] In the same year, a democratic and human rights movement launched by Chinese intellectuals emerged in China which, unfortunately, was soon halted by the Chinese government in the spring of 1979.[9] In 1979, the U.S. State Department's annual *Country Reports on Human Rights Practices* began to include the PRC.[10]

The domestic and international concern over China's human rights situation prompted the Chinese government and scholars to pay more attention to the human rights question in international law. This chapter is a modest effort to analyze the Chinese scholars' views and the practices of the Chinese government. It begins with a concise survey of the Chinese attitude toward the international law of human rights during the Maoist period.

CHINESE ATTITUDE TOWARD THE INTERNATIONAL LAW OF HUMAN RIGHTS IN THE MAOIST ERA

During the Maoist era, not a single article devoted entirely to human rights was published in China.[11] The only extensive coverage of this issue is in Ch'ien Szu's [Qian Si in Pinyin] article entitled "A Criticism of the Views of Bourgeois International Law on the Question of Population," published in 1960. He discussed the issue of human rights together with questions concerning individuals as subjects of international law, nationality, and protection of foreigners.[12] Generally speaking, he took a negative view of the Western concept of human rights and asserted that "imperialism frequently uses the pretext of 'protecting human rights' to intervene in the internal affairs of socialist countries." According to him, "under the socialist system, the elimination of private ownership of the means of production has led to the elimination of the economic basis which gives rise to political and legal inequality, and thereby guarantees the genuine realization of the human rights of the vast laboring people." Moreover, the socialist countries' "suppression of counter-revolutionary criminals and rebellious elements supported and dispatched by imperialism in an attempt to sabotage the people's regime is a necessary measure adopted to protect the interest of the people," and therefore does not involve any human rights issue.[13]

The International Commission of Jurists headquartered in Geneva was denounced by Ch'ien Szu as "imperialist-supported." Its publications entitled *Summary of the Report on the Question of Tibet*[14] and *The Question of Tibet and the Rule of Law*,[15] which considered the Chinese government's armed suppression of the Tibetan "rebellion" as depriving "the Tibetan people of their fundamental human rights and freedom" and that the Tibetan people have been subjected to "massacre, imprisonment, banishment, and forced labor," were denounced as "hypocrisy and shamelessness to the extreme" and as "an excuse to intervene in the internal affairs of China."[16] The same author also denounced President Eisenhower's proposal to organize an "Inter-American Commission on Human Rights" as an attempt by the U.S. to use the Commission "for further control over Latin American countries, since it may, at any time, intervene in the internal affairs of various American countries on the pretext of 'protecting human rights.'"[17]

In conclusion, Ch'ien Szu wrote:

> In short, the 'human rights' referred to by bourgeois international law and the 'human rights' it intends to protect are the rights of the bourgeoisie to enslave and to oppress the laboring people, that is to say, the human rights of the bourgeoisie. Internally, they are used to conceal the encroachment upon the rights and freedoms of the laboring people by the bourgeoisie; externally, they provide pretexts for imperialist opposition to socialist and nationalist countries. They are reactionary from head to toe.[18]

With respect to the question of international protection of human rights and the related question of considering individuals as subjects of international law in order to assert their rights directly under international law, a Chinese writer K'ung Meng [Kong Meng] took a totally negative view. According to him, "the principle concerning fundamental human rights prescribed in the United Nations Charter is that the various member states are obligated to guarantee that individuals under their rule enjoy [such] rights." If an international organization, such as the United Nations, bypasses states and guarantees the human rights of the citizens of these states, it would be intervention in the internal affairs of the states. Therefore, he concludes that all individuals, whether citizens within a state or aliens, are under the sovereignty of the state and are not subjects of international law.[19]

A similar view is shared by late Professor Zhou Gengsheng. He asserted that "expansionist Anglo-American lawyers placed human rights against state sovereignty, thus paving the way theoretically for an imperialist aggressive policy of intervention." They, Zhou observed, invoked the principle of protecting human rights and fundamental freedoms of the United Nations Charter as the basis for the legitimacy of collective intervention.[20] Zhou also criticized Sir Hersh Lauterpacht's view that "to the extent to which 'human rights and fundamental freedoms' have become a persistent feature, partaking of the character of a legal obligation, of the Charter they may have ceased to be matter which is essentially within the domestic jurisdiction of states,"[21] as providing "theoretical bases for imperialist intervention in the internal affairs of other states."[22]

In a 1958 book of selected reference documents on international law, edited by the Office of Teaching and Research of International Law of the Institute of Diplomacy, the thirteen documents selected under the heading of international protection of human rights were: (1) the United Nations Charter (Excerpt of those parts of the preamble relating to human rights) (June 26, 1945) [T.S. 993]; (2) Final Communique of the Asian-African [Bandung] Conference (Part III, Human Rights and Self Determination) (April 24, 1955); (3) the Universal Declaration of Human Rights (December 10, 1948); (4) the Draft Covenant of Human Rights; (5) Resolution adopted by the General Assembly of the United Nations on the Convention on the Political Rights of Women (December 20, 1952) [193 UNTS 135]; (6) Convention on the Prevention and Punishment of the Crime of Genocide (December 9, 1948) [78 UNTS 277]; (7) Draft Protocol on the Revision of the Convention on the Suppression of Traffic in Women and Children and the Convention for the Suppression of Traffic in Women of Full Age (October 20, 1947); (8) Draft Protocol on the Amendment of the 1926 International Slavery Convention (October 20, 1947); (9) Resolutions adopted by the General Assembly of the United Nations on the Convention for the Suppression of the Traffic in Persons and of the Exploitation of the Prostitution of Others (December 2, 1949) [96 UNTS 271]; (10) St. Germain-en-Laye Peace Treaty with Austria (Part III, Chapter 5)[23] (September 9, 1919); (11) Treaty Establishing an Independent and Democratic Austria (Article 7 and Article 26)[24] (May 5, 1955); (12) Resolution of the General Assembly of the United Nations on the Question of Refugees (February 12, 1946); and (13) Resolution Adopted by the General Assembly of the United Nations on the Draft Convention on the Status of Refugees.[25] Since this was merely a collection of reference documents, one can hardly infer that Chinese scholars approved of the contents of these documents. Moreover, except for the United Nations Charter, the PRC during the Maoist period did not join any of the conventions or draft conventions later adopted.[26]

Despite the Chinese scholars' negative attitude toward the concept of "human rights" in international law, on a few occasions, the Chinese official New China News Agency (Hsinhua She or Xinhua She in Pinyin, NCNA), did accuse another country of violating "human rights." For instance, during the period of Sino-Indian conflict in 1962, the NCNA claimed that various measures taken by India, including interference with the freedom of movement of Chinese consulate staff and those who want to visit the Chinese consulate, violated "the code of international law and human rights."[27]

Moreover, while Chinese writers had opposed any interference, whether conducted by a state or by the United Nations, in the internal affairs of the socialist states, a Chinese writer Kuo Ch'un [Guo Qun in Pinyin] observed that the "acts of suppressing national liberation movements basically are not a question of a state's internal affairs [because] such acts violate the fundamental United Nations Charter principles of national self-determination and respect for human rights and also threaten the peace and security of the world." Kuo Ch'un therefore concluded that in such cases "both the General Assembly and the Security Council [of the United Nations] have the duty and authority to handle this matter."[28]

Since the study of international law was virtually suspended together with the study of domestic law during the last stage of Maoist rule, the 1966-1976 Cultural Revolution, there is no way to identify the views of Chinese scholars on the international law of human rights during this decade.

REASONS FOR POST-MAO CHINA'S INTEREST IN THE INTERNATIONAL LAW OF HUMAN RIGHTS

As stated in the introduction of this paper, since 1977 there have been more demands for human rights in China, and therefore it has been necessary for the PRC and its scholars to respond to the issue in order to attack the theoretical basis of those intellectuals who advocate the improvement of the human rights situation in China, to make the concept of human rights less harmful or to accommodate it to the Chinese situation. In May 1979, the CCP theoretical journal *Hongqi* (Red Flag) published an article written by Xiao

Weiyun, Lo Haocai, and Wu Xieyin severely criticizing the concept of "human rights" as of bourgeois origin and always used as a "slogan" by the bourgeoisie.[29] It charges that the advocates of "human rights" do not want socialism, dictatorship of the proletariat, Communist party leadership and the guidance of Marxism, Leninism, and Mao Zedong Thought.[30] The article concludes by saying that it is, therefore, necessary to strengthen the thought and political work of those persons who have been influenced by the "human rights" idea of the bourgeoisie.[31]

Other Chinese scholars do not necessarily share such a totally negative attitude toward the concept of "human rights." In 1979 a law journal published an article written by Wu Daying and Liu Han; while acknowledging the bourgeois origin of the concept of "human rights," they nevertheless pointed out that a thought weapon originally created or used by the bourgeoisie may be used by the proletarian and the revolutionary people by reforming the weapon or giving it new content and significance. The proletarian may use human rights as a weapon to struggle against feudalism or the bourgeoisie.[32] They also pointed out the importance of the human rights question in international intercourse. The reason the majority of the people feel concern over human rights questions is due to their indignation toward the "feudal-Fascist crimes" committed by Lin Biao and the "Gang of Four" and they concluded that most of these demands are proper and reasonable.[33]

The official Chinese position appears quite negative toward the question of "human rights," though it is recognized that a problem exists that must be dealt with. An October 26, 1979 article entitled "Notes on the Human Rights Question," written by "commentator," the pseudonym for a senior Communist official, appeared in *Guangming Ribao* (Enlightenment Daily), the major Chinese newspaper for intellectuals. It states:

'Human rights' is...a slogan with which imperialism and the bourgeoisie attack our proletarian dictatorship and socialist system. Looking at socialist democracy, which combines centralism with democracy and discipline with freedom, from the viewpoint of bourgeois individualist freedom, they attack socialist countries as granting no human rights to their people. They slander measures under the dictatorship of the proletariat (such as the suppression of counterrevolutionaries) as violations of human rights. We must resolutely refute all these attacks and slanders.[34]

But the article also notes that "the proletariat can use the [human rights] slogan as a weapon against the bourgeoisie," therefore, "the proletariat does not negate it in general."[35] Moreover, it also observes that "a very few individuals...make use of 'human rights' to oppose the four fundamental principles, namely, the upholding of the socialist road, the dictatorship of the proletariat, the leadership of the Communist party, and Marxism-Leninism-Mao Zedong Thought...it is necessary to firmly expose and criticize such people."[36]

Except for the reasons stated above, post-Mao China's interest in the "human rights" question is also prompted by the end of its self-imposed "isolation" policy and adoption of the so-called "open door" policy of actively engaging in international intercourse and exchange. To do so, it is necessary to renew its interest in international law in which the law of human rights is a growing area. Moreover, because human rights is frequently invoked or mentioned in international relations, it is a question which the PRC cannot avoid in its foreign relations. Chinese scholar Li Zerei gave three reasons why it is necessary to study the law of human rights:

(1) Respect for human rights is one of the purposes of the United Nations...and our country as a permanent member of the United Nations has the obligation to correctly maintain and execute the "Charter of the United Nations" and related documents on

human rights in order to truly "promote the respect for human rights."

(2) It is only after World War II that [the question of] respect for human rights has become a matter of international concern, so there are many new legal problems relating to the law of human rights waiting to be studied.

(3) Each foreign scholar has his or her own view on human rights, while we should take a Marxist position, viewpoint, and method to study this subject. We consider that only through this process can we give the question of human rights law a scientific interpretation.[37]

In another article published in the CCP theoretical journal *Red Flag*, the importance of studying the human rights question in the international political arena is emphasized:

One aspect of the activities of the United Nations is discussing and reviewing the question of human rights. Countries of different social systems, political interests, and levels of economic development, groups and individuals of different political inclination, all submit their own views on human rights; thus, the question of human rights becomes unprecedentedly wide-ranging and complex. We must seriously analyze and study the complicated struggle around the question of human rights in the current international [arena] and make an effort to insist on our stand and principles in order to maintain world peace and safeguard the right to self-determination and the fundamental human rights of the people of various countries.[38]

CHINESE SCHOLARS' VIEWS ON THE INTERNATIONAL LAW OF HUMAN RIGHTS
Historical Development of the Concept of Human Rights

Almost all Chinese scholars point to the bourgeois origin of the concept of human rights and its ideological basis in the theory of "natural rights of man."[39] They acknowledge the positive aspect of this concept in the bourgeois revolution against the autocracy of the feudal monarchs. The two major documents they frequently referred to are the 1776 American Declaration of Independence and the

1789 French Declaration of the Rights of Man; both advocated freedom, the right of property, and equality among others as natural rights.[40] However, they also criticized that human rights advocated by the bourgeoisie can only be enjoyed by the latter, who own the means of production and thus enslave and exploit the proletarians. Therefore, they have argued that only when the masses of laboring people control the state, and abolish private ownership of the means of production, can they fully enjoy democratic rights, which is broader than the concept of human rights advocated by the bourgeoisie.[41]

The concept of human rights is a part of the municipal law of the bourgeoisie, but with the external expansion of the bourgeoisie, the human rights question gradually entered the international arena, observed some Chinese scholars.[42] A Chinese scholar summarized this development as follows:

In the 1820s, a revolt broke out in Greece to oppose the rule of the Ottoman Empire. When the latter tried to suppress it, Great Britain, France, and other countries raised the flag of 'humanitarianism' to conduct armed intervention. In 1860-1861, France occupied Syria on the ground of protecting the freedom of religion of Maronite Roman Catholics and preventing them from being persecuted. Human rights in fact became an instrument of intervention and aggression of big powers against weak countries. At the same time, there emerged the viewpoint of so-called legitimate intervention on the ground of 'humanitarianism' and others in the theory of international law of the bourgeoisie. Individual scholars even proposed that one of the important purposes of international law is to protect human rights. After World War I, attention focused on [protecting] human rights in the international arena, such as the measures taken by the League of Nations on protecting minorities, the 1926 Slavery Convention [60 LNTS 253] and the 1930 Convention on the Prohibition of Forced Labor [Manley O. Hudson, *International Legislation*, Vol. V, pp. 609-626]. Despite these developments, the concept of human rights was not recognized by international law with corresponding protection. It was not until World War II when the atrocities of Germany, Italy, and Japan aroused the indignation of the people of various countries, that a demand for general protection of human rights was proposed. After the establishment of the United Nations in 1945...respect for human rights was stipulated as a principle of international law.... On December 10, 1948, the General Assembly of the United Nations adopted the "Universal Declaration of Human Rights".... In 1966 it adopted the "International Covenant on Economic, Social, and Cultural Rights" [993 UNTS 3] and the "International Covenant on Civil and Political Rights" [999 UNTS 171] in order to...transform the "Universal Declaration of Human rights" into treaties possessing legally binding force. Both Covenants entered into force in 1976.

Based on the above explanation, [it is clear] that the incorporation of the question of human rights into the scope of international law and thus the emergence of human rights as a principle of international law is a victory of the forces of international peace, democracy, and justice. However, the proposition of incorporating the question of human rights into the scope of international law, internationalizing the question of human rights, and giving international protection to human rights is also an ideal and policy long held by imperialism and thus also accommodates the needs of imperialism...The theories relating to human rights in international law and international protection of human rights basically are a reflection of the traditional ideas of the bourgeoisie and thus possess class bias and limitation.

Since 1961 [the Third World countries have expanded the concept of] human rights by combining the safeguarding of human rights with anti-imperialism and hegemonism...including the concept of national self-determination...and economic sovereignty [in the concept of human rights]....[43]

The Scope of the International Law of Human Rights

According to Chinese scholar Li Zerei, the traditional Western concept of human rights only refers to individuals' civil and political rights. However, the adoption of the "Universal Declaration of Human Rights" by the General Assembly of the United Nations has expanded this concept of individuals' human rights to include economic, social, and cultural rights. This is what Li referred to as the first generation concept of human rights. The second generation concept of human rights expands to include the right of the colonial people to self-determination which is confirmed in Article 1 of the Charter of the United Nations and put into concrete implementation in the 1960 Declaration on the Granting of Independence to Colonial Countries and People. The principle of self-determination was later incorporated into Article 1 of the International Covenant on Economic, Social, and Cultural Rights and the International Covenant on Civil and Political Rights. The third generation development of the human rights concept is the right to development in order to eliminate the poverty and underdevelopment of the newly independent countries caused by colonial rule.[44] At present, according to Chinese scholars, the concept of human rights is not only related to the rights of individuals, but also includes the concept of "collective rights," such as the right of self-determination and the right to development.[45]

The International Protection of Human Rights

According to the textbook edited by Wang Tieya and Wei Min, "the so-called international protection of human rights refers to certain aspects of the cooperation and guarantee by states, in accordance with international law and through treaties, with respect to the realization of fundamental human rights and the prevention and punishment of those acts infringing upon these rights."[46] This means, "like other problems in international law, the international protection of human rights is the result of sovereign states' undertaking the obligations of international treaties or acting in accordance with the generally recognized principles of international law [and] if there are no recognized principles or regulations of generally recognized [principles] of international law or no obligations prescribed by treaties, then the protection of human rights is a municipal law question."[47]

With respect to the contents of the international protection of human rights, Wang and Wei's textbook divides them into the following categories:

The Fundamental Human Rights

The basic documents in this category are the 1966 International Covenant on Economic, Social, and Cultural Rights and International Covenant on Civil and Political Rights. Both treaties were enacted to implement the relevant provisions on human rights of the United Nations Charter and to enable the 1948 Universal Declaration of Human Rights to have legally binding force. They also provide in Article 1 for the right of self-determination by all people and their right to freely dispose of their natural wealth and resources.[48] Wei's textbook also shares this view, but pointed out that the right of self-determination is only applicable to oppressed people under foreign slavery and colonial rule. If a nation within a state demands independence or self government, this is still a matter of domestic jurisdiction of that state and the principle of national self-determination is not applicable to such a case.[49]

The Prevention of Discrimination

The prevention of discrimination question is primarily directed against racial discrimination. There are three important documents in this area, i.e., the Declaration on the Elimination of All Forms of Racial Discrimination adopted by the General Assembly of the United Nations on November 20, 1963; the International Convention on the Elimination of All Forms of Racial Discrimination of March 7, 1966 [660 UNTS 195], and the International Convention on the Suppression and Punishment of the Crime of Apartheid of November 30, 1973 [1015 UNTS 244]. In addition to documents relating to racial discrimination, there are several documents dealing with other forms of discrimination, such as the 1967 Declaration on the Elimination of

Discrimination Against Women, the 1979 Convention on the Elimination of All Forms of Discrimination Against Women [UN Doc. A/RES/34/180], the 1951 Equal Remuneration Convention [165 UNTS 04], and the 1958 Discrimination (Employment and Occupation) Convention [362 UNTS 31] adopted by the International Labor Conference, and the 1960 Convention Against Discrimination in Education [429 UNTS 93] adopted by the United Nations Educational, Scientific, and Cultural Organization.[50]

The Prevention and Punishment of the Offense of Genocide

On December 1, 1946, the General Assembly of the United Nations unanimously confirmed that genocide, i.e., large scale killing of members of a group, is an offense which should be condemned by international law. On December 9, 1948, the General Assembly adopted the Convention on the Prevention and Punishment of the Crime of Genocide [78 UNTS 277], which entered into force on January 12, 1951.[51]

The Prohibition Against Slavery
and Similar Systems and Customs

On September 25, 1926, the Slavery Convention was concluded at Geneva which entered into force on March 9, 1927. In 1956, the Supplementary Convention on the Abolition of Slavery, the Slave Trade, and Institutions and Practices Similar to Slavery [266 UNTS 3] was concluded at Geneva which entered into force on April 30, 1957.[52]

The Prevention and Punishment of Terrorism

Most Western scholars do not include the prevention and punishment of terrorism within the context of international protection of human rights,[53] but the textbook edited by Professors Wang Tieya and Wei Min does. In the textbook, they refer to the Organization of American States Convention to Prevent and Punish the Acts of Terrorism Taking the Forms of Crimes Against Persons and Related Extortion that are of

International Significance, of February 2, 1971 [27 UST 3949, TIAS 8413]; the European Convention on the Suppression of Terrorism of November 10, 1976 [European Treaty Series No. 90], and the International Convention Against the Taking of Hostages of December 17, 1979 [UN Doc. A/RES/34/146].[54]

Others

The textbook edited by Professors Wang and Wei points out that questions relating to the status of refugees, migrant workers, political rights of women, rights of children, freedom of the press and association are also within the scope of international protection of human rights.[55] One area which the textbook does not include in the area of international protection of human rights is the law of development. This is because, as Chinese scholar Li Zerei pointed out, the contents of this right are primarily expressed in resolutions, declarations, or guidelines adopted by those international organizations which have no legislative power, in other words, they are in the nature of what Western scholars have referred to as "soft law."[56] Since the legal contents of the right to development are still in the process of becoming substantive rules of international law, it seems appropriate for Professors Wang and Wei to exclude them at this time from their enumeration of the international protection of human rights.

*The International Protection of Human Rights
and the Question of Non-intervention
in the Internal Affairs of a State*

One of the crucial issues regarding the international protection of human rights is whether a state or an international organization can intervene in a state to ensure compliance with international human rights standards. All Chinese scholars oppose this approach to protect human rights in a state. In the textbook edited by Professors Wang and Wei, this view is considered as "theoretically wrong and practically not feasible." This is because, this book states, "the so-called international character of human rights advocated by Western scholars is based on their theory of considering individuals as subjects of international law and thus setting the principle of state sovereignty against the principle of human rights." However, the book asserts that "the principle of human rights must be subordinate to the principle of state sovereignty and cannot be superior to the principle of state sovereignty," and "only based on the principle of state sovereignty, can the implementation of human rights be realistically guaranteed." However, with respect to those acts which seriously infringe upon human rights, such as taking legislative, administrative, or other measures to implement racial segregation or racial discrimination, engaging in genocide, selling slaves, taking extremely inhuman means to create, expel, and persecute refugees in a large scale way, using violence to take persons as hostages, and engaging in international terrorist activities, the book states that such acts "constitute international crimes" and "necessary measures taken by all states and international organizations to suppress these behaviors are consistent with generally recognized principles of international law and should not be considered as intervening in the internal affairs of a state."[57]

A similar view is expressed in the self-study textbook edited by Wei Min where it is stated that "if any state can arbitrarily use its own standards to judge 'the human rights situation' of another state and then conducts so-called 'humanitarian intervention' on the pretext of 'violation of fundamental human rights,' then there will be no guarantee for the sovereignty of various states."[58]

A Chinese scholar, Liu Fengmin, considers that one of the most serious current problems of international implementation of human rights is the use of the slogan "human rights" as an instrument by a super-power or a big power in a region to intervene in the internal affairs of another state. He also criticizes the U.S. government's use of the "question of human rights" as a bargaining chip in negotiating the solution of certain concrete problems.[59]

Finally, a more sophisticated and articulate analysis of this question is presented by Li Zerei, who observed that international human rights law is composed of three parts, each having a different nature, and that therefore one should not say with certainty that all questions of human rights are or are not within the domestic jurisdiction of a state and should be respectively analyzed and dealt with. According to him, there are two criteria to decide the question of whether a matter of human rights is or is not within the domestic jurisdiction of a state. The first one is whether an act is encroaching on the right of self-determination, right to development, or individuals' human rights as the result of the expansion, aggression, or rule of old and neo-colonialism, hegemonism, or the residual rule of colonialism. If so, then that act is within the sphere of international law and does not belong to the domestic jurisdiction of a state. Under such circumstances, any interferences by international organizations or foreign states on such matters should not be considered as intervention in internal affairs. The second one is whether the criminal acts are done by the remnants of German Nazism, Italian Fascism, or Japanese Militarism or the newly formed Nazi, Fascist, or Militarist states. If so, such criminal acts are not within the domestic jurisdiction of a state.[60]

Consistent with their view on rejecting direct international protection of individuals' human rights in a state, Chinese scholars unanimously deny individuals as subjects of international law.[61]

CHINA'S PARTICIPATION IN INTERNATIONAL CONVENTIONS ON HUMAN RIGHTS

The PRC's acceptance of existing multilateral human

rights conventions is an indication of its official attitude toward the international law of human rights. Before 1980 when Deng Xiaoping had not yet assumed nation-wide control, the PRC participated in none of the human rights conventions. Since 1980, the PRC has become a party to the Convention on the Prevention and Punishment of the Crime of Genocide (done on December 9, 1948 and entered into force on January 12, 1951),[62] Convention Relating to the Status of Refugees (done on July 28, 1951 and entered into force on April 22, 1954),[63] Protocol Relating to the Status of Refugees (done on January 31, 1967 at New York and entered into force on October 4, 1967),[64] International Convention on the Elimination of All Forms of Racial Discrimination (done on March 7, 1966 at New York and entered into force on January 4, 1969),[65] International Convention on the Suppression and Punishment of the Crime of Apartheid (done on November 30, 1973 at New York and entered into force on July 18, 1976),[66] Convention on the Elimination of All Forms of Discrimination Against Women (done on December 18, 1978 at Copenhagen and entered into force on September 3, 1981).[67]

On May 30, 1984, the State Council of the PRC declared its recognition of the following International Labor Conventions ratified by the Republic of China government between 1930 and 1947:[68] Convention Nos. 7 (Minimum Age (Sea), 1920), 11 (Right of Association (Agriculture), 1921), 14 (Weekly Rest (Industry), 1921), 15 (Minimum Age (Trimmers and Stokers), 1921), 16 (Medical Examination of Young Persons (Sea), 1921), 19 (Equality of Treatment (Accident Compensation), 1925), 22 (Seamen's Articles of Agreement, 1926), 23 (Repatriation of Seamen, 1926), 26 (Minimum Wage-fixing Machinery, 1928), 27 (Marking of Weight (Package Transported by Vessels), 1929), 32 (Protection Against Accidents (Dockers), 1932), 45 (Underground Work (Women), 1935), 60 (Minimum Age (Non-industrial Employment), 1937), and 80 (Final Article Revision, 1946).[69]

On December 12, 1986, the PRC signed[70] the Convention Against Torture and Other Cruel, Inhuman, or Degrading Treatment or Punishment (done on December 10, 1984 at New York and entered into force on June 26, 1987).[71] However, as of June 1988, the PRC has not yet ratified this Convention.

The PRC has not yet even signed the International Covenant on Economic, Social, and Cultural Rights and the International Covenant on Civil and Political Rights adopted by the General Assembly of the United Nations in 1966. However, in the 1984 Sino-British Joint Declaration on the Question of Hong Kong,[72] Annex 1, Article 13, paragraph 4, it is provided that "the provisions of the International Covenant on Civil and Political Rights and the International Covenant on Economic, Social, and Cultural Rights as applied to Hong Kong [by the British Government now][73] should remain in force" for a period of 50 years after 1997, the year when the PRC would assume control of Hong Kong. This arrangement would create a strange situation because only part of China (Hong Kong) would be subject to both covenants. In view of this contradiction, there were indications that the PRC intended to participate in the covenants after the Hong Kong agreement.

During the general debate (September 22-October 10, 1986) of the 41st Session of the General Assembly of the United Nations, PRC Foreign Minister Wu Xueqian said in his speech that 1986 "marks the 20th anniversary of the adoption by the United Nations of the International Covenant on Civil and Political Rights and the International Covenant on Economic, Social, and Cultural Rights" and that "these two instruments are of positive significance to the realization of the purpose and principle of the United Nations Charter concerning the respect of human rights."[74] On November 24, 1986, the Agence France-Press (AFP) reported from Beijing that the PRC was likely to sign both covenants soon.[75] On December 15, 1986, the *Chinese Legal*

System Paper published two articles commenting favorably on the two covenants.[76] However, at the time of this writing in June 1988, the PRC has not signed both covenants. While one can only speculate why the PRC declined to do so, it seems reasonable to say that the PRC appears concerned about the educational and promotional consequences of both covenants in the PRC. This concern may be strengthened by the outbreak of student demonstrations, demanding more freedoms and democracy, in various Chinese cities in December 1986-January 1987[77] and the anti-Chinese Communist riots in Tibet in September 1987.[78] Moreover, as will be explained in the next section, many Chinese domestic laws, regulations, and practices are not consistent with the standards provided in the 1948 Universal Declaration of Human Rights and the two covenants to implement and to expand the rights provided in the Declaration.

MAJOR CHINESE LEGISLATION, REGULATIONS, PRACTICES, AND INTERNATIONAL HUMAN RIGHTS STANDARDS

One problem for the PRC's participation in the International Covenant on Civil and Political Rights and the International Covenant on Economic, Social, and Cultural Rights is that some of its legislation, regulations, and practices are clearly inconsistent with certain human rights standards prescribed in both covenants.

According to the Decision of the State Council Relating to Problems of Reeducation Through Labor (August 3, 1957)[79] and Supplementary Regulations Issued by the State Council on Reeducation Through Law (November 29, 1979),[80] a person may be sent to a labor camp by a public security organ (police) for up to four years without judicial review. This rule is contrary to Article 9, paragraph 4 of the International Covenant on Civil and Political Rights,[81] which provides that "[a]nyone who is deprived of his liberty by arrest or detention shall be entitled to take proceedings before a court, in order that the court may decide without delay on the lawfulness of his detention and order his release if the detention is not lawful."

The 1982 Chinese Constitution[82] does not recognize the right to choose a residence.[83] Rural residents need special permission to move to a city. The government may cancel a city resident's right to live there and send him/her to reside in a rural area. This practice is contrary to Article 12, paragraph 1 of the Civil and Political Rights Covenant which provides that "[e]veryone lawfully within the territory of a state shall, within that territory, have the right to liberty of movement and freedom to choose his residence."

The most serious inconsistency between the Civil and Political Rights Covenant and the Chinese law is in the area of criminal justice. The 1979 Chinese Criminal Procedure Law does not recognize the principle of presumption of innocence in criminal trials.[84] This principle is provided in Article 14, paragraph 2 of the Covenant which states that "[e]veryone charged with a criminal offense shall have the right to be presumed innocent until proved guilty according to law." The 1979 Chinese Criminal Law does not recognize the principle of *nullum crimen, nulla poena sine lege* (no punishment without preexisting law making the act a crime).[85] This is contrary to Article 15, paragraph 1, of the Covenant which states that "[n]o one shall be held guilty of any criminal offense on account of any act or omission which did not constitute a criminal offense, under national or international law, at the time when it was committed."

According to PRC election laws, city residents can elect one delegate to the National People's Congress for every 130,000 persons, while rural residents can elect one delegate for every 1,040,000 persons.[86] Since 80 percent of the Chinese live in rural areas, the election law discriminates against the majority of the Chinese people. This discriminatory election law is inconsistent with Article 25, paragraph 2, of the Civil and Political Rights Covenant which guarantees every citizen "the right and the opportunity...to vote and to be elected at genuine periodic elections which shall be by universal and equal suffrage."

The 1982 Chinese Constitution does not recognize the right to strike[87] which is ensured by Article 8, paragraph 1 of the International Covenant on Economic, Social, and Cultural Rights.[88]

If the PRC is going to participate in both covenants, the above stated discrepancies between the covenants and the Chinese legislation, regulations, or practices need to be eliminated, at least on paper. A Chinese scholar, Xu Hong, apparently recognizing these discrepancies, commented generally that "the fundamental spirits of the two covenants are consistent with the principles of law and fundamental policy of our country,"[89] without arguing that the Chinese legal system is not consistent with the provisions of both covenants. At present, it does not appear that the Chinese government is preparing to remove these discrepancies. Moreover, while China also adopts certain international standards in its criminal procedure law, its implementation is far from satisfactory. For instance, the 1979 Criminal Procedure Law provides in Article 32 that "the use of torture to coerce statements and the gathering of evidence by threat, enticement, deceit, or other unlawful methods are strictly prohibited." Despite this official prohibition, torture and ill-treatment of prisoners are a persistent and widespread problem in China. A recent study by Amnesty International, which was based primarily on published Chinese sources, has found that "most torture victims are criminal suspects who are tortured to force them to confess" and "their torturers are usually police officers, or Communist party officials and members of the many informal security units who illegally detain individuals they suspect of committing crimes."[90] For these reasons, it seems unlikely that the PRC will become a contracting party to both covenants in the near future.

CONCLUSIONS

The concept of human rights, according to Marxist theory, is of bourgeois origin but has served a useful purpose, enabling the proletariat to demand certain rights from the bourgeoisie. With the establishment of a Communist state, the people become the masters of themselves; therefore, there should be no human rights problem in a Communist state. During the Maoist period, Chinese scholars and the PRC government generally adhered to this dogmatic view and disregarded the development of the law of human rights in the international arena. With the death of Mao and the emergence of the "Four Modernizations" program and "open door" policy, the PRC can no longer afford to ignore the "human rights" issue at home and abroad. Domestically, there has been more demand for respect for human rights. Moreover, to carry out the PRC's ambitious modernization program, it is necessary to provide a secure environment for the people. Internationally, the PRC is a permanent member of the United Nations Security Council with big power status, and it cannot simply evade the human rights issue. Under such circumstances, it is only natural for the PRC to take a more positive attitude toward the international law of human rights.

In response to this changing attitude toward the human rights issue, Chinese scholars have produced more writings in this area. While generally taking a positive attitude toward the international law of human rights, especially the expanded collective concept of human rights, such as the right of national self-determination and the right to development (bearing in mind the poor human rights situation in China, though greatly improved compared with the Maoist period), it is almost unanimously held in the Chinese writings that the question of individuals' human rights is within the domestic jurisdiction of a state and the theory of considering individuals as subjects of international law, advocated by many Western international lawyers, is rejected.

Realizing that the assertion of domestic jurisdiction to reject Western criticism of human rights violations in China is hardly a convincing argument, Chinese spokesmen have repeatedly asserted that "Chinese citizens enjoy greater freedom now than at any time in the past."[91] Recently, a more sophisticated response to this issue has been made by Chinese scholar Guo Shan:

> In some countries human rights and basic freedoms have not been fully realized due to historical and economic reasons. China supports the international community in showing its concern about large-scale human rights violations in an appropriate manner in order to help improve and promote human rights situations in these countries. But China also believes that in the field of human rights, as with other things, the way one country handles its human rights issue should not be held up as a model for all other countries to follow, neither should it be the sole criterion for judging other countries' human rights situations. China opposes external interference in a country's internal affairs on the pretext of safeguarding human rights.[92]

Until recently, the PRC government took a negative attitude toward international and nongovernmental investigations of alleged violations of human rights in China. However, it now appears to take a more conciliatory attitude. In October 1986, Chinese officials did provide information in answer to a U.S. Embassy inquiry regarding a number of imprisoned priests and others thought to be "political prisoners." They also have been more willing to meet with U.S. government officials and members of professional groups to discuss birth control policies, have provided increased amounts of statistical data, and have facilitated visits to localities. Since 1985 the PRC has participated in the work of the United Nations Commission on Human Rights.[93] Occasionally, Chinese scholars have responded to the inquiry of Amnesty International on the human rights situation in China, though the response is, as expected, to deny any violation of human rights in China.[94]

There are no known organizations within China which monitor or comment on human rights conditions. Outside China, a dissident group, Chinese Alliance for Democracy, keeps an eye on the human rights situations in China and periodically issues reports in its monthly publication *Zhongguo Zhichun* (China Spring).[95]

While the PRC has participated in several important international human rights conventions, it has not yet signed the International Covenant on Civil and Political Rights or the International Covenant on Economic, Social, and Cultural Rights. This is because certain Chinese legislation, regulations, or practices are clearly inconsistent with certain human rights standards prescribed in both covenants, and its domestic human rights situation is far from satisfactory. Also, the PRC seems concerned about the educational and promotional effect of the two covenants inside China, especially among students and intellectuals.

NOTES

1. *White Book on Forced Labor and Concentration Camps in the People's Republic of China*, 2 vols., Paris: Commission Internationale Contre Le Regime Concentrationnaise, 1957, is among the few publications on human rights in the PRC during the Maoist period.
2. See Chalmers Johnson, "What's Wrong with Chinese Political Studies?" *Asian Survey*, Vol. 22 (October 1982), pp. 919-933 and Harry Harding, "From China, with Disdain: New Trends in the Study of China," *ibid.*, pp. 934-958.
3. E.g., see "Prospect and Retrospect, China's Socialist Legal System," *Beijing Review*, Vol. 22, No. 2 (January 12, 1979), p. 27, where the Cultural Revolution period was described as "feudal despotism married to a 20th-century Fascism."
4. Peter Weintraub, "An inside view of China," *Far Eastern Economic Review*, Vol. 96, No. 14 (April 8, 1977), pp. 28-29. See also Jay Mathews, "Letter from Shanghai, Carter's Aid Asked on Rights," *The Washington Post*, April 1, 1977, p. A17.
5. *Ibid.*, p. 29.
6. *Ibid.*
7. Ross H. Munro, "Peking's Controls are Subtle But Real," *The Washington Post*, October 9, 1977, pp. Al, A15; "Peking Sharply Restricts Peasant Travel to Cities," *ibid.*, October 10, 1977, pp. Al, A9; "Dissent Can Bring Death, Writing Wall Posters Isn't for Everyone," *ibid.*, October 11, 1977, pp. Al, A12; "Social Groups in China: Watchdogs for Deviant Behavior," *ibid.*, October 12, 1977, pp. A20 and "China's Rigid Rationing, From Rice to TV Sets, Buying Takes Coupons," *ibid.*, November 27, 1977, pp. Cl, C5.
8. London: Amnesty International Publications, 1978.
9. See generally James D. Seymour, ed., *The Fifth Modernization. China's Human Rights Movement, 1978-1979*, Stanfordville, New York: Human Rights Publishing Group, 1980.
10. *Country Reports on Human Rights Practices for 1979*. Washington, D.C.: U.S. Government Printing Office, 1980, pp. 437-446.
11. See Dong Zhaohong & Lu Xuemen, eds., *1949-84 Faxue Lunwen Muluji* (1949-1984 Collection of Titles of Law Articles), Hanzhou: Zhejiang People's Press, 1986, pp. 141, 611-612.
12. *Guoji Wenti Yanjiu* (Journal of International Studies), 1960, No. 5, pp. 40-49.
13. *Ibid.*, p. 41, translated in Jerome Alan Cohen and Hungdah Chiu,

People's China and International Law, A Documentary Study, Vol. 1, Princeton, New Jersey: Princeton University Press, 1974, p. 607.

14. Published by the Commission in Geneva in 1960.
15. Published by the Commission in Geneva in 1959.
16. Ch'ien Szu, *supra* note 12, p. 42; translated in Cohen and Chiu, Vol. 1, *supra* note 13, pp. 607-608.
17. Ch'ien Szu, *supra* note 12, p. 42; translated in Cohen and Chiu, Vol. 1, *supra* note 13, p. 608.
18. Ch'ien Szu, *supra* note 12, p. 42; translated in Cohen and Chiu, Vol. 1, *supra* note 13, p. 609.
19. K'ung Meng, "A Criticism of the Theories of Bourgeois International Law Concerning the Subjects of International Law," *Journal of International Studies, 1960*, No. 2, p. 51; translated in Cohen and Chiu, Vol. 1, *supra* note 13, pp. 97-98.
20. He cited L. Oppenheim, *International Law*, Vol. 1, 8th ed. by H. Lauterpacht, London: Longmans, Green, 1955, p. 313, where it is stated that the reason for opposing humanitarian intervention by individual states because the [right to intervention] has been abused for selfish purpose "does not apply to collective intervention." This is because, as stated in this book, that "the Charter of the United Nations, in recognizing the promotion of respect for fundamental human rights and freedoms as one of the principal objects of the Organization, marks a further step in the direction of elevating the principle of humanitarian intervention to a basic rule of organized international society...."
21. Oppenheim, *ibid.*, p. 313, n.2.
22. Zhou Gengsheng, *Xiandai Yingmei Guoji Fa Di Sixiang Dongxiang* (Trends in the Thought of Modern British and American International Law), Beijing: World Knowledge Press, 1963, pp. 39, 44-45.
23. Part IV, Political Clauses for Europe, Section V, Protection of Minorities, Articles 62-69 of the Treaty of St. Germain with Austria, September 10, 1919. Text of these articles can be found in Fred L. Israel, ed., *Major Peace Treaties of Modern History, 1648-1967*, Vol. III, New York: Chelsea House and McGraw-Hill, 1967, pp. 1560-1562.
24. Article 7 refers to "Rights of the Slovene and Croat Minorities" and Article 26 refers to "Property Rights and Interests of Minority Groups in Austria." Text of these articles can be found in Israel, Vol. IV, *supra* note 23, pp. 2711-2712 (Article 7) and 2733-2734 (Article 26). It is interesting to note that Article 6 on general human

rights in Austria was omitted from the Reference Documents book.

25. *Guoji Gongfa Cankao Wenjian Xuanji* (Collection of Selected Reference Documents of Public International Law), Beijing: World Knowledge Press, 1958, pp. 99-144.

26. See Hungdah Chiu, *Agreements of the People's Republic of China, A Calendar of Events 1966-1980*. New York: Praeger, 1981, pp. 213-216.

27. See "Indian Government Imposes Increased Restrictions on Chinese Embassy Staff," *NCNA*-English, Peking, November 15, 1962, in *Survey of China Mainland Press*, No. 2863 (November 20, 1962), pp. 28-29, reprinted in Cohen and Chiu, Vol. 2, *supra* note 13, pp. 1019-1020.

28. Guo Qun, *Lianheguo* (The United Nations), Beijing: World Knowledge Press, 1955, p. 15.

29. Xiao Weiyun, Luo Haocai, and Wu Xieyin, "How Marxism Views the Question of 'Human Rights,'" *Hongqi* (Red Flag), 1979, No. 5, pp. 43-44. For a Chinese scholar's view on the development of the concept of human rights in the West, see Shuang Fu, "The Putting Forward of the Slogan of Human Rights and Its Historical Limitation," *Waiguoshi Zhishi* (Knowledge of Foreign History), 1981, No. 5, pp. 4-6, 9.

30. *Ibid.*, p. 46.

31. *Ibid.*, p. 48. A similar view is expressed in Yu Liang, "'Human Rights,' are a Slogan of the Bourgeoisie," *Wen Hui bao (Wen Hui Daily)*, Shanghai, April 8, 1979, p. 3. and Yang Jianrong, "A Concise Comment on the Question of Human Rights," *Xueshu Yanjiu* (Academic Research), 1979, No. 5, p. 76.

32. Wu Daying and Liu Han, "Human Rights Have to be Analyzed Historically and Concretely," *Faxue Yanjiu* (Studies in Law), 1979, No. 4, pp. 10-11. A similar view is expressed in Chen Hanchu, "What is Human Rights?" *Baike Zhishi* (Encyclopedic Knowledge), 1979, no. 5, p. 10.

33. *Ibid.*, p. 13. The authors pointed out that two earlier Chinese Communist regulations in the early 1940s, i.e., before the CCP assumed nation-wide power, did refer to "human rights." *Ibid.*, p. 11. Moreover, on July 2, 1957, Dong Biwu, then President of the Supreme People's Court, referred to "infringement of human rights" in the countryside in his report to the Fourth Meeting of the First National People's Congress. *Ibid.*, p. 12. Two other Chinese scholars also point out that even during the period of so-

cialism (China is now in this stage), there still exists the question of struggling for and protection of human rights. Lin Rongnian and Zhang Jinfang, "Talks on the Question of Human Rights," *Xuexi Yu Tansuo* (Study and Exploration), 1980, No. 1, p. 35.

34. Translated in part in *Beijing Review*, Vol. 22 No. 49 (November 9, 1979), p. 18. See also an article published earlier in the same newspaper where the author considers the concept of "human rights" as having class character and suggest that in the PRC one should use the term "citizens' right." Xu Bing, "On Human Rights and Citizens' Rights," *Enlightenment Daily*, June 19, 1979, p. 4.

35. *Ibid.*, p. 19.

36. *Ibid.*, p. 20.

37. Li Zerei, "A Theoretical Study of International Human Rights Law," *Zhongguo Guojifa Niankan 1983* (Chinese Yearbook of International Law, 1983), Beijing: China Translation and Publishing Corp., 1983, pp. 96-97.

38. Shen Baoxiang, Wang Chengquan, and Li Zerei, "On the Question of Human Rights in International Arena," *Red Flag*, 1982, No. 8, p. 44.

39. E.g., see Xiao Weiyun et al., *supra* note 29, p. 43; Shen Baoxiang et al., *supra* note 38, p. 44; Wu Daying and Liu Han, supra note 32, pp. 9-10; Shi Daxin, "On Human Rights and International Protection of Human Rights," *Anhui Daxue Xuebao* (Zhexue Shehui Kexue Ban) (Anhui University Journal, Philosophy and Social Sciences Edition), 1982, No. 3, p. 52.

40. *Ibid.*

41. E.g., see Shen Baoxing et al., *supra* note 38, p. 48; *Faxue Cidan* (Law Dictionary), Shanghai: Shanghai Dictionary Press, 1980, p. 9, revised ed., 1984, p. 11, and *Jianming Shehui Kexue Cidian* (Concise Dictionary of Social Sciences), Shanghai: Shanghai Dictionary Press, 1982, p. 17.

42. E.g., see Huo Qixhi, "International Protection of Human Rights," in *Zhongguo Dabeike Quanshu Faxue* (The Great Encyclopedia of China, Law), Shanghai: The Great Encyclopedia of China Press, 1984, p. 490 and Shi Daxin, *supra* note 39, p. 53.

43. Shi Daxin, *supra* note 39, pp. 53-54.

44. Li Zerei, *supra* note 38, pp. 98-99.

45. See Wang Tieya and Wei Min, eds., *Guoji Fa* (International Law), Beijing: Law Press, 1981, p. 261 and Wei Min, ed., *Guoji Fa Gailun* (Introduction to International Law), Beijing: Enlightenment Daily Press, 1986, p. 245. Wang and Wei's book is used as a standard

textbook in colleges and Wei's book is used as self-study material under Chinese government sponsored self-study programs.

46. Wang and Wei, *supra* note 45, pp. 261-262. A similar view is shared in Wei, *supra* note 45, p. 245.
47. *Ibid.*
48. Wang and Wei, *supra* note 45, p. 262.
49. Wei, *supra* note 45, p. 247.
50. Wang and Wei, *supra* note 45, pp. 263-264 and Wei, *supra* note 45, pp. 247-248.
51. Wang and Wei, *supra* note 45, p. 264 and Wei, *supra* note 45, p. 248.
52. Wang and Wei, supra note 45, pp. 264-265.
53. E.g., see Theodor Meron, ed., *Human Rights in International Law, Legal and Policy Issues*, 2 Vols., London and New York: Oxford University Press, 1984 and Ian Brownlie, ed., *Basic Documents on Human Rights*, 2nd ed., London and New York: Oxford University Press, 1981.
54. Wang and Wei, *supra* note 45, pp. 265-266.
55. *Ibid.*, p. 266.
56. Li Zerei, *supra* note 38, pp. 103-104. For a study of this question, see Ignaz Serial-Hohenveldern, "International Economic 'Soft Law,'" in Academie de Droit International, *Recueil Des Cours*, Vol. 163 (1979-11), Alphen aan den Rijn, The Netherlands: Sijthoff & Noordhoff, 1980, pp. 169-238.
57. Wang and Wei, *supra* note 45, pp. 267-268.
58. Wei, *supra* note 45, p. 59.
59. Liu Fengmin, "Human Rights Law and Its International Implementation," *Zhongguo Fazhi bao* (Chinese Legal System Paper), July 18, 1984, p. 4.
60. Li Zerei, *supra* note 38, pp. 103-104.
61. E.g., see Wang and Wei, *supra* note 45, pp. 98-100, Wei, *supra* note 45, pp. 74-79 and Li Renzhen, "Looking at the Question of Natural Persons [Individuals] as Subjects of International Law from the Angle of International Protection of Human Rights," *Faxue Pinlun (Wuhan Daxue)*, (Law Review, Wuhan University), 1984, No. 1, pp. 37-40.
62. 78 UNTS 277. On April 18, 1983, the PRC deposited its instrument of ratification which entered into force on July 17, 1983, with reservation to Article 9. All information on the PRC's participation in notes 63 to 67 *infra* comes from *Shijie Zhishi Nianjian 1984* (1984

Yearbook of World Knowledge), Beijing: World Knowledge Press, 1984, pp. 471-479.

63. 189 UNTS 137. On September 24, 1983, the PRC deposited its instrument of accession which entered into force on December 23, 1982, with reservation to Article 14, second part and Article 16, p. 3.

64. 606 UNTS 267. On September 24, 1982, the PRC deposited its instrument of accession with reservation to Article 4.

65. 660 UNTS 195. On December 29, 1981, the PRC deposited its instrument of accession which entered into force on January 28, 1982 with reservation to Article 22.

66. 1015 UNTS 244. On April 18, 1983, the PRC deposited its instrument of accession which entered into force on May 18, 1983.

67. UN Doc. A/RES/34/180. On November 4, 1980, the PRC deposited its instrument of ratification which entered into force on December 4, 1980, with reservation to Article 29, p 1.

68. See *Zhongguo Guoji Fa Niankan 1985* (1985 Chinese Yearbook of International Law), Beijing: China Translations and Publishing Corporation, 1985, pp. 676-720.For those conventions ratified by the pre-1949 Chinese government on the mainland, the PRC does not take the position of automatic succession. If the PRC decides to succeed, it will issue a statement of recognition. See Hungdah Chiu, *The People's Republic of China and the Law of Treaties*, Cambridge, Mass.: Harvard University Press, 1972, pp. 91-96.

69. The text of these conventions can be found in International Labor Organization, *International Labor Conventions and Recommendations, 1919-1981*, Geneva: International Labor Office, 1982.

70. *Multilateral Treaties Deposited with the Secretary-General*, Status as at December 31, 1987, New York: The United Nations, 1988, p. 174.

71. UN Doc. A/RES/39/46.

72. Text reprinted in *International Legal Materials*, Vol. 23, No. 6 (November 1984), pp. 1371-1387.

73. On May 20, 1976, the United Kingdom declared that its ratification of both covenants is applicable to Hong Kong. See *Multilateral Treaties Deposited with the Secretary-General*, Status at December 31, 1984. New York: The United Nations, 1985, pp. 121, 141.

74. "Wu Xueqian's Speech at the UN General Assembly," *Beijing Review*, Vol. 29, No. 40 (October 6, 1986), p. 16.

75. See "PRC Likely to Sign UN Human Rights Conventions," *FBIS-CHI*, November 28, 1986, pp A1-A3.

76. Zhang Daxin, "Concise Introduction of International Human Rights Conventions," *Chinese Legal System Paper*, December 15, 1986, p. 4 and Xu Hong, "Respect Human Rights and Demand Social Progress—Commemorating the 20th Anniversary of the Adoption of the International Covenant on Economic, Social, and Cultural Rights and the International Covenant on Civil and Political Rights," *ibid.*

77. E.g., see Edward A. Gargan, "Thousands Stage Rally in Shanghai Demanding Rights," *The New York Times*, December 21, 1986, pp. 1, 19 and "China Denounces Student Protests As 'Illegal Acts,'" *ibid.*, December 22, 1986, pp. A1, A14.

78. See Daniel Southerland, "Tibet Monks Protest Rule by Chinese," *The Washington Post*, September 30, 1987, p. A28; John Schidlovsky, "At least 6 killed in Tibet protests against Chinese," *The Sun*, Baltimore, October 3, 1987, pp. 1A, 2A; "Curfew imposed after Tibetan protest," *The Sun*, Baltimore, October 5, 1987, p. 2A; "China sends security forces to Tibet after protests," *The Sun*, Baltimore, October 6, 1987, p. 2A; "60 Shout Out Dalai Lama's Name and are Seized in Protest in Tibet," *The New York Times*, October 7, 1987, p. A8; see also "China's Human Rights Record in Tibet," *The Asian Wall Street Journal Weekly*, March 14, 1988, p. 14.

79. For English translation of this Decision, see Shao-chuan Leng and Hungdah Chiu, *Criminal Justice in Post-Mao China, Analysis and Documents*, Albany, New York: State University of New York Press, 1985, pp. 249-251.

80. For English translation of the Regulations, see *ibid.*, pp. 251-252.

81. 999 UNTS 171.

82. English translation in *Beijing Review*, Vol. 25, No. 52 (December 27, 1982), pp. 10-30.

83. This right to residence was provided in the 1954 Chinese Constitution (Article 90, paragraph 2), but was omitted in all subsequent Chinese constitutions (1975, 1978, and 1982).

84. For a discussion of this issue, see Leng and Chiu, *Criminal Justice*, *supra* note 79, pp. 96-98.

85. Article 79 of the Chinese Criminal Law provides: "A person who commits crimes not explicitly defined in the specific parts of the Criminal Law may be convicted and sentenced, after obtaining the approval of the Supreme People's Court, according to the

most similar article in this Law." See Leng and Chiu, *Criminal Justice, supra* note 79, p. 129.

86. See *1983 Zhongguo Baike Nianjian* (1983 Yearbook of Encyclopedia of China), Shanghai: China Great Encyclopedia Press, 1984), p. 226.

87. This right was provided in the 1975 Constitution (Article 28) and the 1978 Constitution (Article 45), but was removed by a constitutional amendment in 1980.

88. 993 UNTS 3.

89. Xu Hong, *supra* note 76.

90. *China, Torture and Ill-treatment of Prisoners*, London: Amnesty International Publications, September 1987, p. 1. For a study of China's criminal justice, see Leng and Chiu, *Criminal Justice, supra* note 79 generally and Hungdah Chiu, "China's Changing Criminal Justice System," *Current History*, Vol. 87, No. 530 (September 1988), pp. 265-268, 271-272.

91. See "PRC Likely to Sign UN Human Rights Conventions," *FBIS-CHI*, November 28, 1986, p. A2.

92. Guo Shan, "China's Role in Human Rights Field," *Beijing Review*, Vol. 30, Nos. 5 & 6 (February 9, 1987), p. 23.

93. *Country Reports on Human Rights Practices for 1986*, Washington, D.C.: U.S. Government Printing Office, 1987, p. 696.

94. See Professor Xiao Yongqing's reply to two French professors' inquiry on mass execution and reeducation through labor (i.e., sending a person to labor camp for up to four years without judicial review) in China, published in *Faxue Zazhi* (Law Magazine), 1985, No. 5, pp. 29-31.

95. See Richard Bernstein, "Student from China Defects to Establish New Rights Journal," *The New York Times*, November 18, 1982, p. A13 and Robert 0. Boorstin, "China Opposition Emerges in Queens, Emigre Ex-Surgeon Expands Magazine Assailing Beijing and Urging Democracy," *The New York Times*, May 17, 1987, p. 7. For a survey of the human rights situation in Post-Mao China, see annual report in *Country Reports on Human Rights Practices* compiled by U.S. Department of State; *China, Violations of Human Rights*, London: Amnesty International, 1984 and John F. Copper, Franz Michael, and Yuan-li Wu, *Human Rights in Post-Mao China*, Boulder and London: Westview Pres, 1985.

TEN

HUMAN RIGHTS AND THE LAW

IN THE PEOPLE'S REPUBLIC OF CHINA

James D. Seymour

> We have twenty million cadres, many of whom at the local level think no laws can hurt or restrain them. It is our job to convince these people that everyone is equal before the law. It may take a long time.
>
> ### *Justice Ministry Spokesman*[1]

This chapter takes issue with two assertions commonly held outside of China pertaining to the closely related subjects of human rights and law. The first is that the Chinese do not care about civil liberties, preferring a legitimate but variant form of human rights. More of this later.

The second has to do with where to place the Chinese legal system, past and present, in terms of the various topologies of law. For example, it is suggested that the Chinese have always preferred "mediation" to the alternatives (common law, statutory law, etc.). It is contended in this chapter, would-be reformers aside, that judicial institutions in the PRC and Taiwan[2] have been so rudimentary that it may be misleading to apply the English word "law" to them. After all, law to us means clear rules consistently enforced by the state, something China is only beginning to see. Although, as in imperial times, the trappings of legal institutions have existed, the people have not trusted them, and have tended to avoid them. These institutions are still rarely respected, even in civil matters.[3] The question remains: To what extent is this situation changing?

In 1986, at the height of the political thaw, senior Shanghai intellectuals advanced the idea that striving for the Four (mostly economic) Modernizations[4] would not suffice; they sought to place an *additional* four modernizations on the national agenda: ideological, political, cultural, and "lifestyle" modernizations. A major part of political modernization was legal reform. As these reformers stated the issue:

> The disregard of law is a major obstacle to reform and modernization. An urgent task for the reform of the political structure is to ensure that "laws are observed," and the first step is to ensure that all democratic rights of the people stipulated in the constitution are secure.[5]

This was not a new idea, of course; such notions have at times been supported by certain officials[6] as well as by many dissidents. (Some *Democracy Wall* writers are now in prison for having made similar arguments.) But it points up the growing support for these ideas. There is a widespread recognition that social modernization is closely related to the questions of law and human rights, or "democratic rights," as the Chinese usually say.[7]

In understanding the relationship between law and human rights, we do well to distinguish between instrumentation and compliance. By "instrumental law" I refer to law as a vehicle for effecting the substantive human rights. Thus, states pass laws to codify rights, such as freedom of expression, which in theory need have nothing to do with national law. In the West these rights were once considered divinely endowed or at any rate "natural." Now, the prevailing view is that they are "human"; sustained in part by the international community though declarations and covenants. But the domestic law of states turns out to be an essential instrument for realizing these rights, even though the rights themselves may be external to the legal system and exist independently of the law.

The situation is different for the rights that are the subject of this chapter. This second law-rights relationship concerns law not as instrument (say, for effecting freedom of speech), but as itself a set of limitations which human rights principles place on the state (for example, to guarantee fair trials). These are largely (but not "merely") procedural questions. Judicial institutions are asked to acquiesce in certain internationally recognized principles. For the law to be fair, it must not be applied arbitrarily. In the administration of justice, restraint is expected of the police, prosecutors, and judges. It is in this sense that I distinguish instrumentation from, for lack of a better term, "compliance."

The compliance requirements of the Universal Declaration of Human Rights appear together (but not as a discrete group) near the beginning of the document. They are stated in general terms. The relevant articles (nos. 5-11) appear below, rearranged in the order in which the subjects will be discussed:

Everyone has the right to recognition everywhere as a person before the law. (*Article 6*)

Everyone is entitled in full equality to a fair and public hearing by an independent and impartial tribunal in the determination of his rights and obligations and of any criminal charge against him. (*Article 10*)

Everyone charged with a penal offence has the right to be presumed innocent until proved guilty according to law in a public trial at which he has had all the guarantees necessary for his defense. (*Article 11, paragraph 1*)

No one shall be held guilty of any penal offence on account of any act or omission which did not constitute a penal offence under national or international law at the time when it was committed. Nor shall a heavier penalty be imposed than the one that was applicable at the time the penal offence was committed. (*Article 11, paragraph 2*)

No one shall be subjected to arbitrary arrest, detention, or exile. (*Article 9*)

No one shall be subjected to torture or to cruel, inhuman, or degrading treatment or punishment. (*Article 5*)

Everyone has the right to an effective remedy by the competent national tribunals for acts violating the fundamental rights granted him by the constitution or by law. (*Article 8*)

Much of this is vague. Where the Declaration becomes specific it invites controversy (for example, regarding the presumption of innocence). Some clarification came in 1966 with the adoption of the International Covenant on Civil and Political Rights,[8] to which we shall make occasional reference below.

Let us examine the performance of the People's Republic of China in the light of the above criteria, focusing primarily on the years since the death of Mao Zedong in 1976. In this chapter we shall be concerned with the extent to which the provisions of the declaration are met *in actual practice,* and will be less concerned with the provisions of Chinese law.

"Personhood." There is perhaps no more hazardous word to translate from legalese than "person." Whether or not the term has much relevance to the subject of human rights,[9] this is not the place to examine what the framers of the Declaration meant by article 6. Nonetheless, the concept does give rise to certain interesting questions with regard to human rights in China, especially during the Mao period. We need only recall the many people who, because of their social backgrounds, ideology, or someone else's whim, were deemed nonpersons. Much of the Maoist thinking along these lines has been laid to rest. Still, the term "coun-

terrevolutionary" crops up in legal rhetoric with worrisome regularity.

Both articles 6 and 10 presuppose the principle of equality before the law. Now that the "class struggle" has been discredited, the Chinese authorities accept this in principle. It is asserted in the current 1982 constitution, having been absent from the 1975 and 1978 versions. The media keep insisting that all people, regardless of party affiliation, are legally equal.[10] As we shall see, much progress remains to be made on this score.

Fair trial. Article 126 of China's constitution asserts that the courts "exercise judicial power independently and are not subject to interference by administrative organs, public organizations, or individuals."[11] On the other hand, Deng Xiaoping has repeatedly inveighed against the notion of separation of powers. "I often criticize the Americans by saying that they have three governments."[12] Deng found support for this position among scholars. According to constitutional expert Zhang Youyu, the idea of a tripartite division of authority "does not accord with socialism with Chinese characteristics."[13]

It would appear that the Communist party is supposed to fall under one of the categories cited in Article 126. Furthermore, there has been considerable effort to give the government independence from the party. To the extent that this is accomplished with respect to the judiciary, some unfairness can be eliminated from trials. But the constitution's preamble calls for the leadership of the Communist Party, and certainly makes no exception of the judiciary. Most local judges probably still think the way one did in 1959, who remarked:

> When cases I handle require arresting and sentencing, have a relatively strong policy nature, or involve village or cooperative cadres, I ask instructions from the party committee both before and during the process of handling the cases, and afterward I report to the party Committee.... Whenever the party committee

gives me instructions, I conscientiously study and thoroughly implement them.[14]

Under such a system, although political dissidents will have the book thrown at them, a party member who is a torturer is often treated leniently.

Indeed, one article in the legal press indicates that the claim that one was merely doing one's job is a "legitimate defense" for all sorts of horrors. "When investigating criminal elements, and particularly those extremely evil and crafty ones who stubbornly deny their guilt, it is all too easy for one's anger to develop into...acts of violence, and into the use of torture to extract a confession." An even more shocking "legitimate defense" implies lenience toward officials who commit rape: "When dealing with cases involving shameful personal secrets, mediation in marital disputes, or the interviewing and educating of women, it is easy to forget oneself and lose one's wisdom. Emotion bursts forth, and [an officer may] harass and fool around with a woman, and even exploit his position as a public security official and rape her."[15]

Although party interference in the judicial process is usually inimical to the interests of justice, this is not invariably so. Sometimes the party steps in and takes action against abuses by cadres. For example, after one local security official, declaring that he was a law unto himself, presided over the torture of an innocent man, instructions were issued by a member of the party Central Committee to the effect that if the charges against the security official were true he was to be subjected to criminal prosecution. The procuracy then arrested the official. But cases of genuine party-imposed justice are rare. Even in this instance local leaders jumped to the official's defense, and he is not known to have been sentenced.[16]

Regarding the right to counsel, the International Covenant on Civil and Political Rights says that a defendant must be allowed "to defend himself in person or through legal assistance of his own choosing."[17] China's constitution does not guarantee access to a lawyer, it simply says that in trials an indicted person has the right to "defense."[18] China had hardly any lawyers before 1979. As late as 1985 a former justice minister declared: "The situation with regard to lawyers is not satisfactory. For one thing, our lawyers are too old and their knowledge is outdated."[19] By now, some progress has been made in training a new contingent of lawyers. In 1986 there were reported to be 3,163 legal service offices and 13,000 full-time lawyers, serving 98 percent of the cities and counties.[20] However, most of these are involved in commercial law.[21] There are few attorneys to handle China's 84,000 criminal cases annually,[22] and the pay is poor.[23] But the fact that there is now a substantial contingent of lawyers is a notable accomplishment considering that there was nothing of the sort a decade earlier.

Unfortunately, lawyers are a politically weak part of the system. Although there is now a lawyers' association, it is quite docile. (One development which would aid in the maintenance of an independent judiciary would be the establishment of a truly autonomous bar association, but the authorities have resisted this step.) Elsewhere in the bureaucracy, a lawyer's role is little understood. There are complaints of lawyers being discriminated against within the legal establishment. They are accused of "playing around with words," "engaging in sophistry," "relieving criminals of their criminal responsibility," and "colluding with and seeking to exculpate criminal elements." There are reports of lawyers being abused or even imprisoned for being too spirited in their defense of the accused. The troubles of lawyers in Hunan province demonstrates the problem:

> Some leading cadres rely on their personal views and authority of office instead of the law, and wantonly and flagrantly interfere

> with the work which falls within the purview of lawyers' re-
> sponsibilities. Court cases should be tried by judicial departments
> according to law.... Unfortunately, some of our comrades have no
> sense of legality. When they are obviously wrong and lawyers
> openly point this out according to law, they will fly into a tower-
> ing rage and invoke their power to suspend the lawyers from
> duties or transfer them to other posts. When blocked by lawyers
> in connection with their abuse of power, some individual leaders
> tend to be shamed into anger and bear a grudge and wait for a
> chance to retaliate. This is intolerable, and contravenes party dis-
> cipline and national law.[24]

Certainly defendants must feel that the situation leaves
much to be desired, especially in politically sensitive cases.
At his 1981 trial, dissident Xu Wenli requested two lawyers
by name, but was told by the presiding judge that they were
not available. Xu then asked that any lawyer from the Legal
Advisory Department be appointed to defend him, and one
was. Nonetheless, at his trial it was Xu himself who presented most of the arguments. To her credit, his lawyer did
make a few legal points on his behalf, such as challenging
the validity and relevance of evidence submitted by the
prosecution.[25]

Important from a human rights point of view is the *timing*
of a detainee's access to a lawyer. Violations of suspects'
rights most often occur during the interrogation stage,
which by law can last up to three months.[26] Unfortunately,
in China one usually does not have access to a lawyer until
the trial is about to begin. The Chinese authorities are aware
that in the West people normally have a right to counsel
during the investigation stage (and in the Soviet Union at
the conclusion of the investigation). But this is not seen as
practical in the PRC.

> The law can only stipulate systems for which the conditions are
> relatively well-matured, and which are actually viable. Were we
> to make stipulations which we could not accomplish, this would
> run counter to our aim of upholding the dignity of the socialist
> legal system.[27]

In other words, having unenforceable laws on the books undermines the law itself, and China lacks sufficient lawyers to provide one to each arrestee. One can derive hope from the fact that the principle of supplying everyone with a lawyer immediately after his arrest is not rejected. However, it has yet to be explicitly embraced.

An added difficulty that people experience in defending themselves is the fast pace at which trials often take place. In order to overcome the problem of pretrial delays,[28] the National People's Congress in 1980 actually removed a provision from the criminal law which had required that the defendant receive a copy of the indictment a week before the trial.[29] Without this minimal right, it is virtually impossible for anyone to defend himself. For the next few years criminal trials tended to be conducted with lightning speed, sometimes with no advance indictment at all. According to Amnesty International, executions were carried out within as few as eight days from the commission of the alleged offense.[30] There has been some improvement since 1984. Bail provisions have been established,[31] and the period between arrest and trial has been lengthened.[32]

Presumption of Innocence. Both the Universal Declaration and the International Covenant on Civil and Political Rights require that a defendant be assumed innocent until convicted. Under Chinese law, there is supposed to be no presumption of either guilt or innocence. However, in practice, guilt is often presumed. An article in *China Law News* candidly admits this: "Some comrades suffer from an occupational malady, namely a powerful sense of their own superiority; they are prejudiced and go by first impressions, and make an assumption of guilt." Indeed, shortly before his trial, Xu Wenli was asked to confess his guilt by no less than the man who would serve as his judge.

The problem can also be seen in the attitude toward "difficult cases," which are defined as situations where "from the evidence compiled there is insufficient basis for ascertaining the facts of the crime, but the possibility that the accused has committed a crime cannot be excluded." It is evident that judges are convicting such defendants, even though there is reasonable doubt. Fortunately, voices have been raised to protest this practice, noting that this inevitably leads to "unjust, false, and mistaken verdicts."[33]

Even in ordinary cases, as distinguished from "difficult" ones, detainees are invariably referred to by the guilt-presuming term "offender";[34] those who refuse to confess are supposed to be treated with special severity. For a Chinese suspect to defend himself is apt to be taken as evidence of lack of contrition. Thus, any attempt to mount a legal defense can be counterproductive.

In the minds of security men, even an acquittal is insufficient to overcome the presumption of guilt, as the following example demonstrates. *After he was found innocent*, a Guizhou engineer was nonetheless trussed up behind a placard declaring him "guilty of corruption and swindling." He was then driven through the streets on the back of a "punishment truck" for the masses to gape at. He was eventually driven to an execution ground to "accompany the executions," after which he was returned to jail. He was released only when the chief of the criminal court happened to discover what was transpiring. What is most revealing about this case is the attitude of the county public security chief: "It would create a bad impression to release someone.... Many prisoners are delivered up [to the courts]; the same number have to be returned [to prison]."[35]

The result of the underlying philosophy of the law and the harshness of the procedures is that an arrest is tantamount to a conviction. Detainees are almost never found innocent. In the province of Heilongjiang, 99.64 percent of the arrests in 1986 were deemed "accurate."[36] One can only guess at how many miscarriages of justice occur; the popular perception is that there are many.[37]

Timely Lawmaking. The process of legislation has proceeded so slowly in China that ex post facto prosecutions have been unavoidable. Although the problem is declining, such prosecutions occasionally still occur. In a 1984 case, a man was convicted of smuggling goods from the Shenzhen Economic Zone to another part of China. (He was supposed to export them.) Such transactions were common, and often facilitated by state-owned firms. Local officials looked the other way, because policy considerations dictated that the zone should prosper—and policy often takes precedence over law. The policy changed *after* the incident in question; the businessman was held accountable anachronously under the new standard.[37]

Nonarbitrary Detention. This relates to many other rights discussed in this chapter. We have already called attention to the devastating term "counterrevolutionary"—offenders to whom no real law may apply. It is not known how many Chinese are deemed counterrevolutionary. The number of these cases declined in the late 1970s, reaching a reported low of 0.5 percent of all criminal cases in 1982.[39] It is possible that they are now on the rise. Wang Mingdi, associate director of the Bureau of Reform Through Labor, has reported that in certain areas of the country counterrevolutionaries numbered one to two percent *of the population.*[40] (That would be a much higher proportion of criminal cases.)

It is also appropriate to note that the International Covenant on Civil and Political Rights calls for a detained person to be promptly informed of the charges, and to be promptly brought before "a judge or other officer authorized by law to exercise judicial power." In China, this requirement is often not met. In Xu Wenli's case, his arrest was not formalized until two months after his original detention.

Civilized Punishment. If there is one "ultimate human right" it is the right not to be tortured. More than capital punishment, torture horrifies people in virtually all national cultures. It is not simply the ultimate discomfort; it is the supreme degradation. We hold no one in such low esteem as we do the torturer, who is seen as utterly antisocial.

Although the PRC constitution contains no express provision on the subject of cruel punishment,[41] it is prohibited by law[42] and disapproved by public opinion. However, as we shall discuss later, torture by China's security personnel is a serious problem.[43]

Article 5 of the Declaration outlaws not only torture but all *degrading treatment*. We noted above the practice of parading people in "punishment trucks," which is common in China. Only on rare occasions have officials or the media raised objections to this practice. However, one writer in *China Law News*, in an unusual aside, did note the current stress on the rule of law and asked where in either the constitution or in other laws is there a regulation allowing such "leftist" practices. "If we want to emphasize rule of law, then we must stop hanging placards on people and parading them through the streets. Such practices originated in feudal society and enjoyed a heyday during the Cultural Revolution; they are illegal and evil."[44]

Capital punishment is widely practiced in China, with perhaps 10,000[45] having been executed since 1983. However, there is no clear international human rights standard precluding the death penalty. The declaration is silent on the subject. Article 6 of the International Covenant on Civil and Political Rights does invite the abolition of capital punishment by declaring: "Nothing in this article shall be invoked to delay or to prevent the abolition of capital punishment...." Countries which do employ the death penalty may only apply it in cases of "the most serious crimes." In executing people for ordinary economic offenses, China clearly contravenes this provision.

International opponents of the death penalty might find ammunition in the fact that too often China executes innocent people. Certainly it was commonplace during the

Cultural Revolution. Since then, such miscarriages of justice have declined, but they have not ceased. Indeed, China's roughshod system of justice makes them inevitable. Reliance on coercive interrogation results in numerous false confessions. Sometimes these confessions are ludicrous but relatively harmless.[46] But one suspects that too often, the results are fatal.

There are other practices—such as prolonged solitary confinement, mass sentencing rallies, and "interrogation by shifts"—which may be deemed unacceptably cruel and degrading.

Remedy for Rights Violations. On this subject, in addition to the Declaration's article 8, the U.N. General Assembly adopted a declaration in 1985 which called for justice for victims of "abuse of power." This requirement is reflected in article 41 of the PRC constitution, which asserts that "citizens who have suffered losses through infringement of their civic rights by any state organ or functionary have the right to compensation in accordance with the law."

We know of a few cases where victims of police abuse have received some compensation. In December 1984 a woman prisoner in Guizhou was "seriously beaten and injured" by a stun-gun wielding deputy chief of the detention center, and she subsequently required three months hospitalization. Although her tormentor only received an intra-party warning, the woman was given "suitable financial compensation."[47] In another case, compensation for seven or eight hours of beating of an innocent man by a local party secretary, et al., included the return of his property plus 80 yuan (about $30) to cover medical expenses.[48] However, compensation appears to be the exception rather than the rule.

This review of China's performance reveals serious shortcomings in meeting the seven "judicial compliance" requirements of the Universal Declaration of Human Rights. Some of the nation's leaders appear to have been making serious effort to improve the situation. They are seeking to modernize the legal system, which was never viable and was in total shambles by the end of the Cultural Revolution. Judging by the gross numbers, they have had some success. Between 1980 and 1982, the courts handled 1.6 million civil cases, and at the end of the period civil cases comprised 76 percent of all cases.[49] The percentage was only 53 in 1977, which suggests that more and more people were turning to the courts to realize their rights. But quantity does not tell us about quality. Achieving a modern legal system is an uphill struggle. Many functionaries are simply not interested in, or do not understand the meaning of, operating within a legal framework.

The Chinese press often blames the sorry state of the law on the nation's habits of patriarchy and feudalism. Presumably these include the traditions of personal rule, and the idea that law is to punish rather than to provide a framework within which everyone must operate. Cadres perceive themselves as inappropriate targets of punishment, and therefore inappropriate targets of the law. Thus, they need not adhere to the law. The eight prohibitions which apply to police and judicial cadres suggest the problem areas:

1.   Making subjective assumptions,
2.   Bending the law for the benefit of relatives or friends,
3.   Perverting justice for bribes,
4.   Attending dinner parties and accepting gifts,
5.   Soliciting or taking bribes,
6.   Engaging in business for profit,
7.   Riding roughshod over the masses, and
8.   Revealing secrets.[50]

But these prohibitions do not address the underlying issues. Even those who are conscious of the law as more than a system of punishments often face the difficult choice of whether to adhere to the law or to obey their superiors in the party. The newspaper *Worker's Daily* gave such a case in Tangshan careful attention. We are not surprised that cadres in the judiciary would hesitate to cross their party superiors. But *Worker's Daily* was unsympathetic.

> The incident in which people like Peng Hong, secretary of the Tangshan Municipal party Committee, and Zhang Jie, president of the Intermediate Court, caused an erroneous litigation is by no means isolated. Today there are a small number of leading cadres who "issue approval slips" and "hand down directives," in violation of the constitution and regulations by the party Central Committee, thus oppressing people with their power and substituting their power for the law. There are also judicial personnel who know the law but refrain from implementing it. Such people are afraid of those in power who throw their weight around; they know that a certain practice violates the law, but they still "obey the man who has the power." In truth, they do so merely to protect their own positions.
>
> The understanding of the legal system by many party cadres remains extremely thin. They are still accustomed to the old way of running mass campaigns, think that "the party secretary is tantamount to the party itself; it's what the secretary says that counts."
>
> Our party and people have suffered considerably under such practices as "substituting power for the law" and obeying "neither law nor heaven."[51]

Although the writer insisted that the law itself, and not the interpretation by this or that cadre, is the embodiment of party policy, it is evident that China's historical legacy to the contrary burdens all efforts to modernize the legal system.

"History," of course, means not only the distant past, but living memory. Cadres know from experience how the political winds can change. A commentator in one legal journal notes:

> Many comrades take a skeptical, wait-and-see attitude toward doing things according to the law. Some are even worried and

scared. They are afraid that if they act according to laws, they might fail to keep abreast of the developing situation. Should *policies* change, they might find themselves on the wrong track. If they act according to laws they might offend the leadership and have to give in under pressures from their immediate superiors. In the end, they might be accused of "right deviation" for "rigid adherence" to the law.[52]

The writer admits, and the anti-bourgeois-liberalization campaign subsequently confirmed, that such officials' fears have plenty of basis. The author himself urges that not enough attention has been paid to the remnant influence of "feudal autocracy," and implies that there has been too much criticism of bourgeois (i.e., Western) legal concepts.

There has indeed been a great deal of controversy about the extent to which foreign standards of law should be allowed to influence China's legal process. A commentary in the party journal *Red Flag* [53] would allow "reference to be made to foreign laws and legal theories," but insisted: "With regard to 'democracy' and 'humanity,' under no circumstances can we let bourgeois legal viewpoints and theories obstruct the implementation of law in our country." In other words, those who possess power want "rights" to be based not on international standards but on what they consider to be China's needs.

But, aside from the vague Constitution, little legislation pertaining to these problems has been passed. This encourages cadres to take a cavalier attitude toward the law. An article in *People's Daily* stated the problem well:

When state administrative personnel violate the law, their infractions are often taken for granted by the masses. Only when the people's rights are seriously infringed upon would they be driven to lodge complaints and "apply for an audience with the higher authorities to appeal for help." In short, because our legal system in state administration is not sound, the people's sense of legality remains very weak.[54]

So it is not that people are unaware of their rights as that there are no legal remedies to realize them, and rarely a politically feasible way to bring errant officials to justice.

The result is a serious lack of discipline among China's security agencies, with abuse of prisoners a more common problem than was hitherto believed. Although such problems are widespread, there have been only a few reports of security and judicial personnel being punished. Some positive examples: A Tianjin judge was dismissed for "perverting the law for selfish interests."[55] In a Shanxi case, some of those responsible for improper divorce proceedings were reprimanded.[56] Lawless behavior by procuratorial personnel has come under fire. Heilongjiang's chief procurator, Yu Jian, observed that although most personnel abided by the law, there were serious lapses. "A small number of personnel have degenerated and became serious criminals.... They caused great damage to the sanctity of the state legal system." Among the wrongdoing was "extorting confessions by torture, framing people with false evidence, ransacking, and illegally detaining and framing people on false accusations."[57]

But it appears that such culprits generally receive little or no punishment, due to political interference in the administration of justice. Even the effort to rid the party of lawless elements is seen in highly political terms. The situation in Shanxi's Luofan County is revealing. Here, we are told,[58] the Public Security Bureau has been "reorganized" and leftist elements expelled. The purge (doubtless part of the then ongoing party rectification campaign) was the party's way of effecting "strict control over the police"—a code word for preventing police brutality. The problem is that eliminating torture does not seem to be an end in itself as much as a vehicle for one faction in the party (Deng Xiaoping's followers) to eliminate their opponents on the left. One wonders how many nonleftist torturers have been spared. At any rate, political conspiracies are a poor way to realize human rights.

Regarding another case, a *Tianjin Daily* commentator[59] urged criminal prosecutions as a tool in cleansing the party of leftists:

> Carrying out the principle of simultaneous rectification and correction of defects means that party organizations at all levels must resolve the problems concerning the persons and events to which the masses strongly object and which have the worst influence. It is necessary to investigate and handle the cases swiftly, deal with those persons concerned severely, and prosecute major and key criminal cases aggressively.

Although the procuracy may sometimes do just that, justice is not always the end result. Party influence and personal networks often undo the work of prosecutors and journalists of integrity. As it is, the court's role is still often purely nominal. This is demonstrated by the fact that party functionaries sometimes have blank paper with the court's seal already affixed. Thus, a party secretary can issue a "judicial" decision virtually without the court being involved at all.[60]

It is evident that a massive effort to educate everyone about law is needed. Indeed, there has been effort along these lines. The press has carried many articles on the subject. Most of China's provincial-level units have their own legal newspapers with a total circulation of 24 million. Some are in non-Chinese (minority) languages.[61] Unfortunately, the law education campaign appears to have been co-opted by conservatives, who see the law not as a protective mechanism for individual citizens, but a means to legitimize their campaign against politically errant intellectuals and students. (Peng Zhen, when asked by foreign reporters whether law takes precedence over policy, said he could not answer.[62] The National People's Congress, over which Peng then presided, is constitutionally charged with interpreting the constitution, with its often conflicting human rights provisions.)

Thus, law is still what it has always been in China: an instrument of control, not a vehicle for codifying rights. History may also explain why there is so much torture, which was routine in imperial China. The Tang dynasty codes gave precise stipulations about carrying out floggings. There were limits, though, and the law also provided for the person carrying out excessive beatings to himself receive strokes equivalent to the excess. Extralegal torture was undoubtedly more common than the "legitimate" beatings. Certainly this was the case during the Ming dynasty, an especially harsh period. People were branded with irons, had nails inserted in their fingers, and vinegar poured in their nostrils. And when it came to capital punishment, the means were sometimes of unparalleled brutality (as would be the case during the Cultural Revolution). Only at the beginning of the twentieth century were such measures as branding and "death by a thousand cuts" proscribed.

The Nationalist (Guomindang) efforts to curb police abuses have generally been half-hearted.[63] The Communists have made a more serious effort to do so, but one must admit that international human rights standards have played little or no role. As we have seen, partisan politics is much more important. While it is obvious that many Chinese subscribe to what we might call international common-law standards of decency, it is equally obvious that many don't, as is the case in most countries. In attempting to rectify these problems, China has the added problem of institutional inertia. It is extraordinarily difficult to remove errant individuals from office, as the following case demonstrates:

> A zealous county court judge in Jiangsu sought to elicit evidence against a man who had allegedly raped his two daughters. After the girls declined to testify, the judge had the girls handcuffed to a pole outside the courthouse. When that failed to produce results he had them jailed for months, even over the objection of the procuracy. The affair attracted considerable attention, and was the

subject of two exposes in the national law press,[64] after which the judge still reportedly remained on the bench.

CONCLUSION

But one need not end on such a gloomy note. Although we have observed the extent of torture and other abuses by China's security personnel, it should be noted that our information comes from the Chinese press, which revealed it as part of a concerted effort to stamp out these practices. Until the Chinese media began revealing this sordid picture, the outside world, even those who focus on such issues, were little aware of the problem. In particular, few facts of post-Cultural Revolution torture were available.[65]

Since late 1984, the picture has been clearer. The Chinese law press, a popular medium, has been filled with accounts of abusive cadre behavior. To cite one typical example: In 1987 a local party secretary in Sichuan compelled 43 peasants to engage in manual labor under the guise of "legal education." People were subjected to corporal punishment, and "even forced to walk on all fours." At night villagers were locked in their rooms. In this relatively mild case of degradation of citizens by cadres, punishment was swift though hardly severe (a suspended one-year jail term).[66]

Thus, it has been demonstrated that when the problem is properly identified, the authorities are capable of taking action. It has been declared that procurators must work to prevent "extortion of confessions through torture, illegal detention, false accusations and frame-ups, and bending the law for the benefit of friends and relatives." Arguments that the public benefits from such practices are erroneous. "On no account can we condone or defend the disregard of state laws, the flagrant violation of citizens' democratic rights and their rights of person, the wholesale extortion of confessions by torture and illegal detention, even to the point of crippling or killing people. Such 'zeal' cannot be tolerated.... The perpetuators must be firmly punished in accordance with the law."[67]

The fact that these issues have been ventilated is a positive sign, and debunks the canard that Chinese do not care about civil liberties. Chinese political culture is compatible with the principles of the Universal Declaration of Human Rights. The problem is that rule of men, rather than rule by law, to a large extent still prevails.[68] Thus, one must be struck by the continuity of past and present. As always, China's "human rights problem" is in part a legal problem. China has taken the first steps toward the realization of a system of law. Before that goal can be fully achieved, however, there will have to be far-reaching political reforms, such as those advocated by the authors of the second Four Modernizations.[69]

NOTES

1. Lu Jian, quoted in the *Hong Kong Standard*, August 18, 1984. In preparing this chapter, I have received help from researchers at the International Secretariat of Amnesty International (London), which I visited in April 1987. Although this assistance is gratefully acknowledged, the views expressed are solely mine, and I am responsible for any errors of fact and interpretation.

2. I refer here to the Chinese Nationalists, not to the Taiwanese. (The latter, having benefited from Japanese tutelage before 1945, often have very different ideas.) For insight into how the ruling elite views law, see the leaked minutes of the generals and their civilian aides of October 17, 1984, translated in *Index on Censorship*, June and October 1985.

3. When it comes to contracts, for example, hardly anyone is aware that law was supposed to be an overriding factor. In a survey conducted by the journal *China Law News* only ten percent of respondents said that people in their units were aware that its economic contracts must conform to the Economic Contract Act. A majority believed that "as long as both parties agree, everything is all right." (*Zhongguo fazhi bao* January 27, 1986, p. 1, U.S. Joint Publications Research Service (hereafter: JPRS) CPS-86-057, p. 34.) Still, citizens are beginning to turn to the courts to uphold their contractual rights. (See note 21).

4. This term denotes modernization of industry, agriculture, defense, and science and technology.

5. Views endorsed at a forum held jointly by *Shehui bao* and the Intelligence Research Institute of the Shanghai Academy of Social Sciences, summarized in *Ming bao* (Hong Kong), September 10, 1986, p. 5, JPRS-CPS-86-086, p. 66.

6. A democratic legal system was promoted in the 1980 "Gengshen" reform program. See Liao Gailong, "The 'Gengshen Reforms' for China," *Qishi niandai*. no. 3, March 1981, pp. 38-48, U.S. *Foreign Broadcast Information Service* (hereafter: *FBIS*), March 16, 1981, especially p. U9.

7. In this chapter, the terms democratic rights (*minzhu quanli*) and human rights (*renquan*) are treated as virtual equivalents. However the term *ren* (human) is more encompassing than *min* (which has connotations of citizenship). To most Chinese who are familiar with the subject, "democratic rights" are those rights

bestowed by the Chinese authorities via the constitution, while "human rights" refers to international standards.

8. The International Covenant on Civil and Political Rights was adopted by the U.N. General Assembly in 1966, and entered into force in 1976. In late 1986 China seemed close to ratifying both this covenant and the International Covenant on Economic, Social, and Cultural Rights (detailed discussions in *South China Morning Post*, November 25, and *Agence France Presse*, November 24, 1986, *FBIS*, November 28, 1986, p. Al), but the anti-bourgeois liberalization campaign apparently made this impossible.

9. *Black's Law Dictionary's* entry under "person" begins with this human-rights neutral definition: "A man considered according to the rank he holds in society, with all the right to which the place he holds entitles him, and the duties which it imposes." A thousand words later we read: "Not every human being is necessarily a person, for a person is capable of rights and duties, and there may well be human beings having no legal rights, as was the case with slaves in English law." It is this which the declaration seeks to reverse. Thus, to say that all human beings are "entitled to recognition everywhere as a person before the law" is simply saying that all human beings have rights.

10. The Party journal *Hongqi* has had several articles on the subject. Note especially Li Buyun, "Adhere to the Principle that All Are Equal Before the Law," June 16, 1986, pp. 24-27, JPRS-CRF-86-015, pp. 42-48. See also: September 16, 1983, JPRS-84675, p. 8.

11. Article 126.

12. *Asiaweek*, March 15, 1987, p. 28. Immediately at issue has been the question of legislative (rather than judicial) independence, for Deng seems to have been trying to curb NPC head Peng Zhen.

13. Quoted in *Asiaweek*, March 15, 1987 p. 28. See also: Heng Shan and Suo Fei, "The 'System of the Separation of the Legislative, Executive, and Judicial Functions' and Socialist System Are Essentially Incompatible," *Guangming Ribao*, May 1, 1987, p. 3, *FBIS*, May 18, 1987, pp. K5-K7.

14. Quoted in D. Clarke, "Concepts of Law in the Chinese Anti-Crime Campaign," *Harvard Law Review*, vol. 98, no. 8, pp. 1890 ff.

15. *Zhongguo fazhi bao*, August 7, 1985.

16. *Minzhu yu fazhi*, no. 7, 1985.

17. International Covenant on Civil and Political Rights, Art. 14, 3(d).

18. Article 125.

19. Wei Wenbo, "Remnant Feudalism Obstructs Rule of Law," *Ta*

gong bao (Hong Kong), May 16, 1985, p. 10, *FBIS*, May 17, 1985, p. W3.

20. *Zhongguo fazhi bao*, July 3, 1986, p. 2, JPRS-CPS-87-02, p. 39. There were also said to be 7,000 part-time lawyers.

21. Actually, it is the expansion of the economy's private sector that primarily accounts for increase in law-related activity. Notwithstanding a severe shortage of lawyers, provincial legal advisory offices have been established to assist people in such matters as contractual rights and obligations. A *People's Daily* report (June 2, 1984, P. 4) notes: "Specialized and key households and economic group ventures have a great need for the advice of legal workers. To perform this new task properly, the legal workers must sweep aside left-wing ideological influences, change their incorrect view that serving as legal advisors is 'not within their proper province,' and eliminate their concern about 'making mistakes if things are not handled right.'" Reading between the lines, one suspects that the once powerful local cadres, usually products of the Cultural Revolution, do not relish their new "bourgeois" task of helping private entrepreneurs protect their contractual rights.

22. This compares with 38,000 civil litigation cases. The figures concerning the number of lawyers (based upon *Zhongguo fazhi bao*, July 3, 1987, CPS-87-002, pp. 39 ff.) ignore the many cases which do not reach the litigation stage, and also do not take account of cases handled by part-time lawyers. The two considerations at least partially cancel each other out.

23. A beginning lawyer in China may receive as little as 60 yuan a month. The top salary (for senior people) is 200 yuan. *South China Morning Post*, April 14, 1985.

24. Commentator article in *Zhongguo fazhi bao*, June 7, 1985, p. 1, *FBIS*, June 21, 1985, pp. K3-K4.

25. Extracts from Xu's account (smuggled out of prison) appeared in *Index on Censorship*, May 1986, pp. 18-25.

26. Article 92 of the Law of Criminal Procedure, supplementary provisions regarding time limits for criminal cases. *State Council Bulletin*, no. 16, July 30, 1984, pp. 547-549, JPRS-CPS-85-001, p. 3.

27. "Democracy and Dictatorship in the Criminal Procedure," *Zhongguo faxue*, no. 1, 1985, pp. 116-123.

28. However, this problem, too, persisted. See editorial, "Strictly Implement Regulations on Time Limits for Handling Criminal Cases," *Zhongguo fazhi bao*, July 9, 1984, p. 1.

29. See Hungdah Chiu, "The 1982 Constitution and the Rule of Law," *Review of Socialist Law 11* (1986) p. 154, citing *People's Daily*, Sept. 3, 1983, P. 3.
30. *Reuters*, October 28, 1984, *South China Morning Post*, October 29, 1984
31. *China Daily*, July 10, 1984.
32. *New China News Agency* (hereafter: *NCNA*), July 5, 1984, *FBIS* July 5, 1984.
33. "Democracy and Dictatorship in the Criminal Procedure," *Zhongguo faxue*, no. 1, 1985, pp. 116-123.
34. On this issue, see the *Chinese Law and Government*, Fall 1988, especially document 14. This special issue concerns cadre accountability to the law.
35. *Zhongguo fazhi bao*, October 7, 1986.
36. Report by Chief Provincial Procurator Jia Chengwen, March 13, 1987, *FBIS*, April 16, 1987, p. S-7.
37. One article discusses six "feudal concepts" which hinder China's legal development. One is the notion that "'The judge sits in court to try cases' and 'has no regret over wrong verdicts.' ...There are cases of obviously wrong verdicts not being corrected when they should be. People have long been dissatisfied with [such] phenomena." (*Zhongguo fazhi bao*, October 13, 1986, JPRS-87-001, pp. 27 ff.)
38. Lee Yee, "Chinese-Style Justice Equals Chaos," *Asian Wall Street Journal*, July 25, 1986.
39. *NCNA*, June 25, 1983; *FBIS*, June 27, 1983.
40. *Agence France Presse*, November 9, 1986, *FBIS*, November 10, 1986, p. Kl.
41. One might interpret the following sentence in Article 37 of the constitution as bearing on the subject: "Unlawful deprivation or restriction of citizens' freedom by detention *or other means* is prohibited...." (Emphasis added.)
42. Article 189 of the Law of Criminal Procedure prohibits not only "the use of torture to coerce statements," but also "the gathering of evidence by threat, enticement, deceit or other unlawful methods." Article 189 of the criminal law itself prescribes a maximum of three years for minor abuses, and maximum of ten years (minimum: 3) for "especially serious" infractions. However, the type of crime envisaged in Article 189 appears to be limited to instances where the main intent is to inflict bodily harm, as distinct from gathering information. "Using torture to coerce a state-

ment" (*xingxun bigong zui*) is outlawed by Article 136, which authorizes three-year sentences (more or less, depending on the gravity) for offenders. Unfortunately, these laws are written with some vagueness, creating loopholes which often permit torturers to escape punishment.

43. See also, *China: Torture and Ill-treatment of Prisoners*, (London and New York: Amnesty International Publications, 1987).

44. *Zhongguo fazhi bao*, October 7, 1985.

45. This figure appeared in the *South China Morning Post* (Hong Kong), December 22, 1986, citing "Western sources."

46. For example, a woman was coerced into fabricating a rape charge, and a man named Liu Ruiyao was apparently tortured until he confessed to five rapes which he had not committed. A police officer (a product of the Cultural Revolution) had fed him details as to the circumstances of the rape, which Liu incorporated in his confession. The policeman was honored with "Third Rank Distinction" for his successful handling of the case. Eventually ("after many setbacks" apparently caused by his protectors) the policeman received a two-year prison sentence.
    For his part, Liu barely escaped execution. The sentence was stayed only fifteen minutes before he was to have been shot. (*Zhongguo fazhi bao*, December 25, 1985, p. 2.)

47. *Zhongguo fazhi bao*, December 16, 1985.

48. *Zhongguo fazhi bao*, May 8, 1985. Eighty yuan is roughly what a worker would have earned in a month. As of the time of this report, six months after the incident, the compensation and restitution had not actually taken place, and the victim was still being tormented.

49. *Hong Kong Standard*, February 14, 1984.

50. From a work report by Wang Yongchen, president of the Tianjin Municipal Higher People's Court, *Tianjin ribao*, May 26, 1986, p. 3, JPRS-CPS-86-059, pp. 73ff.

51. *Gongren ribao*, June 27, 1983, JPRS-84264.

52. Tao Xiren, "Act According to the Laws—the Central Link in Coordinated Development of the Legal System," *Faxue*, no. 8, August 10, 1984, pp. 1-4, JPRS-CPS-85-005, p. 84.

53. September 16, 1983, JPRS-84675, p. 8.

54. Zhang Shangzhou, "Administrative Law in China Should Be Reformed," *Renmin ribao*, January 4, 1984, p. 4, translated in JPRS-CPS-85-017, p. 42.

55. June 9, 1984, *FBIS*, July 5, 1984.

56. July 11, 1984, *FBIS*, July 17, 1984.
57. *Heilongjiang ribao*, April 5, 1984, JPRS-CPS-84-037.
58. *Zhongguo fazhi bao*, October 9, 1985.
59. April 19, 1984, JPRS-CPS-84-040.
60. This situation came to light when a divorce certificate was forged using a brigade secretary's stationery bearing a court seal. (There is no available information to the effect that such devices are used to enable corrupt or abusive police officers to escape justice.) James D. Seymour, *China Rights Annals 1: Human Rights Developments in the People's Republic of China from October 1983 through September 1984* (Armonk, NY: M. E. Sharpe, Inc, 1985), p. 35.
61. *NCNA*, January 4, 1984, JPRS-CPS-84-009.
62. *Beimei ribao*, April 10, 1987, p. 3. A sanitized version appeared in the overseas edition of *Renmin ribao*, April 9, 1987, p. 1.
63. For a Political dissident's participant-observer account of torture in a Taiwan prison, see Chi Wan-sheng, "Dark View from a Taiwan Prison," *Asian Wall Street Journal Weekly*, Sept. 29, 1986. Although at this writing torture by Taiwan's police appears to be on the decline, little has been done to punish those who have engaged in such abuses in the past.
64. One was in *Zhongguo fazhi bao*, July 1, 1985.
65. The little information that was available was summarized in Amnesty International's *Torture in the Eighties* (London, 1984), pp. 185ff. (Cf. the Amnesty report cited in note 42.)
66. *China Legal Daily, Agence France Presse* summary, November 24, 1987, *FBIS-CHI-87-226*, p. 39. (For a separate but somewhat similar case, see Yunnan Provincial Broadcasting Service, April 19, 1987, *FBIS*, April 23, 1987, p. Ql.)
67. *Zhongguo fazhi bao*, January 23, 1985.
68. A bold essay on this theme is: Ni Zhengmou, "A Major Task in the Reform of the Legal System: Eradicate the Concept of the Rule of Men," *Shehui kexue*, no. 10, October 15, 1986, pp. 14-17, JPRS-CPS-001, PP. 42-47.
69. For a similar view, see Zhang Qiong, "A Brief Talk on Reform of the Political Structure," *Zhongguo fazhi bao*, August 11, 1986, p. 2, *FBIS*, August 26, 1986, p. K-27. Zhang argues that political reforms are a prerequisite to "perfecting the legal system." On the other hand, he also says that law "can become an effective means to remove obstacles to the reform of political structure."

ELEVEN

THE LIMITS OF RURAL POLITICAL REFORM

Thomas P. Bernstein

The reformers who came to power in 1978 were deeply dissatisfied with the rural political system. The fused political, bureaucratic, and economic power of the commune had in their view stifled the growth of the agricultural productive forces. Because of this dissatisfaction, rural political reform has long been on the policy agenda. It aims at fostering "democracy," legality, and at reducing overconcentration of power, in order to enable people at the grassroots to "enjoy the right to manage state affairs."[1]

Rural economic reform, i.e., decollectivization and the progressive elimination of restrictions on peasant trade and business enterprise, were themselves intended as a remedy for the excessive power exercised by the rural political apparatus. Economic reforms increased peasant autonomy and thus loosened the grip of political authority over agriculture. Household contracting largely eliminated cadre power over the deployment of peasant labor and gave peasants sources of income over which cadres had no control. The right to engage in private or contracted enterprise and to enter markets gave peasants further opportunities to carry on economic activity relatively independent of political authority. Economic reform showed the intent of policymakers to reduce the scope of political control and domination in the countryside. Moreover, economic reforms had direct institutional consequences. The old, three-tiered multifunctional structure of the people's communes had by 1985 been replaced. The lowest tier, the production teams, became essentially superfluous and largely disappeared. The production brigades were replaced by village administrative and economic committees. The communes were replaced by the *xiang* government as well as a more differentiated set of economic organizations.

These organizational changes were not a substitute for more thoroughgoing economic reform, if only because they left the old power structure in which control was in the hands of brigade and commune party secretaries largely intact.[2] Political reform required the establishment of mechanisms through which peasants could more effectively represent their interests. It required the establishment of ways of protecting their legal rights, an issue of particular significance given the proliferation of contractual relations and of market dealings. And it required devising means of making local political authorities responsive to the new economic situation. Economic reform was not a substitute for political reform, i.e., for the creation of political, legal, and administrative institutions within which the commodity economy could flourish. As Chinese media often pointed out, without political reforms, the economic reforms could not fully succeed.[3] The need for political reform thus arose not simply because of the legacy of the collectivist past, but from the needs of the newly emerging system as well.

Political reform in the countryside must be seen in the context of the impact which economic reform had on rural officialdom. Economic reform had a major impact on rural cadres in the initial stages of reform, when many village cadres withdrew from office, leading to paralysis of party or collective organizations. As the reforms took hold, however, another, far more important consequence arose, in that the economic changes have given rural cadres opportunities to take advantage of the new situation to make money and expand their influence. The reason lies to a significant extent in the partial nature of economic reform. The government continues to be powerfully involved in agricultural production, as with the procurement of the major staples. Marketization is incomplete not only because of the continued role of the state, but because market channels are often clogged, leading to difficulty in the purchase of needed inputs and the sale of peasant products. These conditions, widely reported in the press, enable cadres, who on the basis of their networks have access to information and resources, to engage in profitable economic deals. Cadres have become middlemen, using their connections, and have established ties of patronage with peasant entrepreneurs.[4] They themselves combine official with entrepreneurial roles, using their special access to scarce resources to do business. Sometimes the officials' role in the rural economy is simply that of extorting fees from entrepreneurs or ordinary peasants or of benefiting disproportionately from the contracting out of collective resources. The press has often reported on illegal levies (luantan luanpai). It has also reported on withholding by local officials of valued inputs, such as diesel fuel and fertilizer, which peasants are entitled to purchase once they have contracted to sell grain to the state, but which these officials sell to their favorites.[5] Some of these activities, although corrupt, can be thought of as promoting economic activity; some appear mainly parasitic. They are not of course new; prereform rural politics was by no means free of corruption, patronage, or behavior characteristic of the "second economy."[6] But the reforms have greatly enlarged the scope within which rural cadres can carry on such activities. The country's policymakers condemn all such activities as the "use of power for private gain" (yi quan mou si). From their point of view, this deviant behavior is an instance of a general erosion in the capacity of the center to elicit the compliance of local officials, weakening the utility of cadres and officials as instruments of national policy implementation. Failure to implement national instructions, even when they come in the form of the authoritative annual Document No. 1 of the Central Committee and State Council, is a frequent source of national-level complaint.[7]

Given these problems, political reform ought to aim at making rural officialdom fully accountable. But efforts to do so run up against the maintenance of party dominance. Nationally, political reform has been constrained by the "Four Principles" laid down by Deng Xiaoping in 1979, and so has its local aspect, rural political reform. Adherence to leadership by the Communist Party is the most important of these; the others are adherence to the ideology, the socialist road, and to people's democratic dictatorship. Even as Deng delivered a scathing indictment of the excesses of party dominance, he insisted that the purpose of remedying this situation was to "maintain and further strengthen party leadership and discipline, and not to weaken or relax them." For Deng, party leadership is the key to the country's "unity and stability." Without the party, he fears that the country would once more degenerate into chaos.[8] Party leadership is a particularly crucial issue in the countryside, the locale of half the members (22 million) and of 1.113 million basic-level party branches. In the countryside the party has always been a major means for the maintenance of control, the management of affairs, and the integration of the peasantry.

The principle of adherence to party leadership is an absolute; the interpretation is not. As just noted, Deng himself has sharply criticized the way in which the party has exercised power, and policy has demanded that the autonomy of nonparty institutions be significantly broadened. At times, wide-ranging debate on party control and related issues has been possible. But when, as in 1986, debate seemed to give rise to a challenge to the party's primacy, the campaign against "bourgeois liberalization" was launched. The limitations imposed by the central leaders have meant that political reform has not been structural in nature, in that institutionalized changes in the distribution of political power have not been made. Instead, there have been moderate reforms, including, for instance, a more liberal policy towards debate and participation, as well as efforts to promote legality. The rural areas, as will be discussed below, are no exception to this pattern.

Rural political reform is also constrained by the determination of the central leaders to retain, and if necessary, to rebuild, a strong basic-level political-administrative apparatus. Reformers repudiated the exercise of arbitrary and abusive power during the Maoist era, and they wanted to reduce and even eliminate controls over those areas of rural life that interfered most immediately with development. Early on, however, during the transition to household contracting, when rural leadership disintegrated in some places, policy statements insisted that economic reform did not mean that cadres could abandon their posts and that it was "completely wrong" to believe that peasants no longer required guidance.[9] A situation such as the one reported by John F. Burns from a remote Shaanxi village, in which no one was in charge and peasants didn't even know the name of the local party secretary, yesterday's ever present "petty tyrant," may not be unusual but is as unacceptable to the central authorities as the stifling controls of the prereform era.[10]

Three reasons explain why national authorities want strong rural leadership at the levels of the county, the *xiang* (administrative village or township, i.e., the former commune), and the *cun* (village, i.e., the former production brigade.) The first is the need for capacity to implement national economic plans. To be sure, macroeconomic levers such as prices and markets have been and presumably will increasingly be used. The mix between plan and market is a matter of controversy, but not even the most committed marketeer is likely to want to abandon mandatory planning altogether. In any event, as of the mid-1980s, political and administrative means have continued to be used to insure that peasants behave in accordance with national preferences. For instance, since the abolition of compulsory grain purchase quotas in 1985, mandatory purchase quotas have continued to be assigned, disguised as contracts.[11] Indeed, as long as powerful leaders such as Chen Yun believe that neglect of grain production may lead to chaos (*wu liang zi luan*), cropping patterns are not likely to be left entirely to the vagaries of the market. Agricultural reform leaders such as Du Runsheng have also spoken of the necessity of encouraging peasant investment and discouraging "excessive consumption."[12] A policy goal of altering the balance between peasant investment and consumption could be attained using economic levers, but taxes and other financial incentives would require an administrative system able to reach into the villages.

The second reason has to do with rural development. As China begins to face the long term problems of rural modernization, the necessity of building up the social and physical infrastructure, i.e., schools and roads, has become more compelling, as has the need to upgrade the rural extension network for the diffusion of science and technology. Replenishing the agricultural infrastructure built up in the Maoist era but neglected during the first phase of the reform years is now a matter of increasing national concern, especially in the case of irrigation facilities. Tian Jiyun told the 1986 Rural Work Conference that "to encourage investment in the form of labor, all types of flexible measures should be employed to organize the peasants to take part in agricultural capital construction."[13] Obviously, the requisite political-administrative structure must be in place to accomplish these goals.

Third, China's leaders espouse a series of social and political goals that require organized access to the peasants. These include social goals, such as improvement of social welfare, elimination of the regional and local pockets of poverty that have been resistant to economic reform, improvement of education, and of course, enforcement of the family planning program. Indeed, as long as family planning is a major policy goal, even if the goal is not as stringent as is implied by the one-child family, a mix of administrative coercion and incentives is likely to be necessary, given the conflict of interests that is involved. Another goal that is likely to require administrative intervention is preservation of arable land from encroachment by house builders, and more broadly, by runaway rural industrial growth. China's leaders are unlikely to leave this precious and increasingly scarce asset to the vicissitudes of the market. As of the mid and late 1980s, increasingly loud cries of alarm over shrinkage of arable land presage the likelihood of more administrative intervention.

On the ideological front, while the principle that some can get rich ahead of others seems well established, so is the goal of achieving common prosperity. Party cadres are supposed to pursue it not by redistributing wealth, but by helping the less fortunate in their villages. A "socialist spiritual civilization" is to be built in the villages, which has repressive components such as elimination of "feudal superstitions," i.e., of peasant popular religion, which has widely resurfaced. These goals require an organized political presence in the village of party, youth league, women's federation, and militia. Whether the peasants will be receptive to the implementation of these goals is of course another question. The point is that, quite apart from the normal governmental tasks of tax collection, maintenance of order, and management of conscription, a host of economic, regulatory, developmental, and political tasks are to be carried out. Leadership, if anything, has become even more difficult.

Because of the importance of the local political-administrative apparatus to the implementation of national policy, rural political reforms that might undermine capacity to implement policy are not likely to gain favor in Beijing. Nonetheless, the need for political reform has long been recognized. Policymakers could in principle choose several ways in which to check cadre power. One is to foster the establishment of more independent power from "below," by enabling peasants to organize checks on cadre power. Another is to foster legal accountability. Still another approach is to revive the traditional CCP approach to cadre deviance, i.e., rectification, in which education, criticism, and self-criticism, as well as disciplinary penalties are used to correct cadre conduct. And a third option is to reorganize and rationalize the rural political-administrative system, e.g., by limiting tenure and specifying personal responsibility, thereby raising the efficiency of the cadre force.

Policymakers have pursued all three options to greater or lesser degrees. Some efforts have been made to give peasants a limited voice, and to strengthen the rural legal system. Efforts have been made to rationalize the rural administrative system. A party rectification movement in the countryside designed to clean up abuses began in late 1985 and was completed in the spring of 1987, but the effects were minor.[16] In the sections that follow, three aspects of rural political reform will be examined, namely the extent to which peasants have a political voice, the extent to which legal accountability has made progress, and the extent to which the dominance of party secretaries has been reduced.

INSTITUTIONALIZED VOICE FOR THE PEASANTS

The question of whether peasants should have an organized capacity to protect their interests was raised before household contracting had been fully implemented. In 1980, Liao Gailong, a senior researcher in the party Secretariat's Policy Research Office, taking his cue from Deng Xiaoping's speech on political reform, proposed the creation of independent peasant associations at both the national and local levels. Peasants, he observed, should "have their own independent organizations" to enable them to defend their interests, to democratize grassroots political life, and to check bureaucratic power.[17] At the national level, a peasant association was part of a broader plan to enliven the country's legislature by dividing it into a House of Regional and a House of Social Representatives; peasants would have a voice of their own in the latter.[18] Liao suggested that:

> by establishing such organizations, we can (correct the problem) that the prices of our agricultural products have been too low for a long time, that the price scissors have not been narrowed but have sometimes even widened, that the interests of the peasants are not safeguarded, and that the cost of planting rice cannot be recouped.[19]

Liao voiced confidence that peasant associations would "carry out their work independently and responsibly under the leadership of the party's line, principles, and policies." But his example of the price scissors suggests that an organized peasantry might challenge the fundamental allocational decisions hitherto reserved for the highest policymaking agencies, the Politburo and State Council. Liao's ideas did not get far, perhaps for this reason, or because 1980 was also the year when the Polish government was compelled to recognize Solidarity as a legally independent union. (Liao, it is important to note, had also proposed independent trade unions.) Solidarity represented an unprecedented abandonment of the Leninist principle of transmission belts and deeply disturbed Chinese leaders.[20] His ideas disappeared from the political agenda, although peasant associations were established in some provinces in 1982, but in thoroughly orthodox fashion.[21]

By the mid-1980s, it is worth adding, price scissors became a renewed source of friction between the state and the peasants, because inflation led to major increases in the price of industrial inputs even while the state price for grain did not rise, eliciting much peasant dissatisfaction. Peasant deputies to the National People's Congress raised these questions at the 1988 sessions, asking for redress. Two deputies from Hebei, for instance, said that peasants in their county wanted the NPC deputies to know that grain production was no longer a very profitable undertaking. Chemical fertilizer is now hard to buy and the supply of electricity for farming is very unstable.[22] Peasant interests on matters such as these are clear and unambiguous; perhaps it is for that reason that the regime feels that it cannot afford an organization that could effectively articulate and fight for peasant interests.

If autonomous peasant associations are beyond the pale, to what extent can local people's congresses defend peasant interests? In 1979, direct elections were extended to county-level congresses, the process of selection of nominees liberalized, and a larger number of candidacies permitted. In 1986, these changes were expanded further, with a requirement that one third to twice as many candidates be nominated than the number of deputies' slots.[23] The impact of these changes has been minor. In university districts, student attempts to put up candidates independent of the party were crushed.[24] There are some instances of peasants who reportedly nominate their own candidates, which can be done by groups of ten persons.[25] There are also instances of the defeat of unpopular village deputies at the polls, prompting them to resign their cadre posts because of the consequent loss of face. People's Daily has commented on the morale problems encountered by village cadres who lost elections. In Shaanxi, for instance, in the 1987 elections to county and township people's congresses, 216 candidates did not get elected. In Dingxiang county, Shaanxi, 3 village heads and 10 assistant village heads were voted out of office in the three triannual elections held as of 1987.[26] Dingxiang peasants reportedly commented that formerly no one cared about elections but that they now had become more meaningful. One peasant remarked: "Formerly we felt that it mattered not who was the county magistrate (but now)...we must elect somebody who can do things for us."[27] These examples suggest that in the late 1980s, peasants did have some influence on the election of popular or unpopular local cadres. Possibly, this influence was an improvement over the past, when "village-level elections were neither a reliable nor an effective method for peasants to influence government policy. They were unreliable because they were not institutionalized, and they were ineffective because the elite dominated them."[28] However in 1988, a spate of articles commented sharply that cadre peasant relations had deteriorated. Peasants were angry at cadre corruption, cadre failure to solve their problems, and cadre abuses.[29] Such sentiments would seem to indicate that the 1987 local elections had not become a way for peasants to "throw the rascals out."

What about people's congresses themselves? The following case of assertiveness of a standing committee of a county people's congress is an instructive instance of the policymakers' desire for reform provided that it doesn't change the system. In 1986, a deputy and member of the Standing Committee of the Shaoyang People's Congress in Hunan, himself a *xiang* chief, severely criticized the shortage of fuel. The deputy, Xiao Diaguo, complained that peasants lacked fuel for vehicles, machinery, irrigation pumps, and lamps.

"Since Liberation it has been rare for peasants not even to be able to light their home.... These days, some party members are indifferent to what goes on in the villages. They only care about their well being, but not about that of the peasants. Do they still have the conscience of party members?"[30] Xiao's remarks angered the county party Secretary, who charged Xiao with "antiparty views" and with having unfavorably compared the party with past dynasties. He then ordered the county Discipline Inspection Committee to investigate Xiao for violating the Four Principles. The officers of the Standing Committee of the People's Congress, however, refused to cooperate on the grounds that the investigation constituted improper interference and would have a chilling effect upon the willingness of deputies to speak out.

The dispute reached higher levels, and *People's Daily* Commentator, issued a sharply worded critique, entitled "Comrade, Put Down Your Club."[31] Commentator condemned the party Secretary for illegally intervening in the affairs of the People's Congress, thereby violating the State Constitution, to which the party is subject. People's congresses have the right to discuss and decide matters within their jurisdiction and the Secretary's intervention only shows that "a small number of party comrades" have not learned to respect democracy and the rule of law. The Shaoyang People's Congress officials were completely correct in refusing to cooperate. Commentator seemed to uphold the right of congresses to criticize and articulate peasant interests.

But Commentator then added that all party members, no matter what posts they hold, are obligated to uphold the Four Principles and are subject to the party's discipline if they oppose them. This indicated that the party Secretary's error was not one of principle but one of excessive zeal. By labelling Xiao as a "violator of the Four Principles," the party Secretary had undermined the party's prestige. In saying this, Commentator himself undermined the very principle of legislative independence which he had just upheld. Half of the country's six million deputies are party members and they face the possibility of being held accountable if what they say in session is regarded as a violation of the Four Principles. This crucial abridgment of legislative independence came under fire in 1986, when reform advocates proposed granting deputies western-style immunity and party members serving as deputies the right to differ with the party organizations to which they belong, thereby attenuating the principle of democratic centralism.[32] These proposals show how far the country has yet to go in the establishment of independent legislatures.

A third issue relating to village autonomy arose in the spring of 1987, when the National People's Congress debated the status of village committees (*cunmin weiyuan hui*). These committees, the successors of the production brigades, are constitutionally defined as self-governing mass organizations. Their duties include maintenance of social order, settlement of disputes, and protection of the "legitimate rights and interests" of the peasants.[33] They are regarded as a link between the masses and government, the lowest level of which is the *xiang*. The village committees must fulfill state obligations, but they cannot legally be ordered about. The *xiang* governments must guide them; they do not have the right of leadership (*zhidao* versus *lingdao guanxi*), since village committees are not a subordinate government agency.

The distinction between guidance and leadership is not clear, but whatever the differences higher level units have dominated the committees by "indiscriminately" assigning them tasks.[34] During the 1987 NPC debate on draft regulations for the village committees, the point was made that they should "have the power to turn down assignments given them by any organ, group, enterprise, or institution."[35] This disturbed some NPC deputies, who argued that village committees might refuse to accept the instructions of the *xiang* governments. Tasks such as grain purchase, conscription, and family planning might not con-

sequently be fulfilled. *Xiang* governments would be reduced to ineffectiveness, having lost "their legs in the
villages." These deputies proposed that the village committees should be made into legal organs of government,
subordinate to the *xiang*, thereby insuring proper fulfill-
ment of state assignments.[36] Their proposal required
amending the Constitution's definition of village committees as self-governing mass organizations.

Other deputies, however, defended the constitutional
definition. Several, from Jilin, complained that some *xiang*
governments exercise rigid control over peasant production, issuing orders on sowing, application of manure, and
plowing. Peasants "strongly object" to coercion and arbitrary commands of this type. Deputy Mei Yi from
Guangdong defined the issue as reliance on administrative
coercion versus fostering of peasant self-government.
Guidance requires the *xiang* government cadres to abandon
the old style of issuing administrative orders. Instead, they
must rely on persuasion and on raising of mass consciousness, methods that embody the principle of democratic
self-government. Of course, he added, the village committees must obey the law and fulfill state obligations, but
this can be done without administrative compulsion.[37]

Given these differences, the NPC leadership decided in
April 1987 to table the legislation, requesting the NPC
Standing Committee to find a solution. In late 1987, a draft
was passed. It stipulated that the township government
should provide guidance, support, and assistance to the village committees, which in turn should "assist" (*xiezhu*) the
people's government. Specifically, this meant that the committees should "positively respond to the calls of the
people's governments" at the various levels, educating and
helping the villagers to carry out tasks such as birth control,
military service, tax collections, including grain purchases,
as well as compulsory education.[38] This formulation tilts to

that side of the argument which had opposed enshrining the independence of the village committees into law.

LEGAL ACCOUNTABILITY: VIOLATION OF ECONOMIC CONTRACTS

To what extent have post-Mao legal reforms provided protection for peasants against abuse by rural officials? The issue was raised in 1978 by Hu Qiaomu, then a major spokesman for reform, in lectures to central leaders. How is it, Hu asked, that "certain leading bodies" can arbitrarily order peasants to uproot crops they have planted and grow other crops instead, without being responsible both legally and economically for the ensuing losses?[39] Hu argued that party policies were not enough to correct this situation, and neither were constitutional guarantees. Special laws were needed and special law courts, which would punish violators of peasant rights, as well as a system of enforceable contracts. Peasants would then be able legally to demand compensation for losses and to become "masters of their own destiny," thus making the rural bureaucracy reform politically, even in the absence of legal or constitutional accountability of the rulers of the top.[40] Accountability of local officials would provide the security and predictability essential for successful market reform.

Since Hu Qiaomu's lectures, a new state Constitution has been promulgated, as have numerous laws, including codes of civil and criminal law and procedure, a law on contracts, and a land management law. The scope of citizens' legal rights continues to expand. In early 1987, for example, the Supreme Court empowered citizens to appeal administrative decisions made by police, industrial and commercial bureaus, and tax offices to the courts.[41] The enactment of laws, however, has tended to lag behind the emergence of new needs, an illustration of the reactive policy process that has characterized rural reform as a whole. It was not until the summer of 1988 that "Provisional Rules" were promulgated to regulate private enterprise and private employ-ment, years after both had been practiced widely. Policymakers took their time before taking action, not only because this has been an extremely sensitive issue, but also because they wanted to see how hiring developed before taking action.[42] In the meantime, entrepreneurs had to rely on Central Committee Document No. 1 of 1983 and State Council regulations issued in 1984 that permitted restricted employment of labor.[43] In Wenzhou, Zhejiang, a nationally publicized model of successful market reform, the absence of a law on private enterprise caused large entrepreneurs to feel "uneasy" and to hold back in expanding their busi-nesses. Officials and masses alike "hope" that the state would enact a law that would confer legal status on private enterprise.[44] An "agricultural legal system" (*nongye fa tixi*) is coming into being, albeit slowly.[45]

If laws are to protect peasants, legal assistance must be available. China had 11,389 practicing lawyers in 1982 and about 30,000 in 1986, but only a fraction practice in the countryside, if only because graduates of political-legal col-leges prefer the more exciting work available in cities, especially foreign trade.[46] Zouping county, Shandong had 3 practicing lawyers in 1985 and Fengyang, Anhui, 5; ap-parently not atypical numbers.[47] The paucity of lawyers requires reliance on paraprofessionals. As of 1984, 2,773 legal advisory stations (*falu guwen chu*) had been established in urban and rural China, staffed variably by a trained cadre from the legal system and perhaps 3-5 retired administra-tive cadres or teachers, who had been given a short training course. Twelve of Zouping's 17 *xiang* had established such offices as of 1985, while Fengyang had 25, though only 16 were for peasants. Only one fifth of the country's 92,000 *xiang* had these offices, however, although there is a national program for their establishment. Notaries public also play a significant role in rural legal work, particularly contracts. As of 1984, 2,465 offices for notaries public existed nationwide with a staff of 8,382.[48] In 1985, Zouping had six notaries public, having recently added two.

The gap between the number of potential clients and available help is obviously immense, although it has been narrowing. The vast majority of the tens of millions of rural economic contracts are concluded without legal assistance. The main exception is specialized households who contract with a collective to operate assets such as factories, stores, fishponds, orchards, and the like, usually for a set fee or a share of the profits. These contracts have often been torn up by village cadres, usually because the peasant contractor was thought to be making "too much money." This situation could arise if little was known beforehand about the potential profitability of the undertaking, especially when entrusted to capable managers, or about market conditions. The typical case is of a peasant who contracted to manage an orchard, promised to pay, say, 2,000 yuan per year to the collective, but made 10,000, thereby arousing the envy of cadres and peasants alike (hongyan bing).[49] In order to deter cadres from violating the contract, specialized households seek to have them notarized, thereby acquiring an impressive looking "chop" and a "legal guarantee" (falu baozheng).[50] In Zouping county, 165 documents were notarized in 1981 and 1,810 in the first seven months of 1985, 80 percent being economic contracts.

Notaries public, along with other legal cadres serving the masses, are officers of the state and hence must defend their clients' interests in the light of both party and state policy. Their functions go well beyond those implied by the term, since they check contracts for conformity both to the law and to policy. If they believe the contract to be illegal or if they discern "impure motives," they may refuse to approve it or require changes to be made.[51] Sometimes they themselve may investigate the feasibility of the project, e.g., the availability of essential supplies, in order to reduce the likelihood of contractual default.[52] One notary public in

Liuhe county, Jiangsu, revised 133 contracts, closing loopholes, and thereby contributing to the prevention of conflict.[53]

As these examples show, a major goal of legal help to peasants is to prevent disputes from arising in the first place. Education in law has the same aim. Legal advisors and notaries public are supposed to help eliminate "legal illiteracy" (*famang*). Moreover, cadres have long been accustomed to ordering people about and thus lack an understanding of legal procedure. Popularizing legal knowledge is regarded as a major remedy for this state of affairs. In Zouping, each household is provided with a booklet summarizing 16 laws, while cadres are taught a more complex version of the law, in a program started in 1984 and to be completed in 1989.

With regard to contracts, many cadres and peasants do not understand that when a contract is violated, the law is broken, because they are not accustomed to the idea of contractual obligations. This lack of understanding exists in the village and at higher levels, despite China's rich contractual tradition.[54] Thus, *Zhonggua Fazhi Bao*, the legal newspaper, quotes a Hebei county agricultural official as telling a specialized household, "You are making too much money, and that cannot be allowed," even though his earnings had been based on valid contracts.[55]

Only a small fraction of rural contracts are drawn up with legal assistance, and a still smaller but apparently growing proportion cause conflict. Zouping legal officials estimate that 1 percent of contracts cause disputes, and in Lishu county, Jilin, 140,000 contracts gave rise to only 600 disputes over a three-year period. In 1986, however, the press reported that disputes over economic contracts have occurred "time and again" and have "increased sharply." A Hong Kong source speaks of an "extraordinary increase" in such disputes but does not differentiate between the rural and urban areas.[56]

When a dispute breaks out, the official goal is to find a solution by means of education and mediation, often by village mediation committees, in order to avoid a court case, as in traditional times. Thus, Lishu county's 600 disputes led to only 5 court cases. Examples of how disputes have been settled without resort to courts include a case from a Jiangsu village, in which a peasant had contracted with his brigade to run a plastics factory, whereupon the brigade awarded another contract to someone else to build a second, competing plant. A notary public was called in, who taught the brigade cadres that they had erred in violating the first contract. His words were effective in getting the second project stopped.[57] A second example is of a mediated dispute in Hebei, where four peasants contracted to run a brigade factory and to pay the brigade 1,350 yuan each year. When their income in the first six months rose to 2,500 yuan, brigade cadres cut off the factory's power supply. The contractors complained to the county legal advisory office, which found the cadres to be at fault. Mediation led to an agreement to restore electricity and to cut the contract fee by 120 yuan, thus offsetting lost income.[58]

The state's judicial apparatus at the county level—the county court and its economic section, the procurator, the public security department—appear to play a mixed role in the enforcement of peasant contracts. On the one hand, cases have been publicized in which the courts and associated agencies effectively protected peasants against local cadres. In one Hebei brigade, the cadres had revoked the fruit growing contract of a group of eight peasants, the dispute even leading to damage to the trees. The contractors complained to the commune and to the county's legal office which sent lawyers to the village and ultimately secured a court ruling in their favor. The peasants commented that "with lawyers to speak on our behalf, we really feel we are protected by the law."[59] On the other hand, county judicial officials share to a significant extent the cultural antipathy to law suits, resulting in reluctance or even refusal by county courts to take a case.[60] Sometimes, as in one of the following cases, it is pressure by the county party committee that prevents a contract suit from being heard. Mutual protection networks operate among officials (*guan guan xiang hu*), so that "even judicial departments," in the words of the law journal, may not act to protect peasant rights.[61]

Three cases of court recalcitrance illustrate the difficulties peasant entrepreneurs may encounter in seeking redress. In the first, a notarized contract in Longjing county, Jilin, was "abrogated by a resolution of the Longjing party Committee, thus reducing it to a useless piece of paper...." In this case, a village party branch had initially torn up a contract for an orchard, again because the contractor was thought to be earning too much. The peasant in question, Jin Mengzhe, first complained all the way up to the prefectural party committee but to no avail. He then filed suit, but "regrettably, the county people's court, on the basis of the opinions of individual leaders, rejected the case." Jin appealed to higher courts and also sent a brother to the Ministry of Agriculture in Beijing. These appeals elicited higher-level visitors with whose help the court finally accepted the case. But these interventions angered "certain individuals," who manipulated the court into delaying the hearing. Just as the court was about to hear the case, the county party Committee decided on its own to declare Jin's contract invalid and to order the notary public, who had helped Jin in approaching the higher-level authorities, formally to annul the document. Higher-level intervention was once more required to overturn this patently illegal party decision and to reinstate the case in court, which, as of the date of the newspaper report, was finally about to hear it.[62]

In the second case, the big question "everyone asked was whether a group of farmers would be able to win a case against a State organization." A group of 1,569 households, from Anyui county, Sichuan, sued a state-owned seed company for breach of contract, i.e., for failure to pay the contracted price for rice seedlings. County authorities, including the court, did not respond to their suit. As in the preceding case, the peasants took their case to higher-level courts, but also to the State Council and to the press. The State Council ordered an investigation. Anyui authorities first sought to mediate, but although both sides moderated their claims, a compromise could not be reached. The case finally did come before the Anyui county court. Its judgment favored the peasants, but instead of awarding the 290,000 yuan claimed, the judge awarded about 90,000 including 13,000 yuan in legal costs. Thus the peasants lost money on the deal, but their lawyer remarked: "We went to court not only for our benefit but also for the benefit of the law. We accepted only 90,000 yuan to show our understanding and sympathy for the difficulties our country faces."[63]

The third example of a court unwilling to budge comes from Henan's Loning county, where a peasant, Wang, had contracted for land on which to build a brick kiln. Water damage from mishandled irrigation disrupted production. Because Wang could not deliver the bricks for which peasants had paid in advance, he demanded that the village (*cun*) cadres pay him 1,000 yuan in compensation. They failed to respond and Wang appealed to the county government, which wrote the *xiang* and *cun* authorities, i.e., to Wang's adversaries, asking them to handle the case. The *cun* cadres tried to fob him off with 100 yuan but also threatened him with retaliation should he go to court. Wang brought suit anyway, paid a 63 yuan court fee, but the county court simply sat on the case. Wang thereupon appealed to the prefectural court. This angered *cun* cadres, who now incited peasants to chop down 1,300 fruit trees in a 56-mu orchard that Wang and others had also contracted to run. In addition the *cun* cadres requested the county government to reallocate to other purposes 20-mu of the orchard. This harassment was finally exposed in the *People's Daily*, and although it is not clear from the account whether Wang finally did secure redress, presumably some action followed.[64]

To what extent, then, are cadres held accountable when they violate peasant contracts? First, legal officials charged with protecting peasants, such as notaries public, as well as many other officials at all levels of the system seem determined to protect peasants from contract violations. Further research is needed to establish the extent of these efforts as well as trends. Second, a major reason some peasants are able to find legal protection is not due to the law but to national policy, which favors protection of entrepreneurs, and which results in extensive publicity in favor of victims of abuse as well as in higher-level intervention. Were party and state policy on entrepreneurship to change, it is doubtful that legal protection could be sustained. Third, what is missing from the cases publicized in the media is predictability, regularity, and normalcy. Sometimes a court will act, sometimes not. Sometimes a county party committee will take the initiative in disciplining village leaders who have violated contracts, sometimes it will protect them.[65] Sometimes peasants are successful in appealing to higher-level legal or political authority, sometimes not.[66] Sometimes violators are made to pay fines and compensation; at other times, they are only criticized. All these uncertainties mean that a peasant who signs a fairly complex contract may be better off protecting himself by buying political insurance, such as giving gifts and cultivating good relations with the powerful. Informal networks, patronage ties, and other deals may be more effective than the law. The role played by informal cadre-peasant ties is a measure of how far the legal system still has to go to realize Hu Qiaomu's vision of peasants who are in fact masters of their own fate.

THE ROLE OF THE PARTY

Excessive dominance by local party organizations has been a key target of political reformers. In 1980, Deng Xiaoping spoke of unlimited power concentrated in the hands of the "patriarchal" party secretaries to whom everyone "has to be absolutely obedient" and even "personally attached."[67] Deng also reportedly made the following, harshly biting comment:

> At the grassroots level, we must make up our mind to change the situation in which party members dominate the masses, party branch secretaries dominate all other cadres, and party organizations dominate all other organizations...neither party organizations nor party members have the right to force the masses to accept their views....It is necessary to abrogate all privileges enjoyed by grassroots party organizations. If we fail to...solve all these issues, our party will be in a position antagonistic to the masses. Such a situation has already emerged in some localities and units.[69]

Remedies include party disengagement from policy implementation, which should be left to government and economic units. The party should focus on overall policy and line, ideological education, and on its own organization, thereby ending the problem of "the party not controlling the party." It should foster inner-party democracy, in order to end the "cat and mouse" relationship between superiors and subordinates.[69]

How to attain these changes even while the party retains power is the unanswered question. For instance, a formula for a workable division of the party's role and that of governments and economic organizations has not been found, even though the problem of overconcentration of power is real. As one *xiang* Secretary wrote, to "grasp everything is to grasp nothing." In his case, a company had visited to arrange a business deal, but because the Secretary was absent, other officials were afraid to sign and the deal fell through, thereby losing the township a development opportunity. The Secretary learned from this episode to place greater trust in others and to devise a division of labor in order to share the responsibilities.[70] But even the most elaborate division of functions is not likely to mean much unless it is accompanied by an institutionalized division of power, and this the party has not been willing to undertake.

As of the mid-1980s, the dominance of the party in the countryside has not changed. The displays of party committee power reported in the preceding sections illustrate this point. Territorial party secretaries continue to be the local bosses, and the formal differentiation between party, government, and economic organizations resulted in "three sign boards and one boss," with the masses regarding the new *xiang* governments, which replaced the communes, as mere decoration (*baishe*).[71] Impressions from research done in Zouping and Fengyang counties in 1985 indicate that county, *xiang*, and *cun* party secretaries seemed to be fully in charge. In group discussions, they were accorded deference and their voices carried authority. The one exception to this was a barely literate older village party secretary, whose authority had clearly declined. His situation was a not uncommon example of an older cadre who was no longer able to meet the new challenges of the commodity economy and, thus was slated to be replaced by a younger, better educated person. In the *xiang* and *cun*, party, government, and economic organizations were all housed in one compound, strengthening the impression of unity and close consultation.

The demands of economic development have actually given the role of the party secretary new relevance. In the mid-1980s, an increasingly prominent theme in the scholarly and journalistic press had been the need for services to peasant households. Peasants need help with the timely provision of inputs and especially with marketing. Solutions include establishment of service cooperatives and other joint undertakings (*lienheti*), but an important one, found concretely in Zouping and Fengyang, is for the village party secretary to play the role of "mobilizer for the market." The old slogan, "serve the people," has been adapted to this role: "By serving the people we mean leading organs and leading comrades at all levels in the rural areas should work enthusiastically to help peasants shake off poverty and become rich."[72] The way to do this is to foster development by seeking information on markets, bringing in new technology, and helping with the supply of capital, credit, legal services, etc.[73] The duty of the party cadre, according to a booklet on rural rectification, is to help peasants with their problems of buying and selling, which are "very big obstacles" to the growth of the commodity economy.[74] As peasants reportedly see it, a cadre who fails to provide services "is not a qualified cadre."[75]

Numerous examples of village party secretaries taking the lead in organizing local development have been publicized. One Hebei secretary, for instance, drew up a three-year plan for his village, which included building a school, enlarging an orchard, and reorganizing a collectively owned marble factory.[76] A Jiangsu village party committee led peasants to solve difficulties with the marketing of lotus roots by setting up a service company contractually tied to the peasant households. Formerly, peasants were on their own and couldn't sell their valued product, but now, under party auspices, an organized marketing outlet had been established. Production is planned and peasants are becoming rich.[77] In another Hebei village, the party branch thoroughly organized all households for participation in development projects. Each of the village's fifty party members was put in charge of four households, so that "all measures" can be relayed speedily to each family: "only by having party members take the lead...can the village do everything smoothly."[78]

The examples suggest that the role of the party secretary as the energetic "mobilizer for the market" could well lead to the reimposition of tight control which economic and political reform sought to undo. "Mobilizing for the market," it is important to note, is being combined with a major effort to revitalize the Leninist conception of the vanguard party, in the rectification campaign. The message transmitted in this campaign is that the basic-level party organizations should be the "militant bastions" (*zhandou baolei*) of the party, whose members "march in step" and who are united and disciplined. The task of the "militant bastion" is to implement the party's policy, serve as a link and bridge to the masses, and report mass opinions, demands and attitudes to higher levels. But the fundamental assignment of the "militant bastion" is to lead in the development of the commodity economy and to make everyone prosperous. Party cadres must master the rules of the market, competition, and of innovation. Party members must not think that "trade is crooked" (*waimen xiedao*).[79]

If one current in official thinking emphasizes a mobilizational approach adapted to the new conditions, another is sharply critical of control deemed excessive. A provincial party Secretary who visited the village mentioned above, in which fifty party members regularly mobilized all households, commented that centralization of tasks is "all right" but that it is "imperative to uphold the voluntary principle."[80] In August 1985, *People's Daily* harshly criticized in Jilin province the lack of peasant autonomy "to manage their business activities." Contracts in Jilin are "mandatory plans in disguise." "After a telephone meeting, dozens of townships, hundreds of villages, and thousands of peasant households must go in for simultaneous sowing." Penalties are imposed for failure to comply.[81] In April 1987, deputies from Jilin, it will be recalled, voiced the same complaints, suggesting that nothing had changed in Jilin. "All too many comrades don't know how to tap, kindle, and utilize" the creative initiative of the masses. "Some comrades" issue orders and impose rigid controls.[82]

In 1986, the issue of control, especially that exercised by the party, received intensive, critical attention. A Central Committee and State Council "Circular" called upon local party organizations to ensure that governments exercise their functions "independently."[83] Much debate was devoted to the subject of democratization.[84] In this critical atmosphere, experiments with alternative possibilities were publicized. One such experiment, which acquired the status of a model, was Fuyang county, Anhui. Formerly desperately poor, Fuyang suddenly took off. The commodity economy blossomed, and 110,000 families established workshops that produced one third of the county's industrial output value. Combines in which the state, the collectives, and individuals participated provided the necessary services. Rapid growth and prosperity were achieved without mobilization from above. Reportedly, no one in Fuyang depended on "supervisors." Instead, local authorities created an encouraging environment for enterprise, letting people take the initiative as they saw fit. The authorities followed a formula which has a truly Taoist flavor, i.e., "to...govern by doing nothing."[85]

During the discussions of political reform in 1986, one bold proposal called for abandonment of the concept of the basic-level party organizations as "militant bastions." The author of this idea, Liu Yifei, a teacher in the Chengdu City Party School, argued that the concept had been appropriate during the revolution, but was now in conflict with the party's line, which requires a division of functions between party and government. The notion of "militant bastions" had to be abandoned if the party's monopoly power over basic-level nonparty units was to be ended. Liu proposed that a less mobilizational definition be substituted, e.g., that basic-level party organizations should supervise, coordinate, or guarantee the implementation of the line. But without such an important conceptual change, party organizations will continue to be viewed "as being in charge of everything."[86] This proposal was in striking contradiction to the orthodox Leninist message conveyed by those in charge of party rectification. Liu's idea has not prospered.

If the problem of excessive horizontal party control over nonparty institutions and activities has not been solved, another approach to loosening the political system might be to permit the local party committees greater leeway in setting policy. In 1986, an instance of this found at least temporary approval. The case is that of Wenzhou, Zhejiang, a town with a rich commercial tradition, where markets, trade, and household manufacturing flourished to an unusual degree. Before 1984, development was hampered because peasant households wishing to go into business could not transfer land and engage in such financial transactions as borrowing money at floating interest rates. The Wenzhou Party Committee, not willing to be "bound by upper-level restrictions" and by "what is written in books," permitted entrepreneurs to disregard these restrictions even before they were lifted by Central Committee Document No. 1 in 1984. The party Committee had thus responded creatively to the need of the commodity economy. In 1986, *People's Daily* Commentator hailed these initiatives in glowing terms:

> Though many documents did not affirm these practices and had even clearly called for prohibition, the Wenzhou CPC Committee and the city government saw clearly that these things were conducive to the development of socialist commodity production. Assuming an attitude that called for "not being bound by upper-level restrictions and by what is written in books, but simply being realistic," they gave the "green light" to these practices.[87]

How and under what circumstances the Wenzhou Party Committee actually defied national policy is not clear. Moreover, the significance of the case is attenuated in that Wenzhou was ahead of rather than in violation of policy. When this is the case, "creative initiative" from below has sometimes been approved, e.g., by Mao Zedong, in the case of collectivization in 1955. Still, the treatment of the Wenzhou case seems to have been a real attempt to relax the strictures of hierarchical party discipline. The approval given to the Wenzhou initiative, moreover, is all the more remarkable when viewed against a persistent problem which the central authorities have had of eliciting local compliance. Local officials have distorted national policy, using local rules, regulations, and practices. In 1984 and 1985, these tendencies were nicknamed "Document No. 2," in contrast to the authoritative Document No. 1 of the Central Committee and were criticized sharply.[88]

Had procedural consistency prevailed, Wenzhou's initiative should have been criticized as a case of "Document No. 2." Instead, policy or substantive consistency may have prevailed. The "Document No. 2" represented leftist obstruction of entrepreneurship, which had to be condemned, whereas Wenzhou's policy initiative was, as noted, ahead of policy but in line with the national goal of promoting the growth of the market economy. What this means is that rules defining the independence of local decisionmakers do not exist apart from policy. The Wenzhou initiative, in other words, is not a case of structural reform.

In any event, during the rectification campaign, rural party members have been taught the orthodox line on party discipline. An authoritative booklet castigates "some people with confused ideas" who think that because economic policy had been relaxed, party discipline too could be relaxed. The result is that "a minority of party members" don't pay attention to repeated orders from the center, and believe that they can go their own way, deciding themselves which party policy, which aspect of party discipline, or which state law to obey. "Some party members" have a "selective" (*xuanzi*) approach to implementing party policy. Some say that the "party has its policy and I have my counterpolicy" (*duizhengce*).[89] During the campaign against bourgeois liberalization, moreover, Wenz-hou's status as a model was questioned. Pointedly, a *People's Daily* article spoke of the necessity of proceeding in "everything from reality under the leadership of the CPC central authorities," thus apparently repudiating the Wenzhou Party Committee's freewheeling interpretation of discipline.[90]

CONCLUSION

This examination of three aspects of rural political reform shows that it is not only intellectuals at the fringes of power, but also the country's premier leader who recognize the need for reform. At the same time, Deng and colleagues wish to have their cake and eat it too, i.e., they want political reform provided it does not threaten the party's monopoly of power. What is remarkable is the public recognition of this dilemma and its periodic reappearance on the public agenda. As Su Shaozhi put it in August 1986, despite the commitment of the leaders, "the public's right to take part in political affairs, to speak, and to make policy decisions": has not been "fully insured," because of the lack of "institutionalized provisions."[91]

Institutionalized changes in the distribution of rural political power have not taken place. Peasants do not have a genuine voice of their own, although their actions do of course influence policy. The law restrains rural power-holders to a limited extent, and the party continues to be in control. Yet, important changes have occurred, changes that in China are called *fangsong* or *fangkuan*, relaxation or loosening. Local people's congresses can become more vocal, legal cadres can exert themselves to enforce peasant rights, and those seeking redress can mobilize support from higher levels. Experimentation with looser forms of party control is encouraged, at least at times. These changes are not structural in nature, but they are not insignificant. As they take hold it is conceivable that the changes that have taken place thus far create cumulative pressures for more changes, as people become accustomed to authentic as opposed to mobilized participation, as in local people's congresses.

The question is whether gradual political reform can keep up with the social and economic changes taking place in the countryside. As peasants become more involved in enterprise, their stake in the extent to which the political environment furthers or retards their economic interest also grows. Scattered evidence suggests that peasant political assertiveness is growing, particularly on issues such as prices, corruption, and cadre arbitrariness. The following is an example:

> The government called on the peasants to grow cotton. All right, we worked hard and grew large areas of cotton. However, when the purchasing centers had collected enough cotton, they not only reduced the purchase price, but also refused to purchase any more of our cotton. The peasants waited in a line several li long to sell their cotton, but to no avail....They are simply playing with the peasants....The authorities should give us explanation if they want our money.[92]

The same article quoted a young peasant as saying "is the state not building democratic politics? We peasants also want democracy. We can no longer bend with the wind." He too said that the authorities should give explanations when they take peasant money, and that while it is right to pay taxes, "we cannot help but know that the money from the grain taxes fills the pockets of the 'lords.'"

In 1987 and 1988, reports of peasant riots were published which suggest that at least some peasants are willing to take action on behalf of their interests. In June of 1988, an estimated thousand peasants in a village in the Beijing suburbs clashed with police in protest against the pollution by a petrochemical plant of their drinking water. Reportedly, some of them shouted "Long Live Chairman Mao!"[93] An even more remarkable incident occurred in Cang county,

Shandong, in May of 1987 as reported by a Hong Kong journal which claimed to have had access to an internal party document on the incident. In this case, peasants had been told by the county leaders to grow as much garlic as they could, on the assumption of unlimited demand. This official market estimate turned out to be wrong. When peasants brought a record 30,000 tons of garlic to the purchasing stations, the cadres cut the price from .80 yuan per kilogram to .004 yuan, and then stopped buying altogether. The peasants, enraged and in despair over the loss of income, and further aggravated by various fees imposed by county units, went on a rampage and wrecked party headquarters, some shouting "we are the offspring of Liangshan. It is time for us to rebel." (Liangshan was the lair of the legendary bandits of the novel *Water Margin*.)[94]

What is significant in this story is not peasant willingness to demonstrate, which in itself is not new.[95] What is significant is the relationship to economic reform. Despite the introduction of household contracting and of private enterprise, the county party and government assumed responsibility for the purchasing and marketing of a cash crop, and in the process, for peasant decisions on how much acreage to devote to garlic. When the authorities turned out to have grossly miscalculated, the peasants naturally held them responsible. Lacking channels through which to voice grievances, they rioted. One wonders what the reaction of the peasants would have been had the party-state disengaged from the production of this product. Perhaps they would have found some way of coping on their own. But as long as the party-state is involved in economic decisions vital to the peasants, the peasants necessarily have an interest in what the authorities do. It is from this interest that increased peasant assertiveness and perhaps genuine politicization can be expected to grow.

NOTES

1. "On the Reform of the System of Party and State Leadership," August 18, 1980, *Selected Works of Deng Xiaoping, 1975-1982*, (Beijing: Foreign Languages Press, 1984), p. 304.
2. My rural research strongly points to this conclusion. See my "Local Political Authorities and Economic Reform: Observations from Two Counties in Shandong and Anhui, 1985," paper delivered at Conference on Market Reforms in China and Eastern Europe, University of California, Santa Barbara, May 8-11, 1986.
3. See, e.g., Cui Naifu, Minister of the Interior, in *Zhongguo Fazhi Bao*, October, 1986, JPRS-CPS-87-001, January 13, 1987, p. 17.
4. For some secondary analyses, see Jean C. Oi, "Commercializing China's Rural Cadres," *Problems of Communism*, vol. XXV, no. 5, September-October, 1986, and by the same author, "Peasant Households Between Plan and Market," *Modern China*, vol. 12, no. 2, April 1986.
5. For one of many articles on miscellaneous charges imposed on peasants, see *RMRB* November 17, 1985. For a condemnation of official manipulation of scarce inputs, see *Renmin ribao*, Commentator, April 30, 1987.
6. See for example Chan, Anita, Richard Madsen, and Johnathan Unger, *Chen Village: The Recent History of a Peasant Village in Mao's China* (Berkeley, CA: University of California Press, 1984).
7. Local distortion of central policy came to be called "Document No. 2" as in "Yi hao wenjian yao guan 'erh hao wenjian,'" (No. 1 document must govern 'No. 2 document'), *RMRB* June 12, 1984.
8. *Selected Works of Deng Xiaoping, op. cit.*, p. 324.
9. *RMRB* Commentator, March 2, 1981, *FBIS* no. 41, March 3, 1981, p. L 24, and Yue Ping, "Fangkuang zhengce jue bu shi fangqi lingdao" (relaxing policies definitely does not mean renouncing leadership), *Hongqi* no. 24, December 16, 1981, pp. 11-12.
10. John F. Burns, "A Reporter's Odyssey in Unseen China," *New York Times Magazine*, February 8, 1987, p. 31.
11. *RMRB* August 25, 1985, *FBIS* no. 170, September 3, 1985, *FBIS*, no. 170, September 3, 1985, p. K 12, and Lin Zili, "On the Contract System of Responsibility Linked to Production," *Social Sciences in China*, no. 1, 1983, p. 102, where Lin speaks of contracts as "certificates under the plan."

12. See e.g., *Xinhua*, Beijing, January 26, 1986, *FBIS* no. 29, p. K 8.
13. *Xinhua*, Beijing, November 25, 1986, *FBIS* No. 229, November 28, 1986, p.K 12.
14. *Cf.* "Circular on Strengthening the Work of Rural Basic-level Political Power," CCP Central Committee and State Council, *Xinhua*, Beijing, October 28, 1986, *FBIS* no. 210, October 30, 1986, pp. K 25-27.
15. *RMRB* editorial, July 15, 1981, *FBIS* no. 141, July 23, 1981, pp. K 7ff and *RMRB* February 6, 1982, *FBIS* no. 33, February 18, 1983, pp. K 12ff, for list of ten different duties.
16. See *RMRB* February 8, 1987 and *Xinhua*, Beijing, April 1987, in *FBIS* no. 75, April 30, 1987, pp. K 2-3.
17. Liao Kai-lung, "Historical Experiences and Our Road to Development," *Issues and Studies* no. 12, December 1981, p. 91-92.
18. *Cf.* Falkenheim, Victor, "Political Reform in China," *Current History*, September 1982, p. 261.
19. Liao Kai-lung, *op. cit.*, p. 92.
20. "'Confidential Documents:' 'A Speech of Deng Xiaoping for Restricted Use Only,'" *Pai Hsing*, Hong Kong, no. 122, June 16, 1986, *FBIS*, no. 117, June 18, 1986, pp. W 1-2. This speech was reportedly made on the same day as that published in Deng's *Selected Works*, August 18, 1980. See above, note 1.
21. For articles on such peasant associations, see Radio Wuhan, February 7, 1982, *FBIS* no. 27, February 9, 1982, pp. P 1-2; and Radio Kunming, March 2, 1982, *FBIS* no. 53, March 18, 1982, pp. Q 8-9.
22. *Xinhua*, Beijing, April 4, 1988, *FBIS* no. 65, April 5, 1988, p. 17.
23. *RMRB* January 14, 1987 and *Xinhua*, Beijing, April 2, 1987, *FBIS* no. 63, April 2, 1987, pp. K 21-22.
24. For an analysis of the 1980 elections, see Nathan, Andrew J. *Chinese Democracy*. (New York: Alfred A. Knopf, 1985). Chapter 10.
25. *RMRB*, November 27, 1987, in *FBIS* no. 235, December 8, 1987, pp. 15-16.
26. See note 22 and also, *RMRB* Commentator, November 27, 1987, in *FBIS* no. 235, December 8, 1987, p. 16; *RMRB* Commentator, December 10, 1987, in *FBIS* no. 246, December 23, 1987, pp. 21-22; and *Xinhua*, Beijing, January 9, 1988, in *FBIS* no. 6, January 11, 1988, p. 16.
27. *RMRB*, November 27, 1987, in *FBIS* no. 235, December 8, 1987, pp. 15-16.

28. John P. Burns, *Political Participation in Rural China* (Berkeley: Berkeley University Press, 1988) p. 119.
29. See, e.g., *Nongmin ribao*, October 17, 1987, in *FBIS* no. 208, October 28, 1987, p. 33; and *ibid*, September 26, 1988, in *FBIS* no. 195, October 7, 1988, pp. 12-14. The latter article mentions violent incidents in which peasants take revenge against cadres.
30. *RMRB* Overseas edition, October 7, 1986.
31. *RMRB* Commentator, "Tongzhi, fangxia ni de gunze," November 7, 1986.
32. Zi Mu in *Shijie Jingji Daobao*, August 11, 1986, *Chinese Law and Government*, vol. XX, no. 1, Spring 1987, pp. 87-88. The Organic Law for Local people's congresses, as revised through 1986, states that deputies' speeches are "not punishable by law." See article 29 of the Organic Law, *Xinhua*, Beijing, December 4, 1986, JPRS-CPS-87-001, January 13, 1987, p. 39.
33. *Xinhua*, Beijing, April 2, 1987, *FBIS* no. 65, April 6, 1987, pp. K 9-10.
34. See, e.g., *GMRB*, September 24, 1984, *FBIS* no. 194, October 5, 1984, pp. K 15-18.
35. See note 25, above, and *Xinhua*, Beijing, March 10, 1987, *FBIS* no. 47, March 11, 1987, pp. K 3-4.
36. *RMRB* April 5, 1987, and April 10, 1987, carry reports of the discussions. See also *Liaowang*, Overseas edition, April 20, 1987. *FBIS* no. 79, April 24, 1987 pp. K 10-12, and *Zhongguo Tongxun She*, Hong Kong, April 11, 1987, *FBIS* no. 71, April 14, 1987, pp. K 24-25.
37. *RMRB* April 10, 1987.
38. For the text of the law, see *Zhonghua Renmin Gongheguo Guowu Yuan Gongbao*, no. 27, December 5, 1987, pp. 884-887, as well as RMRB Commentator, November 26, 1988, in *FBIS* no. 229, November 30, 1987, p. 16.
39. Hu Chiao-mu, "Observe Economic Laws, Speed up the Four Modernizations," *Peking Review*, vol. 21, no. 47, November 24, 1978, pp. 19-20.
40. For an analysis of law in China, see Richard Baum, "Modernization and Legal Reform in Post-Mao China: The Rebirth of Socialist Legality," *Studies in Comparative Communism*, vol. XIX, no. 2, Summer 1986, pp. 69-104.
41. *Xinhua*, Beijing, February 11, 1987, *FBIS* no. 28, February 11, 1987, p. K 1.

42. Interview with scholars from a State Council research institute, 1987. For the rules, see *Xinhua*, Beijing, June 28, 1988, *FBIS* no. 140, July 21, 1988, pp. 44-48.
43. See *RMRB* April 10, 1983, *FBIS* no. 72, April 13, 1983, p. K 6, for Document no. 1 on this point, and *Xinhua*, Beijing, March 11, 1984, *FBIS* no. 50, April 13, 1984, pp. K 10ff, for State Council regulations. See also *Zhongguo Fazhi bao* March 13, 1984.
44. *Nongmin RB*, October 11, 1986, *FBIS* no. 213, November 4, 1986, p. K 19.
45. *Zhongguo Fazhi bao*, September 3, 1984.
46. *Zhongguo Tongji Nianjian, 1984* (China Statistical Yearbook, 1984 (Zhongguo Tongji Chubanshe, 1984), p. 11, Edward Epstein, "Law-Long March to the Present, Long Way to go," *Far Eastern Economic Review* March 19, 1987, pp. 103-107; interview with graduate of political-legal college, Beijing, 1985.
47. Mingshui county, Heilongjiang, for instance, also had three lawyers in 1985. See *RMRB* July 21 1985. Information from Zouping county, Shandong, and Fengyang county, Anhui, was gathered in August and September 1985.
48. See *Zhongguo Tongji Nianjian, 1984*, p. 11 and *Xinhua*, Beijing, November 14, 1985, JPRS-CPS-85-118, December 11, 1985, p. 41.
49. One such case was reported in interviews in Zouping. The press is full of them. See e.g., *Zhongguo Fazhi bao*, March 2, 1984.
50. Interviews, Fengyang, Anhui, 1985.
51. *Zhongguo Fazhi bao*, March 16, 1984.
52. *Ibid.*, June 4, 1984.
53. *RMRB* July 6, 1984.
54. *RMRB* March 13, 1986, *FBIS* no. 53, March 19, 1986, pp. K 2-3. On contracts in pre-communist China, see Myron Cohen, "The Role of Contract in Traditional Chinese Social Organizations," Proceedings, *VIIIth International Congress of Anthropological and Ethnological Sciences, 1968*, Tokyo-Kyoto, Vol. II *Ethnology* (Tokyo: Science Council of Japan, 1969), pp. 130-132.
55. *Zhongguo Fazhi bao*, October 31, 1984. See also Lan Cuipai, "Nongcun shixing cheng bao zeren zhi zhong de jige falu wenti," (several legal problems in implementing the contract responsibility system), *Faxue Zazhi* no. 1, 1985, pp. 30-33.
56. See *RMRB* August 3, 1985; *RMRB* March 13, 1986, *FBIS* no. 53, March 19, 1986, pp. K 2-3, and Epstein in *Far Eastern Economic Review*, March 19, 1987, *op. cit.*

57. *RMRB* July 6, 1984. See also *Zhongguo Fazhi bao*, March 28, 1984, case from Heilongjiang.

58. *RMRB* July 6, 1984.

59. *China Daily*, June 9, 1983.

60. Wang Keai and Li Shaokuan, "Lun nongye chengbao hetong" (on agricultural contracts), *Faxue Yanjiu*, June, 1983, pp. 32-37. The authors note that neither judicial nor arbitration organs liked to take these cases.

61. *Ibid.*, p. 37, and *RMRB* August 29, 1983, *FBIS* no. 83, September 1, 1983, pp. K 6-7.

62. *Jilin RB* March 2, 1985, JPRS-CPS-85-058, June 14, 1985, pp. 77-82.

63. *China Daily*, July 3, 1985.

64. *RMRB* June 4, 1984.

65. For a Shaanxi case in which the county party committee compelled a village party branch to correct contract violations and also inflicted inner-party penalties on the branch secretary, see *RMRB* March 24, 1985.

66. *Ibid.*, for a Fujian case, in which a county standing committee of the people's congress investigated violations, and then asked the county public security department and procuracy to handle the case, which they did, resulting in payment of compensation and fines.

67. *Selected Works of Deng Xiaoping, op. cit.*, pp. 311-312.

68. See above, note 20.

69. *Selected Works, op. cit.*, p. 310.

70. *RMRB* July 12, 1985, case from Heilongjiang.

71. *Ibid.* For similar formulations, see *China Daily*, January 16, 1985; *Xinhua*, Beijing, January 22, 1985, *FBIS* no. 16, January 24, 1985, pp. K 20-21; *RMRB* July 12, 1985; and especially, results of a survey of rural party organizations done by the Secretariat's Rural Policy Research Center, *Nongmin RB*, May 16, and 17, JPRS-CPS-86-064, August 19, 1986, p. 33.

72. Radio Wuhan, February 9, 1985, *FBIS* no. 228, November 26, 1985, pp. K 23-26.

73. Radio Wuhan, February 9, 1985, *FBIS* no. 29, February 12, 1985, pp. P 3-4.

74. *Nongcun Zhengdang Fudao Cailiao* (Rural rectification guidance materials), Wu Xiang, et. al., eds. (Beijing: Renmin Chubanshe, 1986), pp 38-39.

75. *RMRB* March 25, 1985, *FBIS* no. 58, March 26, 1985, p. K 6.

76. *Xinhua*, Beijing, June 6, 1986, *FBIS* no. 112, June 11, 1986, p. R 1.
77. *RMRB* January 26, 1984.
78. *Hebei ribao*, August 6, 1986, *FBIS* no. 160, August 19, 1986, p. R 3.
79. *Nongcun Zhengdang Fudao Cailiao, op. cit.*, p. 73 and p. 38.
80. See note 69, above.
81. *RMRB* August 25, 1985, *FBIS* no. 170, September 3, 1985, p. K 12.
82. *RMRB* Commentator, September 14, 1986, *FBIS* no. 186, September 25, 1986, pp. K 18-19.
83. See note 9, above.
84. For a convenient collection of discussions of democratization, see *Chinese Law and Government*, Spring 1987, vol. XX, no. 1 entire issue. For materials specifically on rural China, see *Jingji RB*, September 24, 1986, *FBIS* no. 192, October 3, 1986, p. K 7, and *RMRB* Commentator, November 14, 1986, *FBIS* no. 228, November 26, 1986, pp. K 10-11.
85. *RMRB* September 12, 1986, *FBIS* no. 182, September 19, 1986, pp. K 12-15.
86. *Lilun Nei Can*, no. 7, in *Wen Zhai bao* no. 336, August 7, 1986, *FBIS* no. 157, August 14, 1986, pp. K 2-3. The author's concern is with ending party domination of urban units, such as trade unions and enterprises.
87. RMRB Commentator, July 8, 1986, *FBIS* no. 135, July 15, 1986, pp. K 15-16. Wenzhou received extensive national publicity in 1986.
88. See note 12, above, for a 1984 article on "Documents No. 2." For a similar article published a year later, see *Xinhua* Commentator, *Xinhua*, Beijing, December 18, 1985, *FBIS* no. 245, December 20, 1985, pp. K 21-22.
89. *Nongcun Zhengdang Fudao Cailiao, op. cit.*, p. 69.
90. RMRB February 8, 1987, *FBIS* no. 27, February 10, 1987, pp. K 6-7.
91. RMRB August 15, 1986, *FBIS* no. 162, August 21, 1986, pp. K 3-7.
92. *Nongming ribao*, January 20, *FBIS* no. 25, February 8, 1988.
93. See AFP, Hong Kong, June 30, 1988, in *FBIS* no. 127, July 1, 1988, p. 17. An official account is in *Xinhua*, Beijing, June 30, 1988, *FBIS* no. 127, July 1, 1988, pp. 17-18.
94. Cheng Ying, "Mass Riots on the Mainland Rise One After Another." *Chiushi Nientai* no. 222, July 1, 1988, pp. 38-40, in *FBIS* no. 128, July 5, 1988, pp. 39ff.
95. See John P. Burns, *Political Participation, op. cit.*, 159-163.

EDITORS

ILPYONG J. KIM

Ilpyong J. Kim is professor of political science at the University of Connecticut. Dr. Kim has written and edited six books and published many articles in professional and academic journals on comparative and international politics of East Asia: China, Japan, and Korea. He received his Ph.D. from Columbia University, and has taught in the United States and Japan.

VICTOR C. FALKENHEIM

Victor C. Falkenheim received his Ph.D. in political science from Columbia University. He is presently chairman of the department of East Asian studies at the University of Toronto, a member of the review panel of the Committee on Scholarly Communication with the People's Republic of China, National Academy of Sciences, Washington D.C., and the Editorial Advisory Committee of Pacific Affairs. His publications include chapters in *Citizens and Groups in Chinese Politics, China in the 1980s: Reforms and Their Implications*, and numerous journal articles and papers.

CONTRIBUTORS

THOMAS P. BERNSTEIN

Thomas P. Bernstein is professor of political science at Columbia University were he received his Ph.D. He has held various appointments with universities within the United States and is a Guggenheim Fellow. He has published several books and numerous articles including *China's Rural Reforms, 1978–1987: Breakthroughs, Incrementalism, and Uncertainty* and *Up to the Mountains and Down to the Villages: The Transfer of Youth from Urban to Rural China.*

PARRIS HENRY CHUNG-LIEN CHANG

Parris Henry Chung-lien Chang is professor of political science at Pennsylvania State University. He received his Ph.D. from Columbia University. He is the author of *Radicals and Radical Ideology in China's Cultural Revolution, Power and Policy in China,* and numerous articles in various quarterlies and other publications. He was President of the Mid-Atlantic Region Association for Asian Studies.

HSI-SHENG CH'I

Hsi-sheng Ch'i is professor of political science at the University of North Carolina-Chapel Hill. He earned his Ph.D. from the University of Chicago. He has written several books on China's poltical struggles including *Warlord Politics in China: 1916–1928* and *Nationalist China At War: Military Defeats and Political Collapse, 1937–45* and numerous articles for various quarterlies and other publications. He is the Director of the East Asian Studies Curriculum at North Carolina-Chapel Hill.

HUNGDAH CHIU

Hungdah Chiu is professor of law at the University of Maryland. He received his J.S.D. from Harvard University.

Professor Chiu, who has taught at National Taiwan University and at National Chengchi University in PRC, was a research associate at Harvard Law School for six years. He has written and co-edited many books in English and Chinese and numerous articles in the field of international and comparative law.

LOWELL DITTMER

Lowell Dittmer is professor at the University of California. He received his Ph.D. from the University of Chicago. He has held academic posts at various universities including visiting professor to Peking University, Beijing, The Peoples Republic of China in 1982 and throughout the United States. He is the author of *China's Continuous Revolution: The Post-Revolutionary Epoch* and numerous articles on The People's Republic of China which have appeared in various quarterlies and other publications.

Professor Dittmer is a National Fellow, Hoover Institution and a Research Fellow at the Center for Chinese Studies at the University of Michigan.

SHAO-CHUAN LENG

Shao-chuan Leng is professor of government and foreign affairs and Chairman of the Committee on Asian Studies, University of Virginia. He received his Ph.D. from the University of Pennsylvania. He has held various appointments at universities throughout the United States. He has published numerous books and articles including *Japan and Communist China* and *Law in Chinese Foreign Policy*.

PETER R. MOODY

Peter R. Moody is professor, department of government and international studies, University of Notre Dame. He received his Ph.D. from Yale University. He has received several academic awards and honors including Hoover Institution Peace fellowship and the Pacific Cultural Foundation fellowship. He has held various academic posts at universities in the United States. He has published numerous books and articles including, *The Politics of the Eighth Central Committee of the Communist Party of China* and *Opposition and Dissent in Contemporary China.*

JAMES T. MYERS

James T. Myers is professor, department of political science, University of South Carolina. He received his Ph.D. from George Washington University. He held the post of visiting professor, Faculty of Law, Shanxi University, Peoples Republic of China in 1982. He is a National Defense Foreign Language Fellow and a Member of the National Committee on U.S.-China Relations. He has published several books and written numerous articles.

JAMES D. SEYMOUR

James D. Seymour is associate research scholar at the East Asian Institute, Columbia University. He received his M.A. and Ph.D. both from Columbia and specializes in Chinese politics and comparative human rights. He held various appointments at New York University and the New School for Social Research. He is a member of the National Advisory Committee for Amnesty International and has published several books and written numerous articles on Chinese affairs including, *The Politics of Revolutionary Reintegration* and *The Fifth Modernization: China's Human Rights Movement.*

LYNN T. WHITE, III

Lynn T. White, III is professor of Woodrow Wilson School, Princeton University. He received his Ph.D. from the University of California. He has held a variety of posts at Universities both in the United States and the Far East. He has published numerous books and articles, including conference papers, many on Chinese affairs. He has previously held fellowship of several affiliations related to the Far East.

Index